The Caribbean Heritage—Walker

ERRATA

At the end of page 111, proceed to page 114.

At the end of page 115, proceed to page 112.

At the end of page 113, proceed to page 116.

THE CARIBBEAN HERITAGE

The Caribbean Heritage

by VIRGINIA RADCLIFFE

 WALKER AND COMPANY • NEW YORK

First published in the United States of America in 1976 by the Walker Publishing Company, Inc.

Published simultaneously in Canada by Fitzhenry & Whiteside, Limited, Toronto.

ISBN: 0-8027-0518-9

Library of Congress Catalog Card Number: 75-12189

Printed in the United States of America.

10 9 8 7 6 5 4 3 2 1

For Bob, Ed and Hobby,
three buccaneers who made this book possible,
each in his own fashion

Acknowledgments

Among those who have given invaluable assistance in the course of this book's creation and who have my deep gratitude are Charlotte and Jonathan Blum; Emmanuel Berlinrut of the Bonaire Tourist Information Office; Walter Bussenius; John Connell of the Caribbean Conservation Association; Cheryl Dionaldo; Hendriena van Hoboken of the Curaçao Tourist Bureau; Hector Duval of the Dominican National Tourist Office; Ewen Gillies; Hon. Fritz Jean-Baptiste, Thaïs Capen, Theo Duval and Gerard Sanchez of the Haiti National Office of Tourism; Doctor Hodges of Limbé Hospital, Haiti; Jan Hurwitz; Edward L. Towle of Island Resources Foundation, Inc.; Hu Gentlès, Marcella Martinez, and Winnifred Risden of the Jamaica Tourist Board; Hans Fisher of KLM, Royal Dutch Airlines; Robert Grodé; Wilbur Hollander; Rushton Little; Milton Machlin; Robert F. Marx; Frederick Haupt, III, and Russell V. Keune of the National Trust for Historic Preservation; R. Michael Wright of the Nature Conservancy; Richard Hazlett, Joy Seligsohn and Cornelius de Weever of the Netherlands Antilles Windwards Tourist Bureau; Stuart G. Newman; Joseph Petrocik; Ricardo E. Alegría of the Puerto Ricah Institute of Culture; Vera Rubin of the Research Institute for the Study of Man; James Maduro and Jan Smid of the St. Eustatius Historical Foundation; Robert Devaux of the St. Lucia Archaeological and Historical Society; Morton Sontheimer; Constance Underhill; John A.J. Verschoor; Wolfgang Wagner and Carrie Weisbrod. Many thanks.

Contents

1

Fragments of Green

We are a fragment of green
Floating free in the universe.
We are a note in the lexicon;
Who we are is here.
Every man is an island in the sea,
The whole sea.

A WORD MAP OF THE CARIBBEAN ISLANDS

An island is a restriction and a blast of joy in the imagination. An island is discovered each time someone sights it appearing magically out of the water, its dark or golden shape looming at the edge of the sky. It may have a history no more complex than that of the building of one coral body upon another to form a living reef and eventually an atoll. Or its history may be made of volcanic convulsions, blood, deprivation, criminal politics and genocide and all the other agonies man manages to inflict upon himself in the homelands he chooses. What is different about island homelands is the restriction: the sea. Always there, the sea and its companion winds dictate what we in the twentieth century find, just as they did when the first man and woman and their children ventured into the unknown on a bamboo raft or a hollowed-out canoe.

For notwithstanding our ability to devastate whatever we come upon, we also have a habit of searching for something beyond ourselves, and this is how islands are discovered over and over again. We continue to believe ourselves the first ashore. But once there, too often we don't know what to do with what we find. This is as true today as it was when the West Indies—the islands we are encountering here—were first sighted by Europeans at the close of the fifteenth century. Over and over again through waves of colonists and wars upon wars, the islands were used as tools for foreign ambitions. It would be difficult to find a diarist or adventurer in the centuries past who worried about what would become of the islands themselves once their natural bounty—often fancifully described—was swallowed up by human depredation. The invaders treated these fragile places as if they were mainlands, forgetting or perhaps never understanding the interdependence of their physical and human structures.

Nevertheless, the Europeans did come and have their way, and if it seems to a modern vacationer stretched out on the white sands of a glorious beach that nothing ever happened before he put his reclining chair down, things did happen, on this very beach. They also happened up in the great house on the hill and over on the ruined stone wall and beside the giant water wheel and in the tower that was once a sugar mill. And what happened had an impact on what we in all of the Western Hemisphere are.

The childlike scratchings on a cave wall, the coral-encrusted fragment of a ship's fittings, potsherds and bits of brick are no less valuable testaments to the saga than treasure chests filled with pieces-of-eight. A thousand dramas were enacted in these islands, and their personna left their signatures behind in the shapes of building stones and bottles and clay pipes and fortresses and the gingerbread trim of

Saba, appearing magically out of the water, its dark shape looming at the edge of the sky.

their houses. All too often the markings have been covered up and lost, and every day in the new thrust toward twentieth-century-style competition or in the hope of eradicating the shames of slavery, some visible story is erased out of island memory.

Many of these memories are indeed shameful, some noble, or often simply dreary, which may after all be the chronicle of any lifetime whether it is lived by one person or a whole people.

The West Indian, or Caribbean, story is complicated by the fact that although they are all islands and they are all in one region, each is distinct from every other, harboring an incredible mix of races with complex cultural heritages. Adapting to their own sea-locked landscape, the people of one island may gaze across to their neighbors and recognize them as brothers, yet as somehow different. The land—flat and sandy or mountainous and lush—is enough to cause such differences, and the successions of foreign cultures has added more changes. Within the boundaries of a single island there are always separations caused by geography, history and economics, which in turn are forever in thrall to the sea and the wind. The very quality of a modern island vacation, seemingly subject only to the arrangements of a travel agent and the limitations of one's bank account, is made of all those elements.

The Caribbean islands, each separate from the others, are nonetheless connected by the vast pattern of currents and trade winds. Thus Trinidad has a direct relationship with Jamaica, a thousand miles away.

It may seem that the white sands of the lonely, palm-fringed beach bear no relationship to anything but much desired serenity. But the sea and wind were its parents. Lost in the coral reefs beyond it is the wreck of a sailing ship which has provided a building site for new coral formations. The plantings of sugar cane in the hills above it changed the topography and rainfall pattern. Hurricanes and wars have surged across it; people's faces and ideas have changed and developed. The hotel over on the rocky point once stood on a beach like this one, but it was built of cement taken from the sand and now the rock is all that remains. The vast pattern of currents and trade winds swirling around this shore has even determined what happened on an island a thousand miles beyond the sunset over there in the sea.

On a map, the Caribbean basin is a free-form swimming pool about sixteen hundred miles wide and seven hundred miles long.* Its western and southern rims are solid Central and South America, but the northern and eastern sides are broken like unmatched jigsaw puzzle pieces.

Three long islands—Cuba, Hispaniola and Puerto Rico—stretching from west to east, form the northern edge. Jamaica, ninety miles south of Cuba, completes the group known as the Greater Antilles. The Lesser Antilles chain describes the eastern side, moving southward in a convex arc. Some of these fragments of green are almost like small continents because of the diversity they contain; others barely poke out of the sea.

The Greater Antilles

Cuba, of course, is the largest and, under its current government, the least known to outsiders. Looking on the map like a giant shrimp, Cuba nods westward across the channel to the Yucatan Peninsula and Isla Mujeres.

Tucked under the shrimp's chin is the *Isle of Pines* and further south, the *Caymans*, a chain of sandy, dryish cays sitting on the lip of the deepest known trench in the Caribbean. Treasure ships and their pursuers crossed and recrossed these waters in other years, but little is left in Grand Cayman to speak of its adventurous past. British to the core and friendly to visitors, it is now a haven for a new breed of financier-adventurer and a place where the green turtle, hunted to near extinction, is being farmed by aquaculture.

*A recommended reference map: *West Indies and Central America* (Washington, D.C.: National Geographic Society, 1970).

The Caymans' southeastern neighbor is *Jamaica*, the only large island completely surrounded by the Caribbean Sea. If Cuba looks like a big shrimp, Jamaica is a turtle with its head protruding from its shell, swimming toward Central America. It is about 145 miles long and 35 miles wide, but seems larger because of its rugged topography; it is impossible to drive from one place to another as the crow flies. The result of a very old volcanic upheaval that later sank under the water and acquired a limestone crust, then was thrust upward again, Jamaica's surface is riddled with numberless caves, hillocks and sinkholes that make it look from the air like a green velvet egg crate. Jamaica's history was strongly influenced by this virtually untouched central wilderness. Despite an independent democratic government since 1962, sophisticated bauxite and tourism industries, crowded cities and a thriving cultural life, Jamaica still has a wonderful primitive heart.

At its northeastern point—the turtle's tail—begins the Windward Passage, outlined on one side by southern Cuba

The Virgins are among the "dry" islands of the Eastern Caribbean. This does not detract from their special brand of beauty. The best way to see them is to sail through the intricate waterways past reefs and caves.

and on the other by western Hispaniola. The trade winds blow steadily from the northeast through this much traveled former pirate waterway, which now sees the peaceful sail of yacht races from Miami and the Bahamas. It also feels hurricanes roaring through in the opposite direction, flattening Haitian houses and Cuban cane fields.

An explanation is in order here concerning *Hispaniola*. The average traveler is apt to say, "Hispan-who?" Well, both Haiti and the Dominican Republic are familiar names, but the fact that the two independent countries share an island called Hispaniola, second largest in the Caribbean, always seems to puzzle people. It was called that by the Columbus expedition, and it was the site of the first European settlement in the West Indies. For centuries it was rent by the question of whether the Spanish, French or Independents would have control of it.* Today, Haiti—once called St. Domingue—and the Dominican Republic share its magnificent mountains and valleys. Haiti on the west side occupies about a third, the Dominican Republic with its highly productive agricultural and mineral enterprises, has the central and eastern sections.

In character and ambiance the two nations couldn't be more different, yet there seems to be something almost inherent in the island that invites power struggles and violence, an endless clawing upward for air and liberty. Haiti did it in the most remarkable way; it was the first independent country in the West Indies. Still, its citizens continued to speak French even when Haitians were cutting down French soldiers during their big breakaway from European domination. Today there is much of France in the houses of Port-au-Prince and in the language of the most remote mountain villager and in the somehow chic way each woman wears her dress. "Haiti Chérie," sings the folk chorus, describing the passionate and beautiful country, twisting and turning in chains that are not really there anymore but are still never quite broken.

Its island-mate, once called Santo Domingo, now the Dominican Republic (never to be confused with the Eastern Caribbean island of Dominica) has always had Spanish overtones, and Spanish is the language spoken there today. There have been violent political schisms here too, and Haiti once overran its borders to occupy Ciudad Santo Domingo's palaces and avenues. But Ancient Spanish buildings remain and some are restored and well kept. (See ch. 7.) In most of the other island countries almost nothing is to be seen above the

*English and the United States forces have also occupied it briefly.

The quiet waters of St. Maarten's Great Bay once saw fleets of sailing ships engaged in desperate battles for possession of the 37-square-mile island now shared by the Dutch and the French.

surface of the ground to reflect the time when Spain regarded the Caribbean as its private boat basin.

Next door, to the east, the American Commonwealth of *Puerto Rico* is almost as mountainous as Hispaniola, but its heights are on the whole less rugged. Many of its fertile hills are farmed right up to their summits, where electric poles are installed by dropping them from airplanes—a rather bizarre meeting of the *jibaro*, the small farmer, with instant urbanization.

Much has been written about this smallest of the Greater Antilles and the modern migration of the *Borinqueños* to the mainland and the counter invasions of hordes of Stateside vacationers and industrialists. Through it all a tradition has stubbornly survived underground or emerged like the phoenix in the face of the prevailing belief that Puerto Rico had no indigenous culture. The most lively and innovative of all the islands in the twentieth century context, Puerto Rico has a Spanish pride evident in every day's encounter and in the way it has preserved its landmarks in the midst of Miami-style high-rises.

It is also the easternmost point of the Greater Antilles, an outpost for certain tribes of Indians before the coming of the sixteenth-century Spanish, and a gateway to their ships when they did begin to arrive in numbers. From Fajardo, the fishing village on the east coast, and from the two outlying islands of *Vieques* and *Culebra* (both either partially occupied or lately used as shooting ranges by United States

The Caribbean Islands

ATLANTIC OCEAN

Trade Winds

Turks
and
Caicos Islands

Great Inagua

Île de la Tortue
(Tortuga)

Cap Haitien
(Cap Francais)

Isabella

Île de la
Gonave

• Citadelle

Haiti

Dominican
Republic

Jeremie

HISPANIOLA

Port au Prince

Santo
Domingo

Isla
Saona

Jacmel

Île-à-Vache

Mona Passage

Puerto Rico Trench

St. Thomas
St. John
Tortola
Virgin Gorda

• Sombrero

Puerto Rico
San Juan

Culebra

Anguilla

Mayaguez

Charlotte
Amalie

Anegada Passage

St. Maarten–St. Martin

San
German

Ponce

Vieques

Philipsburg

St. Barth's

Barbuda

Frederiksted

St. Croix

Saba

St. Antigua
John's

• Utuado

St. Eustatius
St. Kitts
Nevis

Montserrat

Guadeloupe Passage

Basseterre

Grande Terre

Basse Terre

Point-à-Pitre

Iles Des Saintes

Marie Galante

Dominica Passage

Guadeloupe

Roseau

Dominica

Martinique Passage

St. Pierre

Martinique

Fort de France

St. Lucia Channel

Castries

St. Lucia

Speightstown

Hurricanes

St. Vincent Passage

Bridgetown

Kingstown

St. Vincent

Barbados

Grenadines

*Tobago
Basin*

EAN SEA

St. George's

Grenada

Point
Salines

Aruba

Oranjestad

Curacao

Bonaire

Canaan

Tobago

Willemstad

Kralendijk

Isla de
Margarita

Dragon's
Mouth

Port of Spain

LA GUAJIRA

Isla la Tortuga

Porlamar

Peninsula
de Paria

Trinidad

Serpent's Mouth

MBIA

GULF OF PARIA

NISH

MAIN

VENEZUELA

armed forces), the Lesser Antilles begin. From there on to the east and south, everything is suddenly geologically different, as if God were keeping nervous watch over a row of boiling pots of the fire-and-brimstone favored by island evangelists.

The Lesser Antilles

All the way down the eastern rim of the Caribbean basin to Venezuela, myriad shapes rise out of the sea, some spewn from volcanic caldrons, others the caldrons themselves. Still others are accumulated coral skeletons of living sea communities that are still building their islands; some are combinations of volcanic overflow and coral reefs. In Grenada there is one place where it is possible to walk a few steps from a black volcanic sand beach to one of pure white coral.

Without consulting a map constantly it is not easy to remember which island is south or east of which. There are so many Saints-This and -That, so many island capitals with similar names, so many confusions like Barbuda, Barbados, Tortuga (several of them), Tortola, Tobago, that an island buff needs to do some homework in order to enjoy them fully.

To keep things as simple as possible, here is how they follow each other down the parabolic course to South America:

Almost directly east of Puerto Rico, the Virgin Island chain begins with the U.S. territories of *St. Thomas*, *St. John* and—due south—*St. Croix*. Twisting to the northeast are British Virgin Islands *Tortola*, *Virgin Gorda* (meaning what it sounds like—the fat girl), *Jost Van Dyke* and *Anegada*, with the reef-encrusted Anegada Passage separating them from a perky loner named *Sombrero*.

The U.S. Virgins were the only West Indian islands held by the Danish monarchy in the centuries when other European powers claimed all the rest. Denmark has left a legacy of street names and architecture and a few feudal families, and twentieth-century America has superimposed its ticky-tacky boxes with all the concomitant values on St. Thomas and St. Croix, if not St. John. Fortunately, as in Puerto Rico, there is a lively rescue movement afoot designed to push back pollution and urban blight and the kind of environment that gives rise to accusations of a new colonialism.

Although they usually appear to be green, the American and British Virgins are among the "dry" islands of the Eastern Caribbean. In many places the rainfall scarcely meets the needs of farms and the population, and the low scrub vegeta-

A typical farm house above Fort-de-France, Martinique. In the mountainous islands, plantations are often almost vertical. Coconuts, bananas, and even sugar may be grown on steep hillsides.

tion on the hillsides cannot retain what water there is. This does not detract from these islands' special brand of beauty, and the best way to see them is to sail through the intricate waterways between the islands and uninhabited cays: St. John's national park and protected mangrove swamps; the caves and natural "fountains" or baths of Virgin Gorda; the now quiet, once jumping pirate island of Tortola; Anegada, the coral reef described by marine biologists as a perfect natural laboratory of rare species of plant and animal life. The American and British Virgins are different from each other, but there is a bond of history and background, and most Virgin Islanders consider themselves one with all of them.

The next island of any size lies to the southeast of the Virgin chain. It is *Anguilla*, flat and beachy, and with occupants who are bitterly unhappy to be grouped politically with certain other islands to the south. Although it is termed British, a close communication is carried on daily with the people of nearby *St. Martin/Sint Maarten*, the lagoon-laced, half-French, half-Dutch 38-square-mile charmer which has changed hands seventeen times and where Peter Stuyvesant lost a leg. A low, very old fieldstone wall divides the French from the Dutch side. The French Department of Guadeloupe administers the affairs of the northeast side with its farms and villages; the southwest section is a member of the six *Netherlands Antilles.* It is a small place to have such a complex setup, but it works and there are no formalities in passing from one side to the other.

From St. Maarten's southern and southeastern shores it is possible to see Saba, St. Eustatius, catch occasional glimpses of St. Kitts and to gaze daily at the peaked silhouette of St. Barthélemy (*St. Barths*). Once Swedish, now French, it is the setting for a fairy tale. Pirates once anchored in the miniature harbor of Gustavia, a town of pink shops and warehouses and well-kept little houses. The island is made of steep green hills and gently curving valleys; adding to its air of picturesque unreality is a pair of idyllic twin beaches with a guest house perched on a wooded island in the bay. Its airstrip seems anachronistic. Administered from Guadeloupe, St. Barths is French-speaking but clings to its own inner life.

The only other island that can be called truly enchanted in this way lies fifteen minutes by air from St. Maarten to the southwest. It is *Saba,* another of the six Netherlands Antilles. Like the tip of a green iceberg, Saba rises out of incredible depths of the sea to a volcanic peak with a single road, hand hewn from the rock, winding up around its heights and over the other side down to the sea again. Immaculately kept, brightly painted wooden cottages, cobbled lanes without a scrap of litter, the sounds of donkeys, roosters, goats and cows, the proud self-reliance of the people, the roster of ship's captains Saba has mothered, are part of an isolated world it is all too easy to romanticize. The Saban's life is hard; it also must be healthful. Many live to well past a hundred years.

Due east of Saba but not within sight is *Barbuda,* whose capital, Codrington, was named for an early English governor. Like Anegada, it is a coral formation with few heights and few people, surrounded by reefs and pierced by a large lagoon. Barbuda and almost all of the northern islands except Saba are "dry."

Now we come to four islands that march down the line dressed in somewhat similar geologic shapes and visible each to the other, yet different in character and political affinities. The first is *St. Eustatius*—Statia—a bumpy two-hour channel ride by small craft and five minutes by STOL plane, southeast of Saba. Another exquisite miniature, Statia is eight square miles of seventeenth- and eighteenth-century history with one lovely little town nestled in the shadow of a great volcanic crater and a harbor that once accommodated as many as two hundred sailing vessels at a time.

The first permanent colony in the Lesser Antilles was established by Sir Thomas Warner at St. Kitts in 1623. His tomb has survived hurricanes and earthquakes, but his church had to be rebuilt about 150 years ago and was again damaged in a 1974 earthquake.

St. Christopher, or *St. Kitts*, is physically a larger version of Statia, with a heritage of hundreds of beautiful buildings. The capital, Basseterre, has some of the most perfect examples of West Indian Georgian architecture in the islands, and the slopes of its plantations are dotted with stone sugar towers of classic design. St. Kitts, Nevis and Anguilla are supposed to form a unit in the West Indies Associated States,* but, as noted before, Anguillans—whose island is located on the north side of St. Martin—want none of it and some years ago staged a "mouse-that-roared" protest widely reported in the press against what they considered thralldom to St. Kitts. *Nevis*, on the other hand, is a loyal baby sister, across a narrows to the south. Named for the clouds that look like snow hovering on its heights, Nevis also has beautiful buildings and many ruins; it has suffered from the same earthquakes and hurricanes and political battering by acquis-

*In February, 1967, Antigua, Dominica, Grenada, St. Kitts-Nevis-Anguilla, St. Lucia and St. Vincent were formed into the West Indies Associated States. Grenada became independent in 1974 and Anguilla's status remains uncertain.

itive European nations as St. Kitts. In the harbor at Charlestown is another of the Caribbean's sunken "cities," buildings sent under the sea by a series of seventeenth-century earth tremors.

Tiny *Montserrat* is British despite the Spanish cast of its name. Another of the "straight up" islands, its dominating volcanic peak rises more than three thousand feet, and it attracts copious rains, something like eighty inches a year. Rocky but lush, its life is still mainly rural and it has managed to keep its looks in the passage of time.

Now we must double back a bit to take in the island of *Antigua* (pronounced An-tee′-ga), which lies roughly opposite Nevis on the eastern frontier of the archipelago. Dry and low-lying like its northern neighbors, Antigua attracts beach-connoisseurs from all over the world and indeed has made tourism a leading industry. It is said that its slopes were once covered with forest which was cut to make way for sugar planting. The result is a rather bleak interior section in contrast to the fine vistas along the shores. England regarded Antigua and St. Kitts as two of its most important colonies, partly because of their geographical positions and partly because of their productivity. They were much fought over and eventually Antigua was made England's principal naval station in the Eastern Caribbean.

The station was situated on Antigua's south coast, looking right out on the Guadeloupe Passage, one of the principal entryways for ships of all nations on their way to the West Indies from Europe. *Guadeloupe* itself is one of the largest islands in the chain, shaped curiously like a pair of lungs—or butterfly wings—named Grande Terre and Basse Terre for some unaccountable reason. Basse Terre is bigger than Grande Terre and is full of high, rugged volcanic mountains, one of which, Grande Soufrière (sulphur) is a kettle of steam. To confuse matters, Basse Terre is also the name of the capital, but the largest city, Pointe-à-Pitre, is on Grande Terre. As a department of France, Guadeloupe also takes in the nearby islands of *Marie Galante, Désirade, Les Saintes* and the farther-up islands of St. Barth's and the French side of St. Martin.

Les Saintes are a group of rocky points emerging from the waters of the channel south of Basse Terre. Here was the second entryway for ships in the age of sail—the Dominica Passage—with the island Columbus named for the Sunday on which he saw it impudently pointing its big toe toward the Saints. *Dominica* (Doe-min-eek′-a) is shaped like the sole of a rather flat foot, although topographically it is anything but flat. Like Guadeloupe it is blessed with crags and waterfalls,

In Guadeloupe it is easy to visualize the world of the pre-Columbian Indian and the seas he braved in his tree-trunk canoes.

a primitive jungle wilderness. Here, more than in any other island, it is easy to visualize the world of the pre-Columbian Indian, the groves he roamed, the primeval animals he hunted and the seas he braved in his tree-trunk canoes. Today, many of the fresh fruits and vegetables used by people on other islands, particularly the dry ones, are transported by schooner from Dominica, and temporary markets are set up until the produce is sold. At the heel of the foot is yet another soufrière, and Martinique Passage to the south was the third of the entryways for frigates and galleons. The notorious Mount Pelée, too terrible to be called a simple soufrière, towers over the north end of *Martinique* and the passage. However, its destructiveness in the most famous of Western Hemisphere volcanic eruptions, in 1902, was turned mostly southwest, where the French colonial town of St. Pierre was engulfed. The only survivor was a prisoner doing solitary time in a cell with extra thick walls.

The convulsions of nature are not the only attractions of this most French of islands, which changed hands during previous centuries somewhat less than most of the others. As the British used Antigua and St. Kitts as bases for their fleets and armies, the French concentrated their West Indian forces at Fort Royal, also called Fort-de-France. Some of the most spectacular sea battles of the eighteenth century—great formations of sail bound closely by the dictates of protocol and wind—were initiated from the anchorage at Fort-de-France Bay, an almost perfect natural harbor. The island has managed to retain many of its traditions, but one that it has fortunately abandoned was the habit, whenever possible, of overrunning *St. Lucia* lying directly to the South.

St. Lucia is another soufrière island. If someone could figure a commercial value of all the sulphur generated in the Eastern Caribbean chain, the unemployment problem might be solved. As it is, the volcanic safety valves spew up steam and provide an idle few minutes for tourists. In archaic times the Indians may have regarded the burning mountains as supernatural beings. St. Lucia is a member of the Associated States but keeps a proud independence and a French nomenclature. Green and capped with hills called *mornes*, its shores are dotted with beaches and photogenic coves.

St. Vincent, twenty-one miles away to the south, is a fraternal twin, looking very much like St. Lucia but by no means identical. Its port and capital, Kingstown, is one of the most alluring small cities in the entire Caribbean, and the island—which floats at the head of the Grenadines chain—is fertile and friendly. Its botanical gardens, begun in 1765, are the oldest in the Western Hemisphere, and some of the rock drawings—petroglyphs—are believed to have been left behind by island dwellers as long ago as 200 B.C. It too has its Soufrière, but most of the other place names on St. Vincent are English.

Now we come to that sprinkling of tiny islands filled with hideaway inlets and beaches and beloved by charter sailors: *the Grenadines*. These southbound miniatures are a part of the Associated States, but their discoverers neglected to call them after saints, so we find a colloquial collection of names: *Bequia, Mustique, Canouan, Mayreau, Prune, Union, Carriacou* and *Kick-em-Jenny*. *Ronde* lies closest to the north coast of *Grenada* (gren-ay´-da), the spice island and sailor's haven that recently became politically independent.

Mountainous and often blanketed in a fine mist called liquid sunshine, Grenada looks almost illusory when approached from the sea. St. George's harbor may be the most photographed of any in the Caribbean. Boats of all styles and sizes form a forest of masts, with the steep streets of the bright-colored Georgian town rising above, sentineled by the old fort on the cliff, often crowned by a rainbow. It is all a balm to the eye, a visual poem, and one hopes that Grenadans, like the other islanders thrusting toward a better life, will realize that a beautiful human environment can be adapted to the uses of that life. Grenada, like Dominica, should also set aside certain places—such as Point Salines with its black and white sand beaches—as national parks.

Now, although we are going against the wind, we must double back to the northeast, where *Barbados* lies due east of St. Vincent. In the centuries of sail, Barbados was protected by the trade winds from attack by occupiers of the other islands and retains a quality of self-possession that, in the midst of a British atmosphere, has persisted into its years of independence. Hilly and rugged on the Atlantic side, its lee-ward shores have many beaches and resorts, while the plains of the interior produce cotton and a surprising variety of green vegetables. Two historic coastal towns in addition to Bridgetown have retained much of their interest, and there is an active movement toward the protection of landmarks and natural resources. Barbado is the word for Bearded Fig tree in Papiamento; fortunately there are still a number of these ancient gnarled and moss-festooned "barbados" growing on the island.

Lying south of Barbados and the Tobago Basin is the big island that quite properly could be called a spinoff from Venezuela. Only the Serpent's Mouth, a narrow strait, separates *Trinidad* from what the Dutch used to call "The Firm Coast," as if all islands were afloat and one could only lose one's sea legs by landing on the shore of South America. Trinidad is pitch and forests and oil, coconut trees, sugar fields and rice paddies, calypso and carnival and East Indian curries. Nowadays its petroleum and natural gas make it one of the few truly industrialized islands in the Lesser Antilles; these resources come out of the ground and are not solely transplanted industries as in other places where refineries have been built.

As in Jamaica and Guyana on the mainland, the presence of East Indians in large numbers is due to the fact that with the decline of slavery in the early part of the nineteenth century, thousands of people came from India and Ceylon as indentured workers for the sugar plantations. The mix today includes more than a third of Asian ancestry; it also produces some of the world's most beautiful women. Trinidadians do a great deal to help themselves, including the building of good roads covered with asphalt from their own pitch lake. While Trinidad, geographically, is almost a projection of Venezuela, its tiny partner in independent government, *Tobago*, looks geographically upward toward Barbados and the Lesser Antillean chain. Elongated and hilly, this is Robinson Crusoe's island, and its beaches could still qualify as the setting for the original story. However, Trinidad and Tobago have been experiencing a cultural springtime matched in the West Indies only by Jamaica and Puerto Rico. Much of their thriving theatre, literary output, art, music, and folklore research are centered around their universities: campuses of The University of the West Indies are located in Trinidad, Jamaica, Barbados and St. Lucia. Puerto Rico has two: The University of Puerto Rico and Interamerican University.

West of Trinidad, *Margarita* and a number of small islands belonging to Venezuela line the banks and basins of that country's north shore waters. A big, bulbous peninsula that is almost an island and is called Paraguaná forms a headland to the Gulf of Venezuela and the city of Maracaibo. In a northern direction are the three southern islands of the Netherlands Antilles, the *ABC's*. *Curaçao* is in the center as befits the seat of government for all six. *Aruba* is to the west and *Bonaire* to the east—hence ABC. All three are salty, sandy and very dry, although Bonaire has a wild, wooded northern section.

They are Dutch in their architecture, schooling and tradition, yet there is evidence that from the times of prehistory

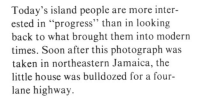

Today's island people are more interested in "progress" than in looking back to what brought them into modern times. Soon after this photograph was taken in northeastern Jamaica, the little house was bulldozed for a four-lane highway.

the inhabitants identified with the people and cultures of the Venezuelan coast. The Spanish possessed them for a while but they had no minerals that were gold in color, and the Dutch West India Company managed to move in rather early to profit from raiding and trading. The perpetual connection to Latin America is maintained by daily close communication and by their shared, special language. Papiamento is one of the happiest tongues spoken anywhere today. It is a witty, fractured mixture of Spanish, Portuguese, French, Dutch and English that the outsider can almost, not quite understand on first hearing, because the speakers always seem to be laughing. Some detractors call it a patois, but in Curaçao and Aruba two newspapers and a number of novels are printed in Papiamento.

Aruba has beaches and oil refineries and divi-divi trees whose backs are perpetually bent by the constant wind. Curaçao, the island with the famous West Indian version of Amsterdam and the Queen Emma pontoon bridge and the gargantuan Shell oil refinery, is civilized and cosmopolitan and quite different from Aruba in character and outlook. Bonaire, often regarded as a stepchild, is really Cinderella, unadorned but beautiful and frequented by visitors mostly for its glorious undersea gardens.

A number of islands offshore from Central America such as *San Andrés* and *Providencia* as well as the three ABC's were not discovered by Columbus but by explorer-adventurers who followed him later. Amerigo Vespucci was one; knowledge of his exploits remains uncertain, but he did make a notable contribution to the saga of the islands and, indeed, to the history of navigation with his development of a method for determining longitudinal position. It might have been well also to have discovered an instrument for determining the accuracy of myths. These waters were peopled by extraordinary beings in the imaginations of tale tellers back in Europe, but even those on the spot believed the tales. In his memoirs, Vespucci claimed he saw giants on the island of Curaçao.

Legends and Misconceptions

Giants, headless people with eyes in their chests, sea monsters whose tails could swamp a ship by a single flip—what marvelous, shuddery, nightmarish conjurations the unknown seas evoked in that adventurous exploration of the mind that was the Renaissance! Even the word Antilles stems from a legend about a lost civilization beyond the mysterious waters of the Atlantic.

trade was a heady new possibility that eventually became an obsession and spawned a powerful middle class in Europe and a plantocracy in the islands.

The Island Heritage

By the end of the eighteenth century, many middle-class Europeans, especially in England, were calling for an end to the infamous slave trade (but not slavery itself). Now that it had brought them wealth or at least comfortable circumstances, they could afford to let conscience prick them. The damage had gone so deep, however, that there was no known way of repairing it. Outnumbered whites in the islands feared the slave revolts that did begin breaking out, and it is quite possible that at the time of the American Revolution many of the island leaders would have struck for freedom for themselves if they had not been afraid to put arms into the hands of slaves.

The successful revolt of the thirteen North American colonies did much to inspire the French Revolution and, in

There is still time to experience some of the islands' moving and beautiful treasures. The flamingos nest on the salt ponds of Bonaire.

turn, the bloody lunges toward republicanism in the islands, especially those held by the French. Haiti succeeded in breaking loose altogether and, despite its subsequent troubled history, stands not only as the first independent but also the first slaveless country in the West Indies.

It is interesting that, except in the Dutch and Spanish islands, abolition of slavery came 15 to 25 years before the Emancipation Proclamation in the United States. But there had been little or no preparation for self-help, and government, paternal or autocratic, still came from over the sea. The development of steamships and the decline of sugar effected great changes in island economies, and the people—now liberated but economically bound—were still dependent on the largesse and decisions of others. It is the same habit of dependence that they are still trying to break a century and a half later. Economic autonomy is not easy to achieve in lands that are sometimes no larger than five square miles. If, for the islanders, the struggle requires a tossing away of their cultural heritage or a disclaiming of it under the mistaken belief that any traces of the past are reminders of colonialism, obviously they will do it. And the average islander, unaware that the crumbling old wall from which he is taking stones to build or repair a house is part of his people's history, needlessly destroys it. Except for a few dedicated individuals, today's island people are more interested in "progress" than in looking back to what brought them into modern times. A chronic lack of funds and expertise hampers efforts to save valuable documents and restore or preserve historic buildings. Politics or the profit motive or both have been responsible for the destruction of more than we can imagine. Hurricanes, earthquakes and fires have done it, and unplanned tourism, with the aid of outside developers, hurried things along. Mainland-style high-risers whose elevators don't work, air-conditioned glass cartons in lands where the trade winds are free-of-charge coolants are a ridiculous trend that it is to be hoped will soon outlive their own unusefulness.

Fortunately more and more historical societies, national trusts and conservation associations are working on ways for their own people and for visitors to use and enjoy what is there. There is still time to experience some of the islands' moving and beautiful treasures, including those that nature bestowed on them eons ago.

2
The Wild

GOD-FACES IN THE CAVES

In a cave at Punta del Este on the Isle of Pines, strange geometric designs are engraved on the rock face. A thousand miles to the southeast near Fontein, Aruba, there is more of such seemingly meaningless graffiti. At Trois-Rivières, Guadeloupe, and Salto Arriba, Puerto Rico, cartoonlike faces stare at the horizon, some with rays springing from their heads. At Upper Icacos, Puerto Rico, and Petit Bordel, St. Vincent, whole figures appear.

Petroglyphs in varying styles but quite often startlingly similar have been found in virtually every island in the Caribbean, most notably in Cuba, Haiti, Dominican Republic, Puerto Rico, St. Croix, St. John, Antigua, Guadeloupe, Martinique, St. Lucia, St. Vincent, Grenada, Trinidad, Bonaire, Curaçao and Aruba. They are part of a legacy of people whose groupings and characteristics and ways of life remained sealed in a time capsule until the late fifteenth century. The truth about them was not necessarily found when the seal was broken. Columbus thought they were East Indians, and the disappointment of the Spanish when they finally realized that these islanders were some other people—and their islands were some place else—led to the put-down "*West Indies.*" Naturally the people who lived there didn't know they were "Indians," and it has taken nearly five centuries to place them in a context of what they really may have been by what they left behind.

Archaeology has arrived late in the West Indies. For centuries what was assumed about the pre-Columbian inhabitants of the islands was derived mainly from diaries and accounts of explorers beginning with Columbus and followed by adventurers and missionary priests, whose observations of the aborigines they encountered were necessarily colored by their calling. Throughout the years since, people have been finding bits of pottery, stone or shell tools, carved figures and petroglyphs, but scientific techniques of inquiry, including carbon-14 dating, have only recently begun to be applied.

The standard story of man's occupation of the West Indies runs more or less as follows: First came the primitive fishing groups called Ciboneys, probably from Florida; next, the peaceful farmer-hunter Arawaks, who migrated from the Orinoco and Amazon in South America up through the Lesser—and West across the Greater—Antilles. They were pursued along a similar route by tribes of fierce, man-eating Carib Indians, who occupied the Eastern Caribbean archipelago but never made it west of Puerto Rico except for occasional raids on Arawak settlements.

Now that more and more scholars, properly trained to investigate the evidence have been probing known sites and discovering new ones, it appears that the accepted pattern is too simplistic and that the story may have begun as early as 7400 B.C. Archaic sites have been found in Hispaniola, Antigua, St. Thomas and Trinidad where two date from 5000 to 3000 B.C. Two others run from 1000 up to the time the Chris-

A Carib Indian couple, as seen through the eyes of an early adventurer in the strange, unreal world of the West Indies.

tian era was beginning in the Middle East. In one of the Trinidad digs, a woman's skeleton came to light; she is thought to be as much as 4,375 years old.

The Busy Sea

Islanders of the archaic period were shell gatherers and eventually became proficient hunters and fishermen. They were at home on the sea and kept contact with their relatives, the Manicuaroid people they had left behind on the mainland of what is now Guyana and northern Venezuela. The proximity of Trinidad to the South American coast would make this interchange logical. One archaeologist who worked these sites theorizes that "an initially hunting-fishing, and subsequently agricultural, pestle and grooved-axe culture moves up the Lesser Antilles into the Caribbean. One element remains, perhaps—to produce elaborate ground stone axes, pestles and the fancy ground stonework of St. Vincent. Another element seems to continue into Hispaniola, where pestles and single and double-bitted axes date from 1000 B.C."* He believes the Caribbean at that time "contained two distinct cultural areas: The Lesser Antilles and Hispaniola."†

In the Pitons of St. Lucia are evidence of the eternal cycle of erupting volcanoes and seismic shudders that continue to alter the profiles of the islands.

*P.O'B. Harris, *Proceedings of the Fifth International Congress for Study of Pre-Columbian Cultures of the Lesser Antilles* (1974), pp. 110-16.
†Ibid.

However, he also notes that the Trinidad Archaic somewhat resembles the Archaic of the Eastern United States, and another student of the Archaic believes that people living in Antigua's Jolly Beach between 1000 and 250 B.C. may have been predated by what is called the Barrera I culture in Hispaniola. It is possible that the earliest people may have come from the north and met the Manicuaroids from South America halfway. So the controversy over where the first men came from continues.

As time went by, the cultural interchange apparently grew ever more complex.* Instead of two big separate waves of migration up the chain of islands, there seem to have been numerous overlaps of "ceramic" with "nonceramic" peoples† and constant travel from island to island in several directions. Ripley Bullen of the University of Florida, who has probed as many caves, mounds and middens throughout the Caribbean as any archaeologist working in this field, believes that the northern islands—the Virgins, Bahamas and Greater Antilles—formed an interacting culture area until the Suazey (Carib) series of people appeared around 1200 A.D.

There is even some evidence that migrations may have occurred from Central America across Hispaniola and over to the eastern islands. The discovery of ball courts in Puerto Rico, St. Croix and Antigua suggests a connection with the Mayans, who built enormous walled structures for their ceremonial ball playing. However, the island arenas didn't have walls and it is thought that the contestants used balls made of rubber from Venezuela, the bounce having a certain religious significance. Did they get the layout for their courts from Central America and their equipment (and gods) from the Orinoco? The history of the Caribbean Indians turns out to be a puzzle that will take an indefinite amount of time to solve, even when archaeologists begin to agree. An educated stab at this has been made through papers given at The International Congress for the Study of Pre-Columbian Cultures of the Lesser Antilles which has been meeting at intervals on various islands since 1967.

According to reports of the participating archaeologists,

---

*A 1975 discovery of negroid skeletons in the U.S. Virgin Islands, dated at about 1250 A.D. has added to a growing body of clues indicating the presence of black Africans in the New World as early as 4000 B.C. Their voyages could have been accomplished by drifting on currents flowing like rivers in the sea from Africa to South and Central America, where most of the finds of statues with negroid features and artifacts with African characteristics have been made.

†In "ceramic" cultures the people had advanced to pottery-making from dependence on chipped stones and shells for their tools and religious images.

the main area of agreement is that the peoples who roamed the Caribbean basin for something like 6,500 years were divided into a long series of overlapping cultures, the principal ones being Archaic; Saladoid (100 A.D.-400+); Cuevas (to 800); Ostione, Palmetto and Calivigny (about 900 to 1200 in some islands); Meillac (to 1400); Suazey (or Carib, after 1200); with numerous offshoots named for the various sites where remains have been found. But any traveler today looking for petroglyphs or pottery sites had better not ask for "terminal Cuevas" or "early Ostione"; he would get a blank stare. The words still used everywhere are Arawak for the type of people Columbus later described as "lovable, tractable, peaceable and praiseworthy," and Carib, a name not

Zemis were a legacy of people whose ways of life and worship remained sealed in a time capsule until the coming of the Spaniards. This artifact was found on Ile de la Tortue off Haiti's north coast.

Legend has it that this wooded cliff
in the Jamaican wilderness is where a
17th century maroon chieftainess called
Nanny poured cauldrons of boiling
water down onto a hapless company of
British soldiers.

only given to the sea of islands but said to be the origin of the word "cannibal," describing their supposed eating habits. Subdivisions of the Arawaks were popularly called Tainos or Borinquens in Puerto Rico, Tainos in the Bahamas and Hispaniola, and Caiquetios down in the offshore islands of Venezuela.

In their hand-hewn, often elaborately carved, canoes propelled by paddles, these people achieved an island-hopping saga that would be the envy of any modern traveler trying to make island plane connections. Their villages were usually built back of a sandy beach. In Grenada a casual visi-

Petroglyphs carved by unknown people on Basse Terre, Guadeloupe, tell a story that when deciphered may differ greatly from the accepted version of Indian life in the islands. Their story may have begun as early as 7400 B.C.

tor can still pick up sherds of their pottery in the eastern coastal marshes, which remain uninhabited. But in many of the other islands, the Europeans later moved into the Indian sites. At Krum Bay and Grambokola Hill in St. Thomas, important archaic sites have been swallowed up by industrial plants. Alfredo Figueredo, curator of the Virgin Islands Museum, notes that the destroyed Grambokola site "would be right where within living memory the best fishing on the southern shore of St. Thomas was found. One may conjecture that it was equally favored in prehistoric times."

Antigua's many-layered Indian Creek site representing several series of cultures is separated from the shore by hills, which differs from the usual pattern. The area itself has gone full circle: After the Indians came eighteenth-century military and naval centers, an exclusive twentieth-century resort, a U.S. satellite-tracking station and, lately, an archaeological laboratory for study of the original series of occupants.

At White Marl in the southern plain of the Rio Cobre, Jamaica, a simulated village has been constructed on the site of a large Arawak settlement and made into a museum. The exhibit building itself is shaped like the circular huts the White Marl people began using around 1000 A.D. Inside the grounds, actual replicas are made of bamboo with conical thatched roofs. These are grouped around a central plaza, which was used for ceremonies. Excavations have revealed the fact that the White Marl people did their cooking in outdoor areas behind their houses, yet it was found that they lit fires inside their huts, as well, possibly as a way of warding off insects or unkind spirits. Their home fires also could have been brought indoors—it was a semitropical climate and the people wore few if any clothes—to keep the coals alive.

In 1968, while archaeologists of an Institute of Jamaica project were digging at White Marl, the locals told them about a cave five hundred yards away. It turned out to be a burial chamber; four skulls, eight partial skulls and three complete mandibles were found, plus about eight hundred other types of human bones. Eleven adult males were buried in the cave along with a very puzzling two-year-old—puzzling because these people were known to have made a practice of skull-shaping. Soon after a child was born, the skull was wrapped to achieve a certain sloping shape they must have deemed attractive. This child hadn't had the treatment and the mystery of why he escaped getting the tribal headache will probably never be solved.

A classic situation did become evident by the discovery of food pots associated with each skull, one containing animal bones and seashells. Well-provisioned trips to the afterlife were certainly not limited to Egyptian kings. White Marl Arawaks, too, must have wanted their loved ones to pass into the next world in a state of affluence as well as grace.

It has been widely held that they had a pantheon of gods and spirits, which some of the petroglyphs may represent, but worshiped no one central Supreme Being. A theory disputing this has been advanced by Columbian scholar José Juan Arrom, who found through roots of language in South America that the environment with which they successfully coexisted was also the source of their worship. This Being, he says, comprised the land (the *cassava* that they grew), the sea (fish which they drew in) and man, who—if he was without grandfather or ancestor—must be eternal and so, master. It was a combination of nature worship and recognition of an anthropomorphic God.

Spanish conquistadores reported seeing rubber balls, now believed to have been made from the sap of the Hevea *braziliensis* trees of the Amazon tributaries. But their religious significance was never as important in the islands as was the worship of zemis, small figures made of stone or conch shell. No ball courts have been found south of Antigua, but zemis turn up at digs in many places throughout the Caribbean dating from about 200 A.D. Fred Olsen, investigating Saladoid pottery at the Antigua ball court site, found conch zemis similar to one of the same period in Guadeloupe at the Morel site. The prongs of the shell were cut off so that it resembled the silhouette of a volcanic cone. It is theorized that these shells represented the "cult of Yocahu," a god who resided in the volcano Pelée. Archaeologist Olsen writes: "It seems probable that the simple, cut-off conch prong was the original prototype of the zemi and that the evolution of the elaborate stone deities with the characteristic hump shaped like a volcano, and whose faces show ear ornaments, can be traced readily over a period of more than a thousand years. The coming of the Caribs is perhaps responsible for the broken stone zemis found in late occupation layers in Guadeloupe and also in Antigua.*

The Caribs were blamed for violent acts far more serious than the breaking up of zemis, although, at the time, their sacrilege may have seemed worse to the Arawaks than the carrying away of their women as concubines. Settlers and Christian missionaries later accused them of gruesomely feasting on whomever they could capture, including the

*Fred Olsen, *Proceedings of the Fifth International Congress for the Study of Pre-Columbian Cultures of the Lesser Antilles* (1974), pp. 11-12.

babies of their subject women. One who doubted this was Père Labat, a French priest who wrote of his experiences with Caribs during a year he spent in the Eastern Caribbean. He contended that their cannibalistic practices were of a ritual nature, deriving from their belief that one gained strength from one's fallen enemy. Some anthropologists today, noting the formalism of their society, tend to agree with Labat.

Although the Carib-Arawak conflict poses the eternal question of what peaceable man is to do when faced with an armed aggressor, both peoples might have survived—if they had been left undisturbed by the Europeans—by merging. The Arawak women might have taken care of that. It is said that when made captive, they refused to learn the Carib language, but that barrier has never stood in the way of procreation.

Neither of the culture divisions created exquisite civilizations such as those the Aztecs, Toltecs, Mayans and Incas founded in the jungles of Central and South America, but their island world was a spectacle for modern man to contemplate. Here was the virgin wilderness: riverbeds lined with species of plants soon to vanish, forests of hardwood, tall

The Virgin Islands National Park, occupying more than two-thirds of the land on St. John, also extends to the underwater reefs that surround it.

mountain peaks wreathed in mist and carpeted with greens of every hue; secret coves along the untouched shorelines where huge green turtles buried their eggs in the warm white sand, oysters hung in the mangrove branches, and langouste, crab, shrimp and snapper waited to be taken from the glassy waters of the offshore banks. There were pineapples and avocados, giant silk cotton trees, the Ceibas from whose twigs the Arawaks said all living things were first created; tree frogs (they still loudly sing "coqui, coqui" at night in Puerto Rico, while in other islands their lyrics vary), alligators like African crocodiles, iguanas, coneys, snakes (the mongoose that has destroyed the snake population of the islands was introduced much later) and insects.

Ants in battalions marched against European man when he disturbed the ecological balance of Puerto Rico and Hispaniola, but the residents before 1492 seemed to have made scarcely a ripple in their environment, adjusting as they did to its bounties and limitations. The Arawaks grew their tobacco and their manioc root for cassava flour, hunted small animals with their dogs, made ornaments out of gold they found in the rivers and fished; the Caribs fished and hunted Arawaks, and the great expanses of the Caribbean basin relaxed in the eternal cycle of god-inspired sunrises and sunsets, devastating hurricanes, erupting volcanoes and an occasional seismic shudder along the fault lines that snaked through the bottom of the sea and the surface crust of islands.

Then, as in the trembling luminous predawn moment when nothing is very clear but everything is somehow ordained, the Spanish arrived.

Genocide

Whatever way we regard Columbus today, as hero or villain, a child of his time or a self-seeking but brilliant innovator, Don Cristóbal Colón was the one who experienced that predawn moment. By an odd coincidence—or was it?—his name came to mean social subjugation, and colonialism in the Western Hemisphere gained purchase when he stepped onto the beach of San Salvador in the Bahamas. For both the Arawaks, whom he found so comely and the Caribs, whom he learned to avoid like the scorpion, his very presence presaged genocide.

He immediately took some Arawaks (also called Tainos) captive to help him find the Great Khan in nearby Japan, which turned out to be Cuba and which probably was already making the world's best cigars.* So, although it may be said that the Arawaks were inadvertently responsible for the modern world's smoking habit, they found few actual ways to revenge themselves against the intruders for what happened to them.

Finding no Khan or gold, Columbus sailed on to the north coast of Hispaniola near the present site of Cap Haitien, where the *Santa Maria* foundered on a reef. He had to leave some men behind, thus establishing the first colony— La Navidad. He returned to the West Indies in 1494 on his second voyage to find they had all disappeared. Considering the friendly attitudes of the local Indian *caciques** and conflicting stories of fights among the caballeros and their cruel behavior toward the Indians, it has been concluded that they invited their own disaster.

This trip also brought members of the Columbus expedition face to face with Caribs living in the Lesser Antilles. It was on Guadeloupe that they discovered to their pious horror that all the occupants of this new world were not docile. At one point the local Caribs vanished from their village at the approach of the Spaniards, who found castrated Taino boys held captive there. The voyagers rescued them, but there is no record that after these Indians were in Spanish hands they were freed.

Very soon afterward came the first battles between the old and new worlds. On St. Croix, a party of seven Caribs fought Columbus's shiploads of men so furiously that they managed to kill one and wound another. While the fleet was in Salt River Lagoon, a tribe of warriors in full, terrifying battle dress—which consisted of colorfully painted bodies and heads half-shaved, half-plumed with a long pony tail— began shooting arrows at the ships. They didn't do much damage, but Columbus's men were unnerved and he decided to sail on without fighting back.

By doing so he discovered Puerto Rico, explored the southern coast of Hispaniola and parts of Jamaica, where the Indians imagined, when they saw beings in big sailing birds, clothed in shining breast plates and plumed helmets, that these were gods who could not die. (Legend has it that they began to mistrust the immortality of the visitors when one Spaniard drowned and after a tense three-day waiting period, didn't revive. In that climate, it must have become apparent a good deal sooner.)

*Both the Carib and Arawak peoples used tobacco.

*An Arawak word generally used by the Spanish to describe an aborigine chieftain or king.

The mortality of the Arawaks was never in question. As soon as the Spaniards began establishing colonies and gold in significant quantities began to be drawn from the rivers of Puerto Rico, Hispaniola and Cuba, the Indians were pressed into a kind of slave labor they could not endure physically or temperamentally. A system called *encomiendas* was developed by Nicolás de Ovando, who came to Hispaniola in 1502 to rule as Royal Governor in the Indies. It involved dividing the Indian lands into estates held by Spanish settlers. The former occupants were held as serfs who must also be converted to Christianity. The Arawaks' belief in a supreme being may have made the new religion possible for them to live with, and the milder aspects of Christianity would have fitted their outlook on life. But this was the period of the Inquisition; to Spanish Christians, it seemed that heresy lurked everywhere beyond Spanish borders. And these aborigines in the islands of the West Indies were outright pagans, fit only to be slaves while their souls were being saved.

Unfortunately, nothing could save their bodies; they began dying of overwork, European plagues and suicide. Through their knowledge of bush medicine, they extracted the poisonous parts of the manioc root and put an end to their sorrows. Between 1492 and 1548 the West Indian population declined from an estimated 300,000 to about 500. In Puerto Rico, then called San Juan Bautista, an abortive revolt by Tainos resulted in the killing of eighty Spanish settlers, whereupon the governor, Juan Ponce de León, ordered the Indian rebels wiped out.

There was one Spanish voice raised against all this. It belonged to the Dominican Bishop and missionary Bartolomé de las Casas, who led his brothers in strong protests to the Spanish Crown. For a time it seemed that the official Code of Burgos* would ease the plight of the Indians, but the settlers went right on exploiting them and in Spain, attention was not paid to the passionately concerned Las Casas until too late, when there were no longer any Arawaks with souls to save.

Ponce de León, as we know, left Puerto Rico for Florida in search of the fountain of youth and was murdered there by Indians.

During the first half of the sixteenth century, while the inhabitants of the Greater Antilles were being decimated, the Caribs in the eastern islands were sharpening their martial arts in proud determination not to let this happen to them.

*A code dealing with the administration and conversion to Christianity of the Indians.

They would make periodic lightning raids against the Spanish settlements in Puerto Rico, which had begun to run out of gold as well as Arawaks. The colonists, without more than nominal help from the mother country, tried to strike back, making several expeditions in the 1530's against the Caribs in Dominica, St. Barth's and Trinidad. The distance covered suggests that during the early 1600's the Caribs still stood a good chance of winning against the intruders.

But before long Spain, despite its efforts to maintain the Spanish Line, was no longer alone in island waters. Privateers and colonists from other European countries appeared and began the long struggle for possession of the islands, braving and sometimes outwitting the Caribs. Small settlements of English, French and Dutch managed to grab toeholds in St. Kitts, Montserrat, Curaçao, Aruba, Bonaire, Barbados and St. Lucia. In the latter island, a certain John Nicol whose ship had strayed off course in 1605 succeeded in trading with the Caribs for such things as pineapples, calabash, papaya, plantains and tobacco, establishing a settlement at what is now Vieux Fort Bay. But the Carib incumbents soon reduced the colony from 67 to 19, and the survivors hastened to row away to Venezuela in a borrowed canoe. Some thirty-four years later, another group of four hundred English was virtually obliterated after one of their vessels, becalmed off nearby Dominica, was boarded by Caribs who thought it French. (They got along better, on the whole, with French settlers.) After a few carefree hours of imbibing from the ship's stores, the visiting Caribs discovered they were about to be hijacked and taken as slaves. They all dived overboard and after making it to shore, called in tribal friends from some neighboring islands. The few settlers surviving the resulting massacre fled to Montserrat.

The first permanent colony in the Lesser Antilles was established by an Englishman, Sir Thomas Warner, who brought his group of twenty-three colonists in 1623 to Sandy Point in St. Kitts near what is now known as Old Road. Soon a French adventurer named Pierre D'Esnambuc was shipwrecked in the vicinity. Although Sir Thomas had already made friendly overtures to the Carib *cacique* Tegreman for peaceable coexistence with his people, Warner contrived to arrange with D'Esnambuc to divide the island between British and French. Tegreman appealed to fellow Caribs in Dominica, who sent a battalion of two thousand war-ready braves. It is alleged that when a Carib maiden called Barbe, who was living with one of the English settlers, alerted him to the plot, the utter destruction of her kinsmen by French and English troops was the result. The scene of the battle was Bloody River, which one may visit peacefully today. It flows near St. Thomas Church at Old Road, where Sir Thomas Warner is buried.

Considering the history of encounters between French and Caribs in the eastern islands, one would not have expected the Indians to trust them any more than they did the English.

In 1650 a French capitalist-adventurer named du Parquet, having purchased three eastern Caribbean islands from the European trading company that claimed to own them, landed on Grenada with two hundred colonists. Since the resident Caribs had not been aware of the transaction, du Parquet traded a few gimcracks and some liquor for their consent that he start a colony.

Taking off for Martinique, another of his purchases, he left his nephew in command. The Caribs began to reconsider and to harass the intruders. An SOS from the nephew to du Parquet brought a rescue company of three hundred soldiers, who quickly destroyed all but forty of the Carib population.

A pantheon of gods and spirits may be found carved on the rocks of almost every island in the Caribbean. Many images, such as these in southern Basse Terre, Guadeloupe, have rays springing from their heads.

Faced with capture and slavery, the surviving forty climbed to a three-hundred-foot seaside cliff and plunged over to the rocks below. The spot has since become known as *Morne des Sauteurs*, The Carib Leap, and may be reached today from the village of Sauteurs on the northeastern coast.

Aside from recent archaeological investigations, such stories, which have assumed the quality of legend, are about all we have left of the Carib peoples. Unlike the Arawaks they had few champions among the Europeans, even counting those who sided with them temporarily. This is understandable; they fought for three centuries to retain their rights in the only way they knew, with uncompromising savagery. Some of their women who did consort with the newcomers achieved a bit of revenge by giving them a local form of gonorrhea, which returning settlers transferred back to the old country, but it is probable that the irony of this was lost on the Caribs. By the end of the eighteenth century only a few were left.

However, on St. Vincent during the years of great sugar-based prosperity, something new was added to the Carib story. It is partly told on a tombstone embedded in the floor of the Anglican cathedral in Kingstown:

ALEXANDER LEITH
Born June 4th 1753
And died February 14th 1798
He lived highly respected and beloved
For his integrity and humanity
And died most sincerely regretted
His death was occasioned by the great
Fatigue he endured during the Carib War
In which as Colonel of the Militia
He bore a distinguished part
The Carib Chief Chattawar
Falling by his hand

This eloquent memorial to a gallant forty-five-year-old English defender of his fellow colonists against the French and the Caribs recalls a chapter that was unlike any other in the history of the island Indians. The St. Vincent Caribs had begun some years earlier to mate with runaway African slaves, presumably from local plantations. They had a good deal in common, and a new race, more determined than ever to retain their freedom, emerged to harrass the British. In the 1770's the settlers tried and failed to exterminate this new and virulent strain of Caribs. The result was a treaty granting the Black Caribs the best land—if they would recognize George III as their sovereign. But when the French attacked

It is believed that the ceremonial ball park at Utuado in Puerto Rico was used by the Taino people for both religion and sport. Its similarity to the ball courts of Central America may indicate early migrations across the Western Caribbean.

in 1778, the Caribs sided with them. Finally, in 1795, they joined the French again against the British.* The fight went on for sixteen months; more than a year later, Alexander Leith died of "fatigue."

Chief Chattawar's followers were deported to Honduras, and it is another of history's ironies that their descendants have become some of the leading citizens of today's Belize. Chattawar himself has emerged a local St. Vincent folk hero. At Fort Charlotte, which stands on a hilltop overlooking Kingstown Bay, the cannons that were turned inward onto the island against the Black Caribs are still in the battlements; there also is a museum with murals by artist Linzee Prescott depicting their saga and that agonizing last battle between Chattawar and Leith.

The determination of the Carib people to survive has persisted through the years since those days, although the twentieth-century may finally toll the bell. Aside from the Honduran Black Caribs, a few people of pure Carib strain still reside in St. Vincent and Dominica. In 1748, the Treaty of Aix-la-Chapelle provided that the Dominica Caribs should be "free from threat of invasion or interference" by the signatory countries. But the agreement was repeatedly broken, and

*The French Revolution—or its "spirit"—set off violent reactions in the islands among slaves and others of the underdog classes.

the Indians retreated to a wild section of the island. When eight of the British island colonies became the West Indies Associated States in 1967—with Dominica as one of them— the 3,700 acres the Caribs were living on were supposed to be theirs. But the Indians say that they have never been given legal title and that squatters are moving in and taking their land. The Dominica government replies that their claims are for a separatist state within a state and that Carib land tenure practices are illegal. A recent appeal to the United Nations by the Indians states that the last remnants of the pre-Columbian habitants are "entitled—indeed bound—to develop our own culture based on our history and background, along our own lines, and are entitled, if we so desire, to avoid assimilation into the general culture of the state."

Traces

Aside from the museums *in situ* at Utuado in Puerto Rico and at White Marl in Jamaica there is almost no interpretive assistance for laymen or students looking for the sites of petroglyphs and Amerindian settlements in the islands. The museums listed in the following pages are usually the best sources of information.

White Marl, described earlier in this chapter, presents an entirely different picture of Greater Antillean aboriginal life from that of Utuado. The huge grounds in Puerto Rico were used for religious ceremonies around the year 1200 A.D., and these ceremonies included the famous ball game. Now fully excavated and restored, the "archaeological park" contains the ball courts, a museum with exhibits of transplanted petroglyphs and artifacts, and landscaping using trees and shrubs indigenous to the area.

New finds, announced in September 1975, have been made in St. Kitts, at the northeast end of Basseterre harbor, which show successive occupation, probably from several hundred years B.C. But at this writing, the skeletons, shell ornaments, pottery and other evidences of various periods are being studied in foreign laboratories, so there is nothing for the visitor to see.

Petroglyphs carved into cave walls and stone outcroppings are in most places still in their original sites for those who care enough to seek them out, but alas, some visitors have been unable to resist adding their own carved initials or imitation pictures. This kind of vandalism and the carrying away of artifacts have been especially troublesome in St. Lucia.

Following is a list of places where the anonymous artists

—who may also have been shamans—have left petroglyphs, which may be simple geometric forms, god-faces or whole-body representations. Some islands include these sites in their tourist bulletins. If the island has a historical society or National Trust, it is wise to apply to it for specific information.

PETROGLYPHS

CUBA   Punta del Este (southeastern point), Isle of Pines.

HAITI   Ile de la Tortue (Tortuga), northwest of Cap Haitien; Dondon Caves, Central Plateau.

JAMAICA   Manchester: road between Milk River and Alligator Pond.

DOMINICAN REPUBLIC   Sierra Prieta Cave, Cotui.

BAHAMAS   Crooked Island.

PUERTO RICO   Salto Arriba; Upper Icacos; Capa, Utuado; Barrio las Cuevas; Barceloneta, Arecibo; East Luquillo.

ST. JOHN   Congo Cay, off northwest coast; Reef Bay in Virgin Islands National Park, and in the hills behind the bay.

ST. CROIX   Salt River Point.

ST. KITTS   Wingfield Estate; Stonefort Estate; Willetts Estate; Hart's Bay.

GUADELOUPE   Trois-Rivières and Capesterre, both on southeast coast of Basse-Terre.

MARTINIQUE   Paquemar, near Vauclin on southeast coast.

ST. LUCIA   Dauphin; Choiseul, Ravine Chute D'Eau.

ST. VINCENT   Indian Bay Point; Barrouallie; Yambou; Petit Bordel; Buccament Bay Cave; Layou; Colonarie.

BONAIRE   Six sites, four in the northeast, two near west coast. The cave at Spelonk contains nearly three hundred markings. The five other sites are at: Pungi; Ceru Grita-Cabai; Pos Calbas; Ceru Pungi; Boca Onima.

CURAÇAO   Hato Grotto near airport. Several other caves in the vicinity bear markings and carvings. Curaçao museum, Willemstad.

ARUBA   About thirty locations along northeast coast including Fontein; Canashito; Ceru Plat.

DIGS

Petroglyphs are not necessarily found at, or even near, the sites of Indian settlements. Because of the vast time span of aboriginal occupation and the overlapping of cultures, it would be quite impossible to visit archaeological digs in terms of their sequence, even if they are currently active. Again it is best to check with the island's archaeological society or museum, if there is one, or with the tourist board.

BAHAMAS   (Columbus' first New World landfall.) Palmetto Grove, San Salvador.

CUBA   Camagüey; Anthropological Museum, Havana University.

JAMAICA   A total of a hundred-fifty sites have been found around the island. Some of these are at: White Marl; Tower Hill; Institute of Jamaica, Kingston.

HAITI   Cabaret, Fort Liberté; islands of Tortue, Cabrit, Vâche, Gonave.

DOMINICAN REPUBLIC   La Romana, southeast coast.

MONTSERRAT   Tronts Bay; Belham River Golf Course.

PUERTO RICO   Villa Taina, Cabo Rojo, near Boqueron Bay, southwest coast; Capa, Utuado; Archaeological Museum of the University of Puerto Rico, Rio Piedras.

ST. JOHN   Coral Bay; Virgin Island National Park Museum, Cruz Bay.

ST. THOMAS   Botany Bay; Krum Bay; Magens Bay; Sara Hill; Nisky; Virgin Island Territorial Museum.

ST. CROIX   Salt River Ball Court; National Park Service Museum, Christiansted.

ANTIGUA   "Nonceramic" sites: Jolly Beach (1100 B.C.-250 B.C.); Salt Pond, north coast; Flinty Bay, Long Island. "Ceramic" sites: Indian Creek Museum and laboratory; Marmora Bay; Mill Reef; Nonsuch; Museum at English Harbour restoration.

ST. KITTS   Basse-Terre Bay.

ST. MAARTEN   Cupecoy Bay.

ST. EUSTATIUS   Golden Rock; St. Eustatius Historical Foundation, Oranjestad.

GUADELOUPE   Morel; The Natural Park, Basse-Terre.

MARTINIQUE La Savane des Pétrifactions, southernmost point near Point des Salines; Anse Trabaud; Museum, Fort St. Louis, Fort-de-France.

ST. LUCIA St. Lucia Archaeological and Historical Society, Castries, lists thirty-eight Amerindian sites, or see *St. Lucia Historic Sites* by Robert J. Devaux, published by the society in 1975; Museum at Morne Fortuné.

ST. VINCENT Sandy Bay; St. Vincent National Trust.

GRENADA Victoria Boulder, Mount Rich; Calivigny; Grenada National Trust, St. George's.

BARBADOS Caribbean Conservation Association, Christ Church; Barbados Museum, Bridgetown; Barbados National Trust, Christ Church.

TRINIDAD The oldest sites found to date are here. The estimate of 7,400 B.C. is partly based on changes of sea level in the Gulf of Paria. Bonwari; St. John; Poonah Road in Central Range.

BONAIRE Onima; Bolivia, north shore.

CURAÇAO Twenty-two sites. See Curaçao Museum, Willemstad.

ARUBA Ceru Noka; Fontein; Sabaneta; Santa Cruz; Tanki Flip.

GUYANA Social History Museum, in process of development.

The principal museums with Amerindian displays and information in the United States are: American Museum of Natural History, New York, N.Y.; Museum of the American Indian, New York, N.Y.; Florida State Museum, Gainesville, Fla.; Yale Peabody Museum, New Haven, Conn.; Smithsonian Institution, Washington, D.C.

SINCE COLUMBUS

In the islands, the wilds that early peoples knew still abide in more places than does the man-made habitat, for it embraces the sea world as well. Not that modern man hasn't tried to win the race for space by every means at his disposal. Whether in greed or innocence, we break the offshore food chain by dynamiting living coral reefs to build marinas and open or deepen harbors. The tidal life cycle is destroyed when we bulldoze and fill in those mosquito-infested mangrove swamps to build hotels or homes or refineries. The natural water filter system of tangled hillside foliage, when burned off to make way for one-crop planting, leaves an arid, thirsty landscape. Bauxite mines strip the red soil bare and choke the rivers; when no one is looking, ships dump oily sludge into the protean sea; causeways that make it easy to drive across bays block the cleansing flow of tides.

And not content with fouling land and sea, we go after the wild residents, as well. To please palates savoring green turtle soup, vast numbers of giant green sea turtles have been maimed simply for the gelatinous ingredient in their lower shell known as calipee, and then left to die. Island alligators have almost totally disappeared into purses and shoes. The nearly extinct Eastern Caribbean parrot, whenever it can be snagged, sells for as high as three thousand dollars to mainland collectors.

Islanders who can make a living selling these items understandably defy poaching laws, where they exist. More often there is no law against shooting doves, taking female turtles and their eggs or slaughtering rare iguanas. Even when the island hunter or fisherman can't sell his catch abroad, the perpetual need for protein in his diet prompts the indiscriminate taking of wildlife without thought of conservation. After all, the island and the sea around it are his habitat, too; he feels entitled to a bit of progging—taking a portion of what has always been his by right of birth.

He is by no means responsible for the most far-reaching destruction. Governmental haste to industrialize, to open job opportunities and provide creature comforts for those who need them most has brought the spoilage practices of the modern mainland to fragile environments that, once damaged, may never be repaired. In Trinidad the great Caroni Swamp is a breeding ground and residence for hundreds of species of birds as well as for crustaceans, fish, reptiles and exotic fur-bearing animals. The local fishing industry in the Gulf of Paria depends in great part on this wild cradle. The scarlet ibis, Trinidad's national bird, inhabits the least accessible mangroves and is officially protected. But Caroni is not a national park and in 1973, to the equal chagrin of fishermen, tourists and ecologists, Shell Trinidad, a division of Royal Dutch Shell, began running a barge through Caroni's waterways to deliver fuel gas to a bottling plant on the other side. Scientists opposed the barge on the grounds that it disturbed the environment in a number of proven ways and that it was a potential firebomb. The situation grew more difficult when the Trinidad government nationalized the oil industry;

many protestors were on the staffs of government projects.

A mediation report in 1974 by the president of the Caribbean Conservation Association, which both sides of the controversy had agreed to accept and which offered practical alternative solutions to the problems, has finally been heeded and a promise made by the oil company. At this writing, the barge continues its regular run. A national-park plan has been advanced within the Trinidad-Tobago government, but no guarantee has been offered that the barge will cease its disturbing invasion of Caroni's ecosystem.*

Sanctuaries

Interestingly enough, the first nature sanctuary in the Caribbean was established back in 1794 at St. Vincent's King's Hill Forest, and sixty-six years later Spain declared 12,400 acres in the Luquillo Forest of Puerto Rico a protected area. But nobody else in the islands followed suit for almost a hundred years, even though Teddy Roosevelt started a precedent in 1903 by designating Luquillo a "forest reserve." (Puerto Rico had become part of the United States in 1898.) The Puerto Rican area now covers 28,000 acres and is part of the U.S. National Park System as an "experimental forest."

In the non-U.S. Caribbean today there are scattered wildernesses that are officially recognized, as in the Dominican Republic, Guadeloupe, Martinique and Bonaire, but the concept of the island national park and, especially, that of the land and sea as one basic identity with multiple characteristics, is only beginning to emerge and is far from being fully understood.

The pioneer and model is the U.S. Virgin Islands National Park. It comprises 9,500 acres of forest land on St. John, most of which was acquired by donations from Laurance Rockefeller during the 1950's; 5,650 acres of protected offshore waters, including the Trunk Bay underwater trail, and the Buck Island Reef National Monument near St. Croix. (See page 71.) By no means was the park born like Venus on the half-shell—it helped that St. John had not been recently commercially developed like St. Thomas and St. Croix—and a long and complex set of circumstances led to its establishment in December, 1956 one of the beneficial af-

*The Trinidad and Tobago Field Naturalists' Club, founded in 1891, has recently increased its sagging membership to 250, largely due to its antibarge campaign. Most of the new members are young, and they are also actively trying to stop the slaughter of nesting leatherback turtles on the beaches.

tereffects being the emergence of the Caribbean Conservation Association. The CCA has gradually picked up membership of a majority of island governments, mostly through the prodding of courageous scientists and dedicated amateurs who had previously been laboring alone. Sparked by the vigorous and innovative leadership of three successive CCA presidents, Mahamad Hanif, John Connell and Edward Towle, who is also president of the St. Thomas-based Island Resources Foundation,* many kinds of conservation and preser-

Buck Island Reef National Monument near St. Croix has been preserved in its original form by the United States National Park Service, a model for other islands wishing to conserve their natural resources.

*A non-profit organization for research and conservation of natural resources and exploration of methods for achieving ecologically sound development in the islands.

vation projects are now moving beyond the dream-stage. Marine parks are being planned or seriously considered for Anegada, Antigua, Barbados, Barbuda, the British Virgin Islands, Dominican Republic, Jamaica and St. Eustatius.

Following a joint study in 1973 by the Island Resources Foundation and scientists of the Dominican Republic, a three-hundred-square-mile marine park on its southeast coast has been projected. Looking across the Mona Passage to Puerto Rico, it will include the semi-arid Isla Saona, Bahia Catalinita and the Bayahive-Boca de Yuma Peninsula with its offshore waters. The plan provides for protection of the manatee, as well as the Haitian Solenodon, giant green and hawksbill turtles, the delicate roseate flamingo, white-crowned pigeon and Hispaniola least parrague.

Projects like this eventually pay off in terms that the indifferent world considers more practical than the saving of exotic endangered wildlife. They make possible studies in tropical medicine of such endemic problems as the bilharzia mollusk vector in island fresh waters and ciguatera poisoning from certain saltwater fish. To do the necessary work before a national park can begin to be a reality, however, money—a great deal of it—is the first requisite, and nobody ever has enough for this kind of thing. Second only to money is the need to combat political indifference and commercial opposition, which are often linked.

Dominica

Dominica, with its mountain rain forests, elfin woodland (cloud forest constantly bathed in mist), lakes, waterfalls, gorges and soufrières, is threatened by logging operations and other random development. The Canadian Nature Federation and other North American groups have been giving technical assistance to the Dominica government in planning a national park program, but nothing much happened until 1975, when John D. Archbold, the American owner of a 950-acre estate in the Dominica highlands donated it to the Nature Conservancy, a nonprofit Washington, D.C., foundation. The direct purpose of this seemingly roundabout gift was to encourage the island government to designate the adjacent 16,000 acres as Dominica's first national park. And it is the first step in the Nature Conservancy's international program to persuade private or corporate owners of such land to join forces with government in saving irreplaceable natural treasures.

The Middleham Estate in Dominica donated by Mr. Archbold and the proposed national park lands are, in the

Petroglyphs in St. Vincent share a cliff
with a more recent shrine which may
have been installed to counteract the
pagan representations.

words of the Conservancy's R. Michael Wright, "a laboratory for botanists, zoologists and a paradise for tourists in search of a true, non-airconditioned Caribbean experience. In direct contrast to the large tracts of forest in the United States dominated by a few species, the forests of Dominica contain numerous different species side by side in a small space (as many as sixty have been found on one ten-acre plot). But the complexity of biological relationships, the numbers of species and the heavy rainfall (up to 250 inches a year) which makes a tropical forest a system of high biological productivity, can also be a threat when man intervenes."

Nature in these parts works very fast to recover from damage, and the forest nutrients soon get recycled into what grows as a replacement. This leaves a fragile soil which, although recently the host of proliferating jungle vegetation, becomes suddenly—under driving rains and blistering sun—"astonishing in its essential poverty, inhospitality and lack of fertility."

The direct importance of this to the average citizen is explained by Dr. Wright: "A tropical rain forest represents the oldest and richest collection of vegetation on earth and contains the ancestors of virtually every modern plant and tree, including the desert cactus. Only by saving such undisturbed forests can the evolutionary process continue and the unparalelled genetic resources contained in the tropical environment be preserved." As for Dominica, "The park and its undisturbed watershed will assure pure drinking water for the capital city and provide potential hydroelectrical power. It will also safeguard against dangers of flood and erosion and provide a bench mark—a picture of how a healthy natural system maintains itself."

Hispaniola

If Dominica is said to be more rugged in relation to its size than the Swiss Alps, the Greater Antilles have some mountains that would look fairly respectable next to the Matterhorn. The Cordillera Central crosses Hispaniola in a northwest-southeast pattern, its rarely traversed heights cutting the sky mainly in the center of the Dominican Republic. Disagreements continue to this day as to the exact heights of some of the mountains. Cordillera Central's Pico Duarte is by recent consensus the tallest mountain in the entire Caribbean, but how tall that is depends on who is talking or writing about it. One source notes 10,417;* another, 10,115 feet.†

Peter Wood, author of *Caribbean Isles* in the 1975 Time-Life Books American Wilderness series, climbed both Pico Duarte and its twin, Pico Pelona, and the altimeter read exactly 9,055 feet for both. According to Mr. Wood, their official height is given as 10,128.

Similarly, Blue Mountain Peak in Jamaica is totted up in every guidebook and official fact sheet as 7,402 feet, while Mr. Wood pegs it at 7,388. All of this may only be of interest to purists and climbers, but it demonstrates the frontier challenges that remain in the islands, even those boasting the appurtenances of modern technology. In all four islands of the Greater Antilles there are wilderness areas virtually un-

*John P. Angelli, ed., *Caribbean Lands*.
†Dominican Republic National Park System report.

touched by man. The Dominican Republic has five *parques nacionales* which, despite the designation, have no facilities for visitors and in places remain unexplored.

The national park idea, so new to islanders, who are inclined to view their familiar landscape as unremarkable, has not yet taken enough shape to accommodate campers and backpackers. Island tourist boards are dedicated to attracting those who will spend money in the hotels and shops. Travelers arriving at island airports clad in blue jeans and carrying a rucksack are immediately assumed by customs and immigration to be hippies—they still use that word!—broke, bent on pot-smoking and disruption. In the Caribbean there

The first nature sanctuary in the West Indies was a botanical garden planted in 1794 on St. Vincent. Captain William Bligh brought seedlings of edible plants, including the breadfruit, to be cultivated here as diet supplements for the slaves of the British islands.

names refer to the time when bands of Maroons, as in eastern Jamaica, harrassed the English colonists and ambushed their soldiers. Those who ventured into Maroon territory rode two on a horse, one rider facing ahead and the other looking back, just in case.

Today, descendants of the Cockpit Country Maroons live mainly along the southwestern edge of this inhospitable wilderness. The karst formations under the dense foliage result in an endless series of sinkholes and hillocks. Jamaica has over seven hundred caves that have been explored or at least counted by local spelunkers, but there could be as many or more in the Land of Look Behind that have never been entered by man. Most of the area occupies the parish of Trelawny south of the coastal town of Falmouth, with some land spilling over into St. James and St. Elizabeth parishes. By automobile it is about two hours away from the busy resort town of Montego Bay, by air about ten minutes, but in another dimension, the distance is ten million years.

Puerto Rico

A much easier wilderness experience awaits nonbackpackers in Puerto Rico, which now has parks all around the island. The largest and best known is in the Luquillo, on and around the mountain called El Yunque, a super-highway drive of about an hour east from San Juan. Massive, rather than tall, El Yunque is laced with well-kept walking trails and provided with guides, interpretive signs and amenities. If it sounds too easy, be assured that El Yunque will provide exertion enough for automobile-soft legs. The wonders of the forest and spectacular views of the eastern end of the island give at least a sense of being transported back before the time of Columbus. And everybody gets rained on at least once during a visit.

Luquillo is really four forests: the Rain, which grows on slopes below two thousand feet and is the most visually spectacular; the Montane Thicket or "Colorado" in valleys and slopes above two thousand feet; the Palm, on high steep slopes and along streams; and the Dwarf, growing only on the highest peaks or ridges. Rain forests are found all through the islands, and they are everybody's idea of the tropics: giant tree ferns, tangled lianas, air plants (epiphytes) —including wild orchids—deep lacy shadows, mysterious bird calls. In the Montane thicket above, the trees are short and gnarled; some are more than a thousand years old. The soil is a carpet of roots, mosses, epiphytes and exotic vines and flowers blooming like candelabra. Occasionally one hears the squawk of a parrot, as rare here as elsewhere in the islands now. The tiny tree frog that usually sings its "coqui" only at night is heard in the forest dusk all day. The palms above are mostly sierras shading masses of low ferns and mosses, and flowered bromeliads. The reward of strong climbers is the Dwarf forest at the top, a thick canopy of windblown trees festooned with beardlike mosses and shading red-flowered bromeliads.

In the forest are rare tanagers and hawks, bare-legged owls and scaled pigeons and quail doves; tiny fish shrimp and crayfish live in the streams and lizards or iguanas dart everywhere on the lower slopes. The Forest Service of Puerto Rico, symbolized not by the U.S. Smokey the Bear but by pictures of a handsome, rugged *guardabosque* in a hard hat, uses the park to determine the best ways to harvest timber and improve future crops. And at Bano de Oro, a "natural" area of 2,100 acres has been set aside to remain in its virgin state forever. Peaks and ridges in certain places are closed to all man's usages to protect the natural runoff of water.

Guadeloupe

Guadeloupe's "natural park" has similar forest characteristics, and the additional attractions of a soufrière, hot springs, waterfalls and lakes. Part of its 74,100 acres remains unexplored, but there are roads and hiking trails of various degrees of difficulty, including one patronizingly named "the Ladies' Path."

Running through the central section of Basse-Terre from the northwest to the southeast, the park culminates in the 4,813-foot Soufrière volcano in the south. Tourist facilities include the Refuge of the Mountaineers Club, a hostel with dormitories and a kitchen. The last time the Soufrière groaned in its sleep was in 1956; at present one can view the old volcano at work in what are called the wet and dry *fumerolles** of the Echelle (ladder), the Colardeau and the Carbet hot springs.

An excellent guide-booklet showing access roads and trails and describing the vast numbers of plant species in Guadeloupe has been published in English and French and is available in the United States through the French West Indies Tourist Office in New York.

Guadeloupe's protected marine park will have two locations: at Grand Cul de Sac Marin, the waters bounded by the coasts where the two island wings almost meet, and at Islet Pigeon off the Leeward coast.

*Gaseous emissions during a volcano's inactive phase.

Martinique

Martinique's mountain forests are the jagged Mornes du Nord, including the awesome Pelée, the rounded, low Mornes du Sud and the north central region brooded over by Morne Jacob with rain forests and gum trees all around. It is not true that if you've seen one rain forest you've seen them all. Martinique's wilds harbor cousins of the American opossum called the manico. The gum trees exude a kind of resin that makes the base for incense. These specific oddities aside, the wonderful fact is that each island's forest land has as much individuality as the place and its people. Martinique has something of the sweep and magnificence of a continent, a sense of living dangerously in itself, for which the Pelée Mountain offered proof in 1902 and the town of St. Pierre suffered in its hubris. (See ch. 3.) There was total devastation in the north; today the slopes are green and growing, as wild and beautiful as ever.

Bonaire

While the land wilderness in the majority of the Antilles is dominated by mountains and rain forests, with as much as 250 inches of rain a year, the islands off the Venezuelan coast, particularly Bonaire, with its meager 22 inches, could be settings for a Western movie. Cattle, in fact, was once their principal commodity, along with the production of salt. Cactuses grow everywhere and, on the eastern side, farms look like ranches. The great dry pans in the south are still being mined and share quarters with the mud-pie-shaped nests of the roseate flamingo. Some good publicity was given the salt company a few years ago when its officials agreed to respect the privacy of these shy, beautiful creatures that fly north to feed at their other sanctuary on the island, Washington Park.

Bonaire (thought to be a variation on an Indian word and not French for "good air") is a study in coral island formation. The dead limestone of the sea-scarred cliffs is bordered by living reefs, an underwater jungle of incredibly complex relationships. Most divers familiar with the best tropical reef locations agree that Bonaire's waters are among the most rewarding. Far less appreciated is the wilderness on land. Washington Park in the northwest, once a 5,928-acre privately owned estate, is as strangely lovely in its own fashion as the misty forests of more northerly islands. The coastline is a series of *bocas*—mouths—where the tides sough in and out with great strength, chewing the rock into strange shapes. At dusk the vista could be a Doré illustration for Dante's *Purgatory*. On higher ground there are hills, Mount Brandaris achieving all of 780 feet, and springs and lakes which alleviate the dryness; the park appears quite green in comparison to the eastern and southern shores. There are acacia, mesquite, cactuses of many varieties, including one that looks like a spiny melon and, in bloom, like a fat candle-holder. The aloe, for centuries a leading prescription for burns and constipation in the local bush pharmacopeia, is prolific enough to be farmed commercially for essentially the same ancient uses, as well as for cosmetics. Bonaire abounds in goats, iguanas, parakeets, mockingbirds, doves, warblers and hummingbirds and parrots (not as rare here as else-where) as well as the crustaceans that cling to the tidewater rocks and the myriad reef life.

Spear fishing is forbidden by law in the offshore waters. Much of the credit for turning them into a protected, if not official, marine park goes to Don Stewart, a sometime charter captain and hotelier who has organized diving for pleasure along conservationist lines instead of the scavenger hunt it has become in too many other islands.

The reef, with its various levels and functions of hard and soft corals, is a continent of nations successfully sharing a common market and protecting the populations in its midst from large foreign predators. Unless man helps, it cannot be protected from the most potentially dangerous predator of all: man himself.

The U.S. Virgin Islands

Two of the three U.S. national parks in the Caribbean are on islands (Puerto Rico and the northern Virgin Islands) that by an odd geologic coincidence may once have been part of a single long mountain range. The land-and-sea park which now occupies two thirds of St. John is a living labora-tory for the observation of natural history in discipline or simple wonderment. Here is demonstrated the vital role of the reef in protecting the shore, the interaction of waves and reefs in building St. John's exquisite coral sand beaches and the extreme differences in shorelines where reefs have been damaged by nature or man.

St. John's hills look like green shadows of people sleep-ing with arms and legs curved around coves and bays and inlets, shoulders and breasts and hips jutting against the sky. On the reefless windward shore, especially at Nanny Point, varicolored outcroppings of the original rock formed a hundred million years ago are perpetually battered by un-deflected waves. At Mary Point's northern exposure, huge boulders, the remains of molten rock extruded above sea level, line the wooded cliffs. Here are cobblestone beaches, tiny inlets where the stones are perfectly rounded. Along the park's northwestern coast, fringe and patch reefs send a con-stant refurbishment to the beaches of tiny particles from the digestive systems of grazing parrot fish and other sources on the living reef. Sea and shore life ranges from the thousands of organisms and fish in the various reef levels to rare hawksbill turtles, some of which nest on the beach, and sand flies, the no-see-ums that maddeningly attack people at the rising and setting of the sun.

St. John's offshore wildlife habitat also includes under-water grass meadows that help slow currents and filter sand, keeping the water "clean" for better reef growth. Sea grass meadows and mangrove swamps offer grazing, nesting and oxygen for underwater and amphibian life. Today's low-profiled land vegetation is partly the result of yesterday's sugar, cotton, indigo and tobacco growing. Virgin forests were cleared to make way for these crops, and erosion erased the topsoil. Some original species of trees and shrubs survive, but lignum vitae, the hardwood glory of the Virgin Islands, was in such demand for use in ships' masts during the era of sail that it has almost disappeared. The remaining trees that grew on land too steep for planting were cleared for the mak-ing of charcoal.

What is mostly seen today is second- or third-growth foliage and species of trees that were introduced from else-where, such as the wild tamarind and South American genip. Extensive regrowth has in many places become a jungle that almost engulfs the plantation buildings responsible for the wild's disappearance in the first place.

As in most parks of the United States system, there are trails—underwater too—and interpretive displays, making it easier to comprehend what the environmental relationships are all about. But anyone contemplating a visit to St. John or to the Buck Island Reef National Monument at St. Croix, forty miles to the south, will find much pleasure and advance information in the 1974 publication *Virgin Islands National Park: the Story Behind the Scenery* by Alan H. Robinson, illustrated with color photographs by Fritz Henle and others. Robinson not only "explains" the park, but reveals how little we still really know about climatic and other natural changes as opposed to those made by human beings.

Although the United States National Park System has some management problems due in part to lack of funds, the national park idea may be the best solution to date for preventing destruction of the earth's remaining wilderness. And the U.S. has done much to light the way.

But Caribbean islands with their sharply limited space and expanding populations have a formidable barrier to overcome. Commercial enterprises that give employment to the people also tend to mismanage shoreline and prime inland acreage unless enlightened advance planning has been done, and this is rare.

The ideal national park in the islands would occupy space carefully allocated for certain kinds of development and for the use of citizens and visitors, designed to conserve offshore areas, the beaches, wetlands, watersheds and forests. The prospect of this happening is obscured by numerous clouds. The fact that so many islands are trying, is a rainbow over the sea.

3

Larceny on the High Seas

They were called privateers, smugglers, buccaneers, zeeroovers, filibusters, freebooters, corsairs or pirates. Whether they were inside the law or in defiance of it depended on whose law you were talking about. If a man and his ship held a commission from an island governor or his European sovereign to prey upon Spanish colonies and shipping, his king called him a privateer, but the Spanish called him a pirate. If he was English, Dutch or Danish he was probably even worse; he was a *corsario Luterano*, a Protestant (Lutheran) pirate. And if England and France happened to be at war, which was the case at least half the time, a French privateer or filibuster was a pirate to the English and vice versa.

The activities of this wide-ranging fraternity began in the early 1500's and continued for more than three centuries. They encompassed illegal trading and smuggling, which filled a great need for colonists of all nations, and also out-and-out hijacking of treasure ships and assaults on cities of the Spanish Main, or the slave castles* of the African coast. Privateers sometimes banded together as an unofficial navy, protecting the new European island colonies against the Spanish, who didn't want to lose forever what they had already allowed in many places to slip through their fingers.

It was an individualistic, dog-eat-dog, loosely put-together tribe of disenfranchised bondsmen, hunters, opportunist soldiers and sailors, Huguenots, refugees, runaway slaves, criminals, mutineers, gentlemen, a few women and on occasion, island governors. Sometimes they cooperated with each other and, just as often, feuded on nationalistic or religious grounds. Few souvenirs exist to commemorate them, and they usually saw to it there was nothing much left of any

*Great stone castles on the west—or "Guinea"—coast were built as depots for captured Africans being processed for passage into slavery in the New World.

town they plundered. That they buried their instant assets in great brass-bound chests deep in island sands is mostly a fable kept alive by novelists and the few caches that have been found. Actually, old wells and cisterns are more likely places to find such items because townspeople and planters tended to drop their valuables hurriedly into the nearest hole as they ran from marauders bent on extracting every ounce of their tradeable treasure.*

Ships sunk during the centuries after Columbus were the real sources of buried treasure and appropriate monuments to these children of fortune. Most of them lived unbelievably rugged lives on islands and aboard every kind of vessel, from single-masted barques or *filibotes* (probable origin of "filibusters") to the prize three-hundred-ton galleons they managed to waylay. Their enemies were rough seas, contrary currents, reefs, rocks, hurricanes, government edicts and other human beings. Sometimes they were clever enough to use

*An exception was the occasion of Francis Drake's massive pillage of Santo Domingo. The city's treasure and jewels were brought to him as a ransom. (See ch. 7.)

According to his biographer, Exquemeling, Sir Henry Morgan was the most avaricious, licentious, yet brilliant commander of all the buccaneers. The old sea dog later sued for defamation of character.

these hazards to their advantage, as did piratical colonies in the Virgin Islands that settled in and employed the surrounding reefs as weapons, luring ships into shallow waters and onto the treacherous coral heads. In the much-traversed Anegada Channel northeast of Tortola and Virgin Gorda, some 134 ships lost between 1523 and 1833, lie buried in the coral banks. These have been documented by archaeologists Robert Marx and Edward Towle, who admit there may be many more.

Quite often when one ship sank, it became a hazard to the next luckless craft passing through, and the result was something like a multicar pileup on the throughway. It is known that this happened with some Spanish treasure ships off Bermuda, where robbing of shipwreck victims and free diving for underwater treasure became virtually a profession for the inhabitants, who were called "wrackers."

Spanish hard goods such as *reales*, gold or silver ingots and jewels were not the only negotiable securities heisted by Caribbean pirates. Slaves might be a major part of a prize ship's manifest, and they brought a good price in every island ($150 in most places, a bargain $135 in Curaçao). Since the slavers themselves were more often than not carrying contraband goods, a boarding by pirates was simply a case of a thief catching a thief.

The Treasure Routes

During the early days, as Spain penetrated deeper and deeper into mainland Central and South America (the Spanish Main) few hazards other than bad weather and faulty navigation menaced the plate fleets or (*flotas*) hauling gold and silver back to Seville. (Cadiz later came to be the port most used for West Indies enterprises.)

The most important of the *flotas* was the *Tierra Firme*, so called because it was the Spanish name for southern Central America. These ships generally made their first landfall at Guadeloupe, Dominica or Martinique, depending on which island was sighted first. Englishman Thomas Gage, who had become a priest in Spain and who wrote a lengthy memoir of his picaresque adventures as a Dominican missionary in the new world, described the leisurely summer passage of the *Tierra Firme* from the Canaries as a continuing social event, with passengers visiting each other on the various ships and organizing galas, concerts and card games. Groups of Dominican and Jesuit missionaries, who were on their way to service in the Indies and the Pacific, engaged in highly competitive choral singing and theatrical contests. On arrival at Guadeloupe, passengers and crews traded with the Caribs, washed their clothes on the beach (which must have been a relief after seven weeks at sea), took on water and tried to convert the residents. One of these was an escaped slave who had set up housekeeping with a Carib wife. Teams of Jesuits applied intense pressure to persuade him back into the ranks of the saved, and just when victory seemed at hand, his Carib friends attacked the beach, killing some Spanish, wounding others, while still others drowned trying to reach their ship. All lost their laundry.

The *Tierra Firme* usually headed southwest after leaving the central Leewards, called at Cartagena and finally put in at Porto Bello on the Isthmus of Panama. This drink-em-up, shoot-em-up Wild-West-style town staged a massive trade fair whenever the plate fleet arrived. Stalls were set up for merchandise of all kinds from Spain's far-flung colonies and traders; precious metals formed into wedges for transport were often used as currency. Pearls, jewels, hides, tallow, lard, dyewood, cochineal (dried insects used for dye), indigo, hardwoods—especially the super-hard lignum vitae much prized for ship's masts—and tobacco were among the cargoes loaded aboard the galleons which became successively larger each year. Tortoise shell was especially valuable for combs and furniture veneer. Cowrie shells were sent by the tons to be used in the African slave trade as a form of money. Sometimes people became part of the cargo; they were homesick planters, wives and children wanting passage on the ships that were presumably safe because they were sailing back to Spain in a convoy.

The *Nueva España* Flota—named for what is now Mexico—sailed from Cadiz at another time of the year but made similar landfalls in the eastern Caribbean before proceeding northwest past the southern shores of St. Croix, Puerto Rico, Hispaniola and Jamaica. Then it would head past the Bay of Campeche to Vera Cruz, where a fair similar to the one at Porto Bello was held.

On their return journeys, both fleets made pit stops in Havana before hazarding the passage through the Turks and Caicos or the difficult Exuma Sound to the open Atlantic. One would think that the only danger of attack on these treasure ships would come when they were heading east, fully laden. But on the trip out from Spain they carried much more than the ballast of blue cobblestones that paved the streets of San Juan Bautista and other New World cities. Because trade with any country but Spain was forbidden, they brought the officially sanctioned needs of life that everyone hungered for.

As soon as the Lesser Antilles began to be colonized by nations other than Spain, the *flotas* were attacked both going and coming by privateers, pirates and other members of the contraband fraternity, and so they had to change their habitual routes. The *Tierra Firme* began making its first Caribbean sighting off Tobago, then sailed through the passage north of Trinidad and along the Venezuelan coast past Bonaire, Curaçao and Aruba to Cartagena. *Nueva España* would sight Anguilla north of St. Maarten, then head for the Anegada Channel. If the ships passed safely through the reefs, they would pause at San Juan and then make for the Mexican coast via Hispaniola, Jamaica or Cuba.

By taking these new routes, Spanish navigators vainly hoped to avoid boarding parties. It wasn't easy, when the Dutch West India Company, for one, was paying stockholders a 50 percent dividend on what could be captured from the plate *flotas*. As for the Spanish colonists, their mother country's insistence that all supplies be brought from home and that taxes be paid on all goods, made a few deals on the side with smugglers inevitable. As early as 1552 the English naval commander Sir John Hawkins began openly trading with them, while his queen coolly entertained the Spanish ambassador as if she weren't fully aware of what was going on. Thus, as so often happens with unrealistic laws, enemy began making deals with enemy.

The situation was not eased by Catholic Spain's determination to crush all heretics, particularly those daring to poach its preserves west of The Line. The cruelty and outright butchery visited on any Protestant or even a French group of settlers or refugees discovered in Spanish territory didn't precisely fall under the heading of piracy, but such massacres did lead to violence and piratical acts in retribution. A typical revenge was taken by Dominique de Gourgues in Florida, when in 1565 he and a hundred-fifty men and some Indian allies raided a French colony that had been taken by the Spanish, shot or strung the Spaniards up from the highest trees and went on to seize three treasure galleons, reportedly tossing everyone on board into the sea. Thus, as in this instance, privateers—and often their governments back home—justified illegal or under-the-table activities on "moral" grounds.

Sir John Hawkins was an outright slave merchant who was responsible for starting tribal conflicts on the Guinea coast that produced more slaves for the New World markets, then he would ship the victims to the Spanish Main, where he sold them to the colonists before the local governors discovered what he was up to. His marketing plan made excellent profits for his backers until the third of these voyages, in which he sailed with his cousin Francis Drake in command of one of the ships. As they approached Mexico, Hawkins's flagship, the *Jesus of Lubeck* was badly battered in heavy seas, so they put in at San Juan de Ulúa, Mexico City's Caribbean port. Hawkins managed to capture a small fortified island in the harbor where he made repairs on the *Jesus*. Discovering that the *Nueva España* fleet was expected in a few days, he quickly arranged with the town officials to get supplies and promised not to attack any of the Spanish ships then in the harbor. But the fleet arrived several days early, carrying the Spanish viceroy. Hypocritical letters were exchanged between the two fleets, and while the polite ink flowed, the Spanish attacked the little harbor island, forcing the English to take to their ships, where they kept on fighting.

Hawkins was determined not to lose the gold and other treasure he had collected during the voyage and, at risk to his own life, he managed to collect it all in one ship, the *Minion*. Meanwhile, Francis Drake, aboard his ship the *Judith*, disappeared into the Caribbean, leaving his cousin to limp home, rich, but with a crew of only fifteen starving survivors. The men Hawkins had to leave behind as hostages were subjected to the tortures of the Inquisition; some were made galley slaves or burned at the stake. It was a sorry ending to a lusty mercantile enterprise, and its long-term result was that England and Spain stopped pretending they were friendly. Now

Fort Charles, first built in 1656 as one of five forts guarding the pirate city of Port Royal, was leveled in the great earthquake of 1692. It was soon rebuilt and today is one of the few well-preserved relics of Jamaica's early military might.

it was every country for itself in the Caribbean. Although Francis Drake was criticized in some quarters for leaving Hawkins in the lurch, by 1565 he had become Spain's bitterest public enemy.

As navigator, elusive raider of Spanish towns, a pirate and world explorer, and nemesis of Philip II's invincible Armada, Francis Drake's propaganda value to England was immense. His hatred of "Popish" Spain probably lay behind most of his actions in the Caribbean, although outwitting his prospective victims and winning their gold became an enjoyable game in its own right: "To singe the beard of the Spanish King" was the phrase at the time. To give him due credit, it was said that he never attacked a foreign frigate unless it tried to attack him first, and he showed mercy on the men whose ships he sank.

By 1595, when he and Hawkins, who was now old and ill, sailed through a channel in the Virgin Islands (Drake's Passage) to attack El Morro at San Juan, he was a living legend. When word spread that he was heading west to the Indies, colonists everywhere built hasty fortifications, and householders disappeared into the bush with all the worldly goods they could carry.

Sir John Hawkins died before the unsuccessful attack on Puerto Rico, and from then on, Drake's star began to set. His failure in San Juan was the beginning of a series of reverses, and he died on board his ship off Panama, where he had hoped to make one last raid on Porto Bello. Ironically, he was buried at sea near Nombre de Dios, the Panama town in which had been established his reputation as *El Draqui*, scourge of the Spanish empire.*

Feared as he was during his heyday, Drake's was by no means the only name invoked to terrify Spanish colonial children into behaving. Dutch raiders roamed the southern Caribbean in revenge for Spanish repressions at home, and their ships hijacked not only treasure galleons but entire islands. They occupied Aruba, Bonaire and Curaçao and plundered shore towns all along the Spanish Main, eventually occupying some of it. Thomas Gage described a raid by two Dutch privateering ships upon a small Spanish coastal vessel that was taking him and his worldly goods (which were considerable for a man sworn to poverty) to Porto Bello. It soon became apparent that he was the victim of the *zee-roover* Diego El Mulatto, who was himself half Spanish but was now a commander for the Dutch.

---

*Marine archaeologists claim they found Drake's coffin during an expedition in Panamanian waters in the summer of 1975.

El Mulatto had been getting full satisfaction for the cruel treatment he said the Spanish afforded him when he was a slave. In concert with a bloodthirsty friend called Peg Leg (*Pie de Palo*), his steady stream of piratical feats included the utter destruction of Campeche. The entire coastline was in such terror of sending out any shipping because of El Mulatto that it is remarkable that the captain of Gage's little vessel set sail at all. He lost his entire cargo of hides and provisions, and the passengers were stripped of everything but some pieces of eight that Gage had hidden in his bed quilt. When the boat had been picked clean, El Mulatto invited everybody to a dinner party, serving the food he had just relieved them of.

Diego El Mulatto and Pie de Palo were typical of the adventurers who gained fame during the seventeenth and eighteenth centuries by virtue of the widespread publicity accorded them in books—remarkable in an age when most people were illiterate and books costly for those who could read them. Gage was one of the authors whose memoirs were popular in Europe. Another was a mysterious "surgeon" named Alexander Oexmelin—or John Exquemeling—who had learned his trade as an indentured servant to a doctor. He wrote *De Americanenische Zee-Roovers* (*The Buccaneers of America*), which was eventually translated from the original Dutch into French, English and Spanish, and which, in paperback, is still in print after three centuries.

The Buccaneers

Much of what is known about the breeding grounds of the group of sea robbers known as buccaneers came from Exquemeling's account, and although his anecdotes were probably much changed, even distorted, by translators of the period, his descriptions of the land and the life that was lived there, his own included, are so vivid and detailed that it is easy to believe he was a gifted reporter as well as amateur naturalist.

The land he wrote about was the island of Hispaniola, particularly the northwestern section of what is now Haiti. This wilderness, which included the small offshore island of Tortuga—now Ile de la Tortue—was partially populated by French planters despite the well-established sovereignty of the Spanish. There were also many unfortunates from all nations, indentured servants who were European whites sold into five- and seven-year periods of virtual slavery. As one of these, Exquemeling wrote bitterly about the system and its cruelties.

In the interior villages were many people of mixed races: some part black and Spanish, others part Indian. Those of combined black and Indian blood, he said, were called *alcatraces*—pelicans—a strange appellation for men who were able to slay a wild hog or steer with one thrust of the spear. Squads of such hunters—"the cowkillers"—came to the aid of the Spanish at Santo Domingo in 1655 when the English forces of Admiral Penn and General Venables tried to take the capital. Discouraged eyewitnesses of that debacle claimed that the cowkillers were so fierce and accurate that their spears would slide right through a man and come out the other side, leaving a gaping hole. (The failed Santo Domingo engagement led the English forces to invade Jamaica, with the intent of "liberating" at least one of the Spanish islands.)

The cowkillers of Hispaniola made a good living from their sloppy profession; apparently their garments were covered with blood most of the time as a result of killing and skinning animals and they seldom bathed, so that anyone downwind of them suffered acute discomfort. They sold their meat to planters and passing ships, and their method of smoking it in barbecue huts on racks made of green sticks, called by the Indians *boucans*, was the origin of the word *boucanier*. How they became seagoing privateers and pirates was the burden of Exquemeling's tale.

As early as 1602 a certain Pierre Le Grand took a crew of Tortugans out in a small boat which seemed no menace to the admiral of a Spanish flagship when he spotted it on the horizon. But the buccaneers' main weapon was surprise. After swearing an oath of loyalty to each other, they sank their boat and clambored aboard the treasure ship "with no other weapons than a pistol and a cutlass each. They encountered no resistance, and made for the cabin where the Captain and some others were playing cards. Instantly a pistol was clapped to his breast and he was compelled to surrender the ship. Meanwhile, others had gone to the gun room and seized the arms. Some Spaniards who tried to prevent them were shot dead."*

Exquemeling reported that Pierre Le Grand kept as many Spanish sailors as he needed to run the ship and set the rest ashore. His successes must have helped inspire the planters and hunters of Tortuga to imitate him as they watched his band begin a lively trade with their spoils, selling hides and tobacco to merchant ships anchored at Hispaniola ports. With the money they bought arms and ammunition and with their increasing fleet of prize ships, they began har-

*A.O. Exquemeling, *The Buccaneers of America*.

assing Spanish shipping all over the Western Caribbean.

The Spanish retaliated with several attempts in the 1620's to wipe out the ranks of buccaneers on Tortuga, at the same time destroying great herds of wild cattle, the commodity that had kept the hunters reasonably law abiding until then. Deprived of their source of trade, the cowkillers turned to piracy in earnest and developed a kind of law among themselves: the "Custom of the Coast." Much has been made of this informal yet strict code of "honor," but it was actually a practical system of sharing that also took into consideratón the buccaneers' necessary adjustment to life without women. Contraband was divided according to an hierarchy, with the captain, the hunters (of the meat provisioning the ship), the carpenter and the ship's surgeon receiving predetermined amounts. If a man had lost an arm or a leg, an eye or a finger in the action, special bonus shares were awarded him before the general apportioning began. Despite such rules, French and English buccaneers were not well organized and there was a great deal of infighting among them.

They were most active in the western and southwestern Caribbean, where Spanish trading and supply ships moved back and forth among the settlements. The Bay of Campeche saw constant traffic of this sort, as did the trade routes to the South American coast. Pierre François, Bartolomeo el Portugues and Roche Braziliano (Rock the Brazilian) were three buccaneers whose exploits along these coasts were described in detail by Exquemeling, who also inadvertently revealed that these ruthless characters always seemed to emerge from their adventures either broke or in bondage or dead. In one instance, Pierre François pretended his barque was a Spanish coaster in order to surprise a Spanish flagship guarding pearl-diving operations off the Colombian coast. Following the usual practice, he sank his own boat and kept the Spanish flag flying on the ship he captured, but in his haste to escape a pursuing man-of-war, his pirates overloaded the mainmast and it came crashing down to the deck. Their makeshift rigging was not good enough to permit their escape, and François had to surrender his booty of pearls worth 100,000 pieces of eight.

Bartolomeo, the Portuguese cutlass-wielder whose portrait shows him as an archetypal villain with a wicked eye and curved mustachios, was escaping in a prize he had captured, when contrary winds forced him into the path of three avenging Spanish ships, one of which took him prisoner. Discovering he was going to be hanged onshore, he dived overboard with two wine bottles as water wings and hid in the Yucatán jungles without food or weapons. His luck held as he finally made it to a port town, where he found, as if by magic, a buccaneer ship from Jamaica. A coup of revenge was planned for the ship that had captured him; he and his new companions took it and sailed along the south of Cuba, heading for Jamaica. There, however, their prize ran aground near the Isle of Pines on the reefs of Los Jardines and may still be there. Bartolomeo and the others had to paddle to Jamaica in a canoe.

As for Roche Braziliano, he was a swaggering character who liked to live it up until he had spent every last real he had earned. His antisocial behavior became more and more outrageous with every successful raid. According to Exquemeling: ". . . he behaved as if possessed by a sullen fury. When he was drunk, he would roam the town like a madman. The first person he came across, he would chop off his arm or leg, without anyone daring to intervene, for he was like a maniac. He perpetrated the greatest atrocities possible against the Spaniards. Some of them he tied or spitted on wooden stakes and roasted them alive between two fires, like killing a pig—and all because they refused to show him the road to the hog-yards he wanted to plunder."*

Roche's cruelties may have been more barbarous than those practiced by other buccaneers, but all contemporary reports indicate that their heady sense of being above the law led many of them to hideous excesses. At one point Roche was captured and shipped to Spain, where he swore he would never return to the New World. But his word meant nothing and he was soon back in Jamaica, "devoting all his energy to every exploit which promised to harm the Spaniards."*

The most notorious of all those bent on harming the Spaniards and lining his own pockets in the process was, of course, Henry Morgan, who had Exquemeling to thank for his reputation as the most daring, cruel and outrageous pirate of all time. Exquemeling shipped on as surgeon with Morgan's expedition to seize Panama, and his published recollections later prompted the old sea dog to sue him for defamation of character.

Whether Morgan was any worse than the others would be hard to judge; being a natural leader, he found more opportunity than most to indulge in the ruthlessness inspired by his greed. Certainly his name is inextricably bound with the Jamaican city of Port Royal, called the "Sodom of the West Indies" by more than one observer. This and other such appellations were usually applied, to be sure, by contem-

*Ibid.
*Ibid.

porary preachers; one can imagine the thundering voice of doom in the pulpit of St. Paul's, calling on the Lord for retribution against the sinners of the town. The fact was that at least one of these gentlemen of the cloth was not averse to taking a tot of brandy before noon with influential friends in one of the town's many taverns. Six years after Penn and Venables took Jamaica away from the Spanish, the burgeoning city had a drinking establishment of some kind for every ten of its people.

The rise of Port Royal in the second half of the seventeenth century was a natural result of English Jamaica's need for protection against the Spanish, who hadn't given up hope of getting the island back. As a trading center, Port Royal also offered a means of making a far better living than the struggling plantations could offer. Over in Western Hispaniola, the French* were becoming so deeply ensconced that English buccaneers turned to Port Royal as a place to fence their captured Spanish treasures with local merchants and spend their money on the pleasures of the city. If the early governors of Jamaica had been against this kind of commerce it couldn't have developed, but the attitude of the time was: "Let's trade with the Spanish colonies if they will let us, but since we know they won't, anything goes."

Charles II was King of England by this time, and although he wanted the West Indian islands to be profitable, English military and naval protection was spotty and capricious. As a result, the Jamaican Establishment opened its doors to anyone who had a ship, no matter where or how he had picked it up. Even the illustrious Commodore Christopher Myngs, who had more or less official instructions to raid Santiago de Cuba as a "defense" action, returned to Port Royal with enough loot to warm any out-and-out pirate's black heart. Henry Morgan was one of Myngs's captains.

Morgan's early life followed the classic pattern of white servants in the colonies as described by Exquemeling. A young Welshman seeking his fortune in England's port cities, he was kidnapped and shipped as an indentured servant to work on a Barbados plantation. Descriptions of a servant's life in Barbados at that time make it easy to understand how General Venables could raise an army of volunteers there in 1655 for his raid on Santo Domingo. Morgan was one of those who joined up.

He continued on with Venables' army after the rout at

---

*In 1697 The Treaty of Ryswick finally granted Western Hispaniola to France and it became known as St. Domingue. The eastern two-thirds of the island remained Spanish Santo Domingo.

Santo Domingo and helped with the easy takeover of Jamaica. When the island proved to be an unruly prize, Morgan went to sea as a privateer under Myngs and later as an aide to Edward Mansveldt, the most famous Dutch pirate of the time. With the encouragement of Governor Sir Thomas Lynch, Mansveldt and his ship's company-of-all-nations decided to raid Panama's Porto Bello at fair time. The venture was mostly unsuccessful, and Mansveldt, old by contemporary standards, escaped to Tortuga to evade retribution from his Port Royal creditors. He died soon afterward and Morgan became Jamaica's top sea rover. England had been at war with Holland and France, and the moment that struggle was decided, Morgan, who had been keeping his skills sharpened by local raids along the Spanish Main, began plotting a major coup. The current governor, Sir Thomas Modyford, helped by awarding him a colonelship in the army, a valuable asset in his planned shore raids against the Spanish.

After an inauspicious beginning against a colony in southeastern Cuba, Morgan made his name by sacking Porto Bello, Maracaibo and Panama City. His excesses there were evidence that he was indeed the avaricious, licentious, torture-loving but brilliant commander Exquemeling said he was. During these adventures, however, the European chess game went on, and, as usual, the fortunes of the colonies changed according to who on the Continent was moving which chess piece. The landmark Treaty of Madrid in 1670 recognized—at last—that England had a right to the West Indian territories it then occupied, thereby making invalid all the rationalizing in Jamaica and other English-held islands that the "Spanish Peril" was an excuse for raiding Spanish territories. Some odd heads got cracked from this: Modyford, accused of encouraging piracy, spent the next few years pacing the Tower of London, but arch-pirate Henry Morgan was rewarded with a knighthood and the lieutenant-governorship of Jamaica. It was a triumph for the former indentured servant, but it also proved to be the end of his career. When you are lieutenant-governor, you don't get around the way you did when you were a commander of a fleet of buccaneers bent on destruction, rapine and treasure.

Another restraint on Morgan was the new look of Law and Order in Jamaica. Port Royal continued to be a privateer haven for those who had letters of marque or influence with the government, but everybody else was now called pirate. When Morgan returned with his new titles to serve under Lord Vaughn, the new governor-general, he found that the planters and merchants were still openly dealing with buccaneers and other questionable types. Under instructions from the English Crown, he lost no time in forcibly nudging his former companions into a more legal way of life.

So pious had he become that he gave a set of silver—a tankard and plate in the most exquisite hand-wrought design —to St. Peter's Church at Port Royal, presumably to be used in the sacrament, but obviously used for other services in his own earlier life. These pieces may still be seen at St. Peter's for a small sum to the concierge. No one knows whether they really belonged to Morgan, but it's fun to imagine them part of some cache of loot from a plate fleet.

Morgan's former cronies may have held his new respectability against him—certainly those he sentenced to the gibbet could have had little love for him. But he must have moved through the town without fear, for history and contemporary observers agree that he began frequenting the taverns, to the detriment of his health. (Anyone's liver would become a sieve if the reports about the local kill-devil rhum* were accurate; apparently it made today's island overproof

*Most of the Caribbean islands had their own versions of "kill-devil rhum." Port Royal's was reputed to be among the most lethal.

That the people of Jamaica's seventeenth century "sin city" lived well was proved by Robert Marx and his team of divers, who uncovered hundreds of silver, pewter, and ceramic pieces in their underwater excavation of Port Royal during the late 1960s. With Marx (right) is Jamaican diver Caynute Kelly.

"white fire" a soft drink in comparison.) Morgan died of his complaints in 1688 and was given a proper funeral, but his grave has never been found for reasons that will soon be obvious.

The Drowning of Sin City

As noted previously, between 1655 and 1692 Port Royal functioned as merchant port, protection, anchorage and capital of Jamaica. Spanish Town, a few miles inland to the northwest, was the nominal capital, but the island governor and most of the top officials as well as Jamaica's leading merchants resided in the city at the tip of Palisadoes sand-spit. Kingston, across the harbor, was a primitive village.

The Spanish had used the peninsula, which was a long, snakelike outcropping of limestone, mainly as a shipyard, and the houses they built were of only one story. Paying no attention to occasional shivers of the earth, the English built up Port Royal like a contemporary city back home, with houses crowded together along streets nostalgically named High, Thames, Queen, York, Tower and the like. A number of these buildings were skyscrapers of four stories, and there were impressive municipal structures such as the Custom House, Court House, the Exchange and the prisons—Marshallsea for men and Bridewell for "land-ladies"* and other lewd types. The Custom House, also called the King's Warehouse, was the governor's office and chancery court and overlooked the huge harbor that lay to the north.

Interspersed with the many taverns and brothels were places of legitimate business, for in spite of the raffish side of trade, a thriving commerce was carried on with the North American colonies and with Africa. Many a captured African tribesman arrived at Port Royal after a trip across the Atlantic jammed into a filthy slaver, only to be shipped out again for a continuation of hell in the Spanish mines of South America. Many remained in Jamaica to be sold to plantation owners, and from all that we know now, their lives were no better under the English or French.

Merchants, public officials and the clergy as well as artisans and ordinary townsmen lived in the crowded little city, presumably somewhat segregated among themselves according to class. Archaeologists working in the nineteen-sixties and early seventies have found innumerable evidences of the good life that was enjoyed by residents and the constant swirl of transients in and out of the city. Monogrammed silver and

*Brothels often served as rooming houses.

Potsherds and other seemingly worthless fragments found at shipwreck sites can be of immense value to archaeologists in learning about the past. All too often, such clues are destroyed by treasure hunters bent only on finding a fortune.

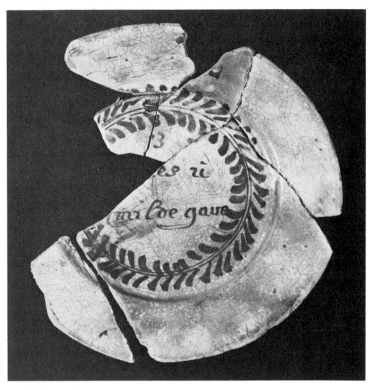

pewter flatware, fine imported porcelains, watches and jewelry, wigs, butter (petrified after nearly three centuries), liquor bottles and pipes—thousands upon thousands of delicately shaped white clay pipes.

There were several kinds of food markets—for beef, pig, turtle, fish and fresh vegetables, which were sold every morning at the wharves much as they are in many islands today. If the picture of buccaneers roistering with their wenches is the prevalent one we have of Port Royal, it may be surprising to learn from archaeological evidence that the city and its people were remarkably healthy. And although schools weren't mentioned in any contemporary descriptions, we know that there were families with children. Port Royal functioned rather well during its brief time of fame.

If the vengeance of the Lord as threatened by the clergy is to be blamed for Port Royal's short life, then He has been waging a vendetta against the West Indies since the Archeozoic era with a series of seismic slips and shifts, volcanic eruptions and yearly hurricanes.

In Jamaica on June 7, 1692, the air was warm, sticky, the sky overcast and the sea becalmed. Ships were unable to move for lack of wind, which frustrated a band of French corsairs attempting an attack on the north coast and halted pursuit of them by the Port Royal warship *Guernsey*. Two years before there had been a few alarming quavers of the earth that destroyed some property; in the Eastern Caribbean the shock waves had been far more severe.

In Port Royal the morning of June 7 progressed normally from early market activities toward lunchtime. The harbor was busy despite the weather, the usual commercial bustle clogged the streets and at King's House there was debate about the French invasion menace. Some people were already having drinks in the taverns . . .

At 20 minutes to 12, a fault in the Caribbean Sea north of Jamaica began to move, causing the sea to slosh back and forth between Jamaica and Cuba eight times before the main series of shocks was over. Two mountains in the center of the island had their tops sheared off; plantations and settlements all over Jamaica were leveled, as was Spanish Town, but because Port Royal was the most densely populated place, and subject to a tidal wave as well as the movement of the earth, there has long been the impression that it was the only place destroyed.

Archaeologist Philip Mayes, who conducted land excavations for a time in the late 1960's, says the earthquake shock caused the sands literally to flow from underneath the town. Only a small area remained,* centered around the present site of St. Peter's Church. Presumably the land that stayed above water didn't include Henry Morgan's grave.

Eyewitness John Uffgress, a merchant who was enjoying a dram of toddy at his favorite tavern when the earth began to shake, ran out to the street and saw people "with lifted-up hands begging God's assistance. We continued running up the street whilst on either side of us we saw the houses, some swallowed up, others thrown on heaps; the sand in the streets rose like the waves of the sea, lifting up all persons that stood upon it and immediately dropping into pits; and at the same instant a flood of water breaking in and rolling those poor souls over and over; some catching hold of beams and rafters of houses, others were found in the sand that appeared when the water was drained away, with their legs and arms out."*

One of the two English defense ships, H.M.S. *Swan*, had been undergoing careening at the time and may have been tossed by the tidal wave over the roofs of houses and then swept out to sea again. Some accounts tell of people clinging to such a vessel. Others note that many of those who were

*Archaeologist Robert Marx estimates the area as ten acres.

*In a manuscript in the Jamaican archives, Spanish Town. Quoted in Robert F. Marx, *Port Royal Rediscovered*.

saved were rescued by ships in the harbor, although it isn't clear how these ships avoided capsizing or being swamped. As in all such catastrophes, there were weird escapes—people trapped in earth fissures during the first tremor and released in the second or third.

The inscription on a tombstone in the churchyard of rebuilt St. Peter's church may still be marveled at by visitors:

Here lyes the body of Lewis Galdy Esq., who departed this life at Port Royal the 22 December 1739 Aged 80. He was born at Montpelier in France but left that country for his religion and came to settle in this island where he was swallowed up in the great earthquake in the year 1692 & by the providence of God was by another shock thrown into the sea & miraculously saved by swimming until a boat took him up. He lived many years after in great reputation, beloved by all that knew him and much lamented at his death.

The town's other houses of worship—Anglican St. Paul's, the Roman Catholic chapel, Jewish synagogue, Friends' Meeting House, Baptist and Presbyterian churches (attesting to Port Royal's relaxed attitude toward religion and somewhat belying its reputation for utter godlessness)—all disappeared in one of the subsequent quakes that continued to rock the city after the first, most spectacular shudder.

It was recounted that while some of the survivors were praying or searching for their families, others seized the opportunity to loot what remained of the shops, homes and storehouses. One clergyman wrote: "The dead were robbed of what they had about them, some stripped, others searched, their pockets picked, their fingers cut off for their rings, their gold buttons taken out of their shirts. So that the richest are now the poorest, and the meanest of the people are now enriched by the losses of others, which loss duly to estimate and value, is more difficult than to reckon the number of people lost."*

The reckoning has been that about two thousand perished in the earthquake, and no one knows how many others died in the aftermath of disease and violence. As for the buildings that had slid under the water, many were still visible from the surface at first; others were only partially submerged. The wrackers—many of them escaped slaves from the pearl fisheries off South America—soon picked drowned Port Royal clean.

Stories were told of sea monsters, giant squid and serpents that guarded treasure under collapsed walls, and the

*Ibid.

legends became more and more romantic as time passed. There are still people who claim they have heard the bell of St. Paul's tolling mournfully whenever the currents were right.

What was left of the town began to be rebuilt. Fort Charles and St. Peter's were restored, and the daily activities of traders, adventurers, pirates and the military continued as before, if with a good deal less glamour. Subsequent fires and earthquakes contributed to Port Royal's change in character. As the centuries went by, storms and tides reshaped the sand-spit, river drainage and harbor dredging filled the outer bay with silt, suffocating what was left to be seen of the under-water ruins. Eventually Port Royal lapsed into a dreamy period, becoming a simple fishing village livened only by its reputation—despite the presence of a police training station —as a good place to go if you wanted to drop out.

In the early nineteenth century a naval hospital was built with bricks found in the water. Although there had been spo-radic efforts by individuals through the years to explore the site, nothing scientific was attempted until 1959, when a Na-tional Geographic Society-Smithsonian Institution spon-sorship brought Edward Link, his wife Marian, Mendel Pe-terson of the Smithsonian and a team of U.S. Navy frogmen to Port Royal's waters for a six-week exploration. They used sophisticated equipment and the talents of Captain P.V.H. Weems, a navigational expert who mapped the sunken areas. For the first time the problems of uncovering parts of build-ings, artifacts—and possible treasure—could be realistically assessed. They did bring up a number of valuable items, including a watch that had stopped at 18 minutes to 12. But six weeks were simply not enough. Robert Marx, who was engaged by the Jamaican Government in 1965 to delve seriously into the problems of underwater Port Royal, ob-served that twenty years would scarcely be long enough to uncover properly all the secrets time and the tides have buried.

Two Jamaican divers and a group of dedicated volunteer restorers made up the Marx team, working for three years with scrounged and makeshift equipment, the divers encoun-tering sharks, manta rays and sea urchins, the restorers working in the drafty old Naval Hospital ruin under kero-sene lamps. As so often happens in such a pioneer effort, remarkable results were obtained. A vast collection of pieces detailing the life and times of Port Royal were mainly brought up in the underwater phase of the project including one of those elusive hoards of Spanish gold pieces. Land operations were later begun with British assistance, and these are still going on. But the land archaeologists Philip Mayes and Tony Priddy, found themselves as frustrated by water-level problems as the divers had been with the problem of silt. They had to drain the excavation areas by means of specially designed pumps. Then at the moment they began uncovering a real find—remains of a church and a longboat —real-estate litigation involving nearby hotel property forced the discovery literally back underground. The whole find had to be covered up.

Port Royal today is well worth visiting, but don't think you will find a Colonial Williamsburg. Methods of artifact preservation may be observed in the Naval Hospital laboratory and display rooms, but no way has been found to preserve the underwater walls that remain standing. Although many announcements have been made of plans to turn both the submerged section and what is left on land into a museum *in situ*, most of the present-day town remains a low-income village with its own provincial way of life. The other place to browse for Port Royal memorabilia is the Institute of Jamaica on East Street, near the harbor in old downtown Kingston. In the collection are remarkable items of ship and

Archaeologists searching for the secrets of the drowned city of Port Royal were nearly drowned as water seeped into every excavation. A well-point system of water drainage finally had to be installed.

shore life recovered by Link, Marx and Mayes, as well as reproductions of documents from the archives of Spanish Town.

Jamaica has taken great care to preserve valuable documents that have helped in reconstructing a portrait of pre-1692 Port Royal, as well as other historic places in Jamaica and the Caribbean. For instance, much of what we know about Henry Morgan after he became respectable, and of the crackdown on piracy at Port Royal, is found in laws and letters. One such document was an egregiously hypocritical letter Morgan wrote to the secretary of state in London in 1682.

La Trompeuse

In his letter Morgan said that the Protestant commander of a ship, *La Trompeuse*, which belonged to the King of France, wanted to settle in Jamaica to escape religious persecution at home. Morgan claimed that he had insisted that if Captain Paine were allowed to settle in Jamaica he would have to take an oath of allegiance and naturalization papers (how times had changed!), and that he would have to send his ship back to France. He concluded: "If I have done amiss I hope my good intent will excuse me; if the French Captain has wronged anyone (which I am not aware of) his estate is here to make good."*

That was the start of a pirate tale that took *La Trompeuse* to Honduras, Hispaniola, the coast of Venezuela and West Africa and eventually to the harbor of Charlotte Amalie, St. Thomas. Shortly after Morgan penned his letter, two Port Royal merchants hired the frigate to pick up logwood in Honduras, but it was waylaid by Jean Hamlin, a French filibuster captain, and his brethren, and turned into a man-of-war. After that, according to the Jamaican governor, Sir Thomas Lynch, *La Trompeuse* took "seven or eight of our vessels, barbarously used our men, put a full-stop to our trade, and compelled the men of war to set out. A sloop came in yesterday from Antigua and Tobago that was captured by her and robbed of all. There are a hundred and twenty desperate rogues on board her, 20 or 30 of them English."*

Why Captain Peter Paine was blamed for all this is not clear, but he was shipped to French Hispaniola and then to

*Quoted in Isador Paiewonsky, *La Trompeuse in the Harbour of St. Thomas.*

*Ibid.

France and probably prison. It was Jean Hamlin and his great and good friend Gov. Adolph Esmit of the Danish Virgin Islands who were the leading players in the *La Trompeuse* drama from then on. Henry Morgan seems not to have been blamed in any way for harboring the ship in the first place.

During the next year Lynch claimed that pirates were swarming all over the Western Caribbean and that *La Trompeuse* alone had captured sixteen to eighteen ships. He sent out two naval vessels after her, one of them the *Guernsey* (the same ship that nine years later was on patrol against the French at the time of the earthquake).

But Jean Hamlin and his illegally acquired flagship proved a damned elusive pimpernel. Governor Lynch's fury may be imagined when his captains, with two hundred men aboard each pursuing frigate, failed to find the pirate ship, which was apparently dealing with offshore settlements along Hispaniola just as the buccaneers had done in years past with the tacit cooperation of the Jamaican establishment. Only now it was against Jamaican law, and English—not Spanish—ships were the unwitting prizes. On February 22, 1683, Lynch wrote to the Secretary to Lords of Trade and Plantations in London:

"Our frigate, I doubt not, will make an end of *La Trompeuse* if she has not already done it, for six or seven vessels which have come during the last three days from the coast report that they saw nothing of the pirate. To ensure the destruction of *La Trompeuse* and sow dissention among the pirates, I have sent Captain Coxon to offer to one Yankey [slang for Dutch pirate] men, victuals, pardon, naturalization and 200 pounds in money to him and Coxon if he will go after *La Trompeuse*."

Meanwhile, the *Guernsey* spent three months trying to catch up with Hamlin, who had apparently paused in St. Thomas before sailing on for Barbados. In desperation, the governors of Jamaica and the Leewards pleaded for help from the British government and were rewarded with the arrival in St. Thomas of the frigate H.M.S. *Ruby* whose Captain, Richard May, must have suspected from the beginning that Governor Esmit in St. Thomas was playing profitable games with Jean Hamlin. Meticulously correct but pointedly worded letters passed back and forth between May and Esmit, whose choice of those on whom he bestowed hospitality was becoming an increasing source of worry among the English officials in Nevis, St. Kitts and Antigua as well as Jamaica.

Captain May didn't find *La Trompeuse*, which was next

thought to have departed for the Gold Coast of Africa, where she was joined by cronies and her command began increasing the fleet of marauding ships by taking prizes. By this time she was armed with 30 guns and 120 men, and did not miss a single opportunity to relieve Jamaica-bound slavers of every bit of gold and provisions her masters could lay their hands on. Hamlin was described as having used thumbscrews and much worse to persuade crew members of the captured ships to reveal the whereabouts of treasure. The pirates would strip a captured ship of anything they could use, including slaves, fittings and sometimes skilled members of the crew. After a particularly rich series of raids, Hamlin would scurry back to St. Thomas, where, according to one witness, Governor Esmit "sent refreshments to the pirate, who, in return sent silks and satins and arranged with him a private signal."*

Sometimes, during working hours, *La Trompeuse* flew French colors; at other times the "King's jack and pennant like an English man-of-war" enabled her to draw near her prey before she was found out, to the horror of all who realized too late she was the dreaded pirate. Jean Hamlin and his cohorts went on with the Africa-St. Thomas run, bagging seventeen ships off the Guinea coast until July 30, 1683, when Capt. Charles Carlile arrived before the port of St. Thomas in the H.M.S. *Francis*, two days after *La Trompeuse* had been received as usual into the harbor by signal to the governor.

Captain Carlile's log reads in part:

"The pirate fired at me and the castle ashore also. Stood off. Sent a boat ashore with a letter from Governor Stapleton [Nevis] to the Governor [Esmit] desiring his assistance." Apparently, a shot was fired from shore against the English ship, because Carlile sent a protest letter to Esmit, while, as he noted in his journal, he "Made all haste to prepare fireworks hoping to burn the pirate this night before she could be moved up into the bay. Letter from the Governor inviting me ashore on business. He had a great mind to get me ashore and in custody before the pirate's consort, which is daily expected, should come in. He sent me a present of fresh meat and an invitation to dine with him tomorrow. Got my fireworks fixed to burn the pirate tonight. At 7 P.M. shoved off in the pinnace with nine men, towing another boat with five men more. The pirate discovered us before we reached them; we exchanged shots with them and then boarded and took possession. The crew escaped. Fired her in several places and lay on our own oars close by to see that none came off to put

*Ibid.

out the fire. When she blew up, she kindled a great privateer that lay by, which burned to the water's edge.''*

Esmit must have been beside himself, for *La Trompeuse* was loaded with treasure, such as some twenty-four thousand pounds of silver, which he could have relieved her of before the attack by Carlile. In a report, Andreas Brock, secretary for the Danish Virgin Islands, claims the reason he didn't was that "he did not want people ashore to see what the ship had." Brock further noted that "The pirate Hamlyn is housed here the whole time in the fort . . . Esmit would not deliver the said Hamlyn to the English. Furthermore, Esmit sent Hamlyn together with his comrades and pirates out of the harbor with a barque and fishing nets belonging to the Company [West India & Guinea Company, Copenhagen]. They sailed around the island and went into Mosquito Bay. That same evening, Esmit sent rifles, ammunition and provisions overland to the pirates as well as five chests and boxes. . . . Later the pirates sailed away in the barque."

Hamlin was thought to have headed for French Hispaniola, where he could have resumed his career among the brethren. But he was never heard of after he left St. Thomas, and whether he was killed, drowned or was reformed—an unlikely possibility—may never be known. While he thrived, he outdid all the other pirates in ruthlessness, cruelty—and cleverness.

As for Esmit, the burning of *La Trompeuse* was the beginning of the end. Hamlin wasn't the only renegade he had harbored, and complaints from the British and French colonies about "that nest of pirates" in St. Thomas finally reached high places in Denmark. He had obtained the Virgin Islands governship with the help of his beautiful English wife, Charite, who was a born lobbyist and helped him at the Danish court to snatch the post from his brother Nicholas. After the scandal of *La Trompeuse* broke and his other piratical activities became known, Charite went to court again on his behalf, but failed this time and returned to St. Thomas to share his discreditation. Her letters show her to have been loyal and loving to the end. Although he was later acquitted of charges and eventually returned to his Virgin Islands post, his luck had changed. At last, when everything else had gone against him, he sailed for Europe and tried to talk the King of Sweden into invading the Virgin Islands and taking them for Sweden, but that scheme failed, and, like Hamlin, Esmit simply disappeared.

It would be interesting to know whether Esmit tried to

*Ibid.

St. Pierre, on the northwest coast of
Martinique, began as a pirate city and
ended in 1902 as a New World Pompeii
when the angry Pelée Mountain ex-
ploded in an avalanche of fire and lava.

bring up the *La Trompeuse* treasure from the floor of St.
Thomas harbor. Sir William Stapleton at Nevis wrote the
Lords of Trade and Plantations in London on May 14, 1684,
that "a fortnight ago the Governor of St. Thomas sent his
wife and two sloops away with what gold and plunder he
has." Esmit tried later to get the treasure from a Spanish
galleon sunk off Hispaniola, but twenty-six other ships got
there ahead of him and they were all finally driven off by an
armed English frigate.

SHIPWRECKS AND
OTHER BURIED THINGS

From 1492 until the middle of the nineteenth century,
when the introduction of steam power lessened dependence
on the wind, some four thousand ships sank under the waters

of the Caribbean, the Gulf of Mexico and the neighboring Atlantic. They were pirates or fell prey to them, or to reefs, rocks, storms or their own faulty navigation, and they were most vulnerable in the most traveled sea lanes off the coasts of Central America, Florida and the Bahamas. There was a tendency to steer close to land masses, and in these waters, rocks and lethal coral heads lay in wait for the unwary, for ships blown off course or forced into the shallows by enemies.

Hurricanes and heavy tropical storms often wrecked dozens of craft anchored in a harbor. The terrible 1780 hurricane sank six ships in Montego Bay alone. A gale could break frail rigging into bits within minutes, split a hull apart and sink it in less than an hour. The Spanish government kept careful records of cargo and equipment aboard the treasure galleons and their armed convoy vessels, and when news came of such a disaster, sent salvage crews out to try to recover whatever they could. But many a ship simply disappeared, crew, cargo and all, into the vast reaches of the ocean, leaving no hint of where to begin a search. After consulting Spanish archives, Robert Marx described the cargo of the *Notre Dame de Deliverance*, lost in this manner in 1755, as consisting of "1,170 pounds of gold bullion carried in 17 chests, 15,399 gold doubloons, 153 gold snuff boxes weighing six ounces each, a gold-hilted sword, a gold watch, 1,072,000 pieces of eight, 764 ounces of virgin silver, 31 pounds of silver ore, a large number of items made of silver, six pairs of diamond earrings, a diamond ring, several chests of precious stones, plus general cargo consisting of Chinese fans, cocoa, drugs and indigo."*

Although obviously only a small proportion of ships wrecked in the Caribbean area carried such a grand collection of treasure, enough of them did to make treasure hunting in the twentieth century a tempting fantasy, a popular sport and a potentially profitable business. However, the decision to go treasure hunting opens a Pandora's box of problems.

Most cultures have some legend of a serpent or a monster guarding a hoard of treasure that is under a curse and will bring woe or death to any human being who tries to recover it. For the amateur and even the professional, the obstacles to recovering—and profiting from—shipwreck treasure are as multitentacled as the Port Royal octopus, as fearsome as the Nibelung Fafnir. The techniques of modern diving should have made things easier, but they haven't.

*Robert F. Marx, *Shipwrecks of the Western Hemisphere*.

First there is the basic decision: Does a shipwreck old enough to be potentially valuable in learning about our predecessors belong to the public domain and the realm of archaeology, or is it a matter of finders, keepers? Unfortunately, people who wouldn't dream of vandalizing a historic monument on land don't give a second thought to carrying off anything they find under water. Yet coins and precious stones or metals and art objects are but a minute part of a sunken ship's total rewards in terms of evidence yielded of the customs of the period. For the historian, everything found on or around a wreck—sometimes scattered for miles in all directions—contains valuable information. The finds may be as seemingly innocuous as tobacco leaves, shoe buckles or pieces of rigging. Having no monetary value, they can only be regarded as souvenirs or trash to a treasure salvor or a casual diver, but to the trained archaeological detective they could conceivably provide an entirely new version of what happened at a given time and place.

Suppose, for example, that one of these finds turned out to be part of a ship that crossed the Atlantic to the Western Hemisphere before Columbus? Although this is a remote possibility, what can and does happen under the proper circumstances is that knowledge is gained about manufacturing advances, shipping customs, clothing, dietary habits, armaments, religious observances and other aspects of life. If all this evidence can be studied by those who understand how to interpret it, it can form an important mosaic of information about our predecessors.

Florida, the Bahamas and a few islands such as Jamaica have strict laws governing the recovery of what is considered treasure, but the "unimportant" finds that interest only scientists can easily get lost through everyday attrition: offshore wrecks are visited by succeeding waves of pleasure divers, and very soon anything of scientific interest on them is carried away. As for the long list of as yet unlocated wrecks, there is some still hope.

This is so because locating a wreck in the less obvious spots is a science in itself. In the archives of Europe's maritime countries, historians have discovered what ships were lost, approximately where and how (if possible), and what was on their manifests, and they have published the results of their research. That makes it a bit easier for the amateur, but, then, before locating a wreck in the open water, he needs to equip himself with an expensive boat and complex electronic equipment, hire experts to assist him and carry all the appurtenances of a professional diving expedition. And if he is searching the reef structure near the shore, he must be as careful of being wrecked himself as the original navigator of the earlier vessel.

After all these preparations, suppose he finds some interesting shapes on the sea bottom. If a reef is nearby, whatever is there is probably encrusted with coral and unrecognizable. It takes a trained eye to determine what should be left in place and what should be brought to the surface. If the find is out in the ocean and was wrecked by a storm, it is probably scattered in pieces on the ocean floor. If it is in shallow water, teredo worms will have consumed every inch of wood not buried in the mud. Expertise in interpreting finds under all of these conditions will be necessary, and, as already indicated, the number of experts in the field is more or less limited to professional salvors and marine archaeologists.

Stories—some true—continue to be told of island fishermen who have come across fabulous treasures while lobstering or trawling. They couldn't know—nor can the average amateur—the market value of their finds; once again, expert advice is necessary. All of this makes a case for the importance of archaeology and also should point up that it is impossible to keep a treasure find a secret.

The average wreck probably will have no recognizable treasure at all. If it was scuttled by some buccaneer in order to board a prize ship, nothing of monetary value would have been left on it. If it was a messenger—an "advice"—boat, it was built for speed and carried nothing that would slow it down. And a convoy ship carried cannon and other armaments, but was forbidden to transport treasure. Merchantmen were laden with supplies for the colonies going out, and produce from the plantations going home. Slavers were filled with their black gold, and sometimes ivory, going west; heading north and east on their return, their holds contained puncheons of rum.

However, enough treasure ships were sunk and unsalvaged to keep modern adventurers' appetites whetted. Also, with the amount of smuggling, privateering and piracy that prevailed from the early sixteenth century on, the valuables that went unlisted in ships' manifests or on Crown record books cannot be estimated. Private citizens affluent enough to travel carried their fortunes with them for obvious reasons; those moving to the colonies sometimes shipped all their household goods, since they would never see again anything they left behind. So, despite the odds against finding these items, a vast and tantalizing amount must still lie undiscovered, protected by silt and coral overgrowth.

Who has the right of salvage remains a tangled knot in

the territories of islands lacking legislation on the matter. If, for instance, a find is made and after a complicated series of deductions, dating of coins, cannon and other artifacts, and after deciding whether or not the goods belonged on a ship or were merely brought aboard from somewhere else, it is determined that the vessel was a Spanish treasure galleon—does it belong to Spain? Can the island in whose waters it was discovered claim ownership, and if so, what is the offshore limit? This too is a subject that should be explored thoroughly before any salvor, amateur or professional, sails with his metal detector in search of economic independence. And if, while touring the islands (especially out-of-the-way cays), a colorful, bearded character buys a round of drinks for everybody in the tropical harbor tavern and then furtively shows his cache of doubloons, saying all he needs to find the fabulous treasure of the *Mary D* out there in the channel is a bit of the old scratch—beware. The doubloons are probably brass, and even if he does know where real treasure is, he's not about to share it with anyone.

Actually, such small-time con men are on the fringes of some really large-scale, fully-equipped professional enterprises concentrated around the coasts of Florida and in Bahamas waters, where so many ships have been lost trying to reach the open Atlantic. A new age of piracy has dawned, oddly enough as a result of a U.S. law forbidding treasure hunting within a three-mile limit from the mean high-water mark. It supersedes a Florida State law which had set the limit as three miles beyond the fringe reefs of the coast—a much wider area—but which allowed the state to award salvage contracts within the limit to individuals.

In 1964 a sensational find off Vero Beach of a wrecked Spanish fleet by a group known as Real Eight and headed by a well-known salvage diver, Kip Wagner, had resulted in the recovery of treasure worth six million dollars. The Florida legislation was enacted to prevent a gold rush from ravaging further discoveries, as happened with the Wagner find, and provided for archaeological supervision of wreck sites. But many salvors with sophisticated locating equipment claimed the state was using their information on site locations to award contracts to certain favorites. The battle raged in the courts for ten years until the new U.S. regulation was passed. What the closer limit has done is to place some of the most potentially rich wreck sites beyond the U.S. line and into international waters. Those professionals who had contracts with Florida find them no longer valid, and it is now a free-for-all.

What will be left for the archaeologists will be poor

pickings indeed. A professional salvage operator whose only interest is in treasure is not going to save artifacts of archaeological interest, even if he recognizes them when he finds them. Nor is he going to make grid maps or use any other of the techniques necessary to establish specific data about the find. Worse still, many of these people use blasting and heavy raking machinery to make their work easier. Reefs are damaged, the environment seriously disturbed and the remains of the wreck rendered useless.

It is to be hoped that, as in classic pirate lore, excessive greed will defeat the villains eventually. Already, people are disappearing mysteriously; boats are being sabotaged. Legislation apparently has only confused the issue, and the small islands that have enacted offshore limit laws have no marine police to enforce them. If a treasure-guarding monster god exists, now is the time for him to get to work.

The Angry Mountain

In the Caribbean there is, in fact, a trilogy of gods whose anger shapes the islands. The tropical storm and the hurricane have driven uncounted ships to their graves, swept across defenseless islands, leveling towns and plantations, mercilessly destroying life but shaping new land forms. The hurricane of 1780 caused major destruction throughout the eastern archipelago. Today's storms, two hundred years later, can be just as lethal.

Earthquakes, as we have seen, managed to change the face of the islands in 1974 as they did in 1680 and 1692. The third god is the volcano. When it appears to be sleeping, men farm the slopes of its cone, or build cities at the base. Warning signs that the god may be stirring go unheeded and the fertile volcanic soil offers an irresistible temptation. The district around a soufrière is often the most valuable real estate in the entire island.

So it was in St. Pierre in Martinique. The city sat at the edge of a wide bay on the northwest coast, four miles from the cloud-haloed 4,428-foot peak known as the Pelée Mountain. St. Pierre began as a haven for corsairs and privateers, a French cousin to Jamaica's Port Royal, preceding it by twenty years. D'Esnambuc, the man who had talked Thomas Warner into sharing St. Kitts with him, had come here and started a plantation on the rich green slopes. The town grew as a port for needed supplies brought in by as many as two hundred ships a year. The vessels, legal and illegal, with their captains, crews and cargoes lent a liveliness to the atmosphere. Denounced as a godless city, like Port Royal, St.

Pierre also had numerous churches. The Jesuits were prominent, and a school for girls—the first one in the islands—was founded in the 17th century by Ursuline nuns. St. Pierre came to be called the money box of Martinique and throughout the seventeenth century vied with Fort-de-France in the south for the right to be the island's capital.

In the early 18th century as the era of piracy began to fade, St. Pierre became a center for intellectuals and artists as well as for first families. Its climate was healthful. The town's huge cobbled square, the Place Bertin, had graceful fountains and landscaping. There was a handsome theater three stories high with a facade of seven arches formed by ionic columns in bas relief; twin curved stone stairways with wrought-iron railings led to the entrance gallery. Troupes of players were imported from France to entertain the elite.

Throughout the city there were tree-shaded walks, and in 1803, magnificent botanical gardens were planted on the Ursuline estate. By 1900 the former pirate port had developed into a gem of French civilization with a sophistication rare in the West Indies and an increase in population from about two thousand in 1660 to almost thirty thousand. Its cultural amenities were supported by the surrounding sugar estates, and it had fifteen rum distilleries, a foundry and a large cooperage. The bay was always filled with ships.

Until 1792 everyone had thought Pelée was an extinct volcanic crater. No one knew then that it had erupted and buried a Carib village hundreds of years before,* and when on January 22, sulfur spewed out of a series of holes, burning trees and spreading a horrid odor throughout the area, people were curious but not particularly uneasy. The god, in fact, was only turning over in his sleep and didn't stir again until August 6, 1851. This time he groaned and coughed and sent ashes down on St. Pierre and Le Prêcheur further up the coast, then settled down again for another forty-eight years.

It was in 1899 that signs of rage—sulfur flames—appeared above the crater, which had a diameter of three thousand feet. The fires increased in size for the next three years, and on April 24, 1902, a pillar of black smoke rose into the air. It was awe-inspiring and exciting; for miles around people watched the phenomenon as it changed from day to day as if it were a marvelous entertainment; some even hiked to the peak to have a closer look. The big crater filled with boiling water and birds were found dead in the sea. Ash began raining on St. Pierre, and on May 4, the Rivière

*Remains of the Carib settlement were found recently by archaeologists.

Blanche, which coursed down the slopes, overflowed, breaching the dam and sending an avalanche of mud and rocks to the shore. In its relentless sweep, it buried the Guerin sugar factory and killed twenty-five people.

St. Pierre and the surrounding countryside were now becoming blanketed by choking ashes and the rivers were all overflowing. Still, most people, including the island's governor and other responsible officials, believed St. Pierre was a safe place to wait out the emergency. Many country people hurried into town to take refuge. Each day the mountain produced a new spectacular event. On May 7 an explosion like a giant bomb sent huge chunks of fiery rock into the air; the crater was giving away. By the next morning a shaft of inky smoke rose out of the mountain. At two minutes after eight an explosion with the intensity of an atom bomb split the mountain top into bits, and the mushroom cloud enveloped everything on the southwest slope to the sea: all of St. Pierre and everyone in it except for one man, a prisoner in a dungeon named Ludger Sylbaris.

Those who were aboard ships in the bay or who had the foresight to take refuge in small boats were the unhappy witnesses of a tragedy swifter and more destructive than the Port Royal earthquake. The deadly black and burning cloud, laced with lightning streaks, had killed twenty-eight thousand people, among them the governor and his lady, in the space of three or four minutes. On the mountain top it left a "needle," a chimney rising almost five thousand feet above the crater top.

During the summer the volcano continued to be sporadically active, sending another destructive burning cloud down the opposite slope to kill more thousands who had no place to hide from the terror. After that, until October 30, 1904, Pelée sputtered for a while, then retired for another twenty-seven years. In 1929, the mountain awakened in as vindictive a mood as ever, but this time the fury of the burning cloud was expended directly into the sea. The last time there has been any sign was in 1933. If the fifty-year cycle of activity in the past has any significance, it may soon be time for a new Pelée watch. The story of St. Pierre also may give pause to other islands whose soufrières are "extinct," for in 1902, the volcano of St. Vincent also had a nightmare. Not much has been written about this catastrophe because it didn't destroy a beautiful city, although it did claim almost two thousand souls.

People began to return to the ruins of St. Pierre, as people do after a war—and the town looked as if it had indeed been targeted by an atomic explosion. Stumps of trees and shells of buildings were a kind of visual foreshadowing of Hiroshima. Today St. Pierre is a museum of sorts, with its ruined theater and remains of other buildings as evidence of its proud past. There is also a collection of weird mementos of the volcano's incredible deeds: twisted glass, stone turned to glass, items saved from the rubble.

Since the disaster, the subtropical greenery has grown lush again, covering the slopes of the mountain with velvet. In St. Pierre, new buildings have sprung up among the ruins and in the harbor fishermen put out to sea at dawn as they have always done. But like Port Royal, St. Pierre is a town living on memories, no longer identifiable as its former self.

4

The Great House on the Hill

Crumbling masonry walls whose gaping doorways afford a glimpse of the cobalt sea beyond; broken roof beams with the soft wind sighing through; remnants of field-stone fences sprouting weeds or split apart by strangler fig and liana; ruined round brick towers silhouetted against the sunset sky —these are the ghostly testaments of the islands, romantic and beautiful, speaking silently of nearly three centuries of European devotion to Profit.

Before and reaching into the Industrial Revolution, profit was the goal and mover of peoples, the motive for travel and conquest, for ruthless political maneuvering and the relentless oppression of others and for the construction of a remarkable collection of aesthetically and functionally perfect buildings. Profits extracted from the islands were totted up in the account books of European mercantile companies, seagoing traders and privateers, town merchants and country planters and even in the books of an ancient fraternal order.*

Almost every maritime nation of Europe formed its own "West India Company," usually chartered by the Crown, which might also be a major shareholder. Sometimes the company would occupy entire islands for its enterprises and settlers, as did the Danish West India and Guinea Company in St. Thomas in 1672 and St. John in 1694. In this case, the corporate name revealed the company's labor policy as well, for "Guinea" was the common word for the coast of West Africa and included what is now Ghana, gateway for the slave trade.

A profit could only be made if overhead costs were kept down. Mining, cattle or agricultural land was acquired by colonists gratis at first, courtesy of the aboriginal inhabitants. But it was costly getting out to the islands, and every

*For a time in the seventeenth century the Knights of Malta owned St. Croix.

piece of equipment and the barest requirements of life had to be imported. Jungle had to be cleared, trees felled, woodwork hewn, every foot of stonework fashioned by hand. If island goods were to be shipped abroad on a vast enough scale to be profitable, a low-cost, malleable work force was a prime requisite. This came to be true on the southern colonial plantations of the American mainland as well, but the institution of slavery—all-pervasive as are its leftover effects today—did not then geographically involve the lives of everyone in the United States, but in the islands its influence was total.

It had become the way of life there in 1492 when the first Spanish explorer realized he could enslave an Indian. Christian Spain was at that time finally ridding itself of a long Moorish occupation; it was accustomed to Moslem slave practices, and the triumph of Christian rule didn't change the economic facts of life in its New World colonies. Thus, before the Indian work force in its island and mainland colonies began to give out, it already had another to replace it. The slave trade in Africa had been launched in the fifteenth century by Portuguese mariners.

A CRY OF LIFE

To insure its Western Hemisphere colonial monopoly, the Spanish Crown began awarding contracts to certain slave traders who were often financed by the affluent Dutch. The holder of such a contract, an *asiento*, was supposed to have exclusivity in the islands, but pirates and privateers soon appeared on the scene, and when other European nations began establishing island colonies, they too depended on the slave traders. Well into the nineteenth century, these slavers controlled the fate of sixty to a hundred million people uprooted from the African continent.

How many of them perished during the "middle passage"—the horrendous journey from the Guinea coast to the New World—is not known. Slave ships were packed to the gunwales with human beings in neck or ankle chains. Often they were forced to stand because there was no place to sit or lie and were given filthy food and, if they were lucky, an occasional sloshing down with sea water; it was said that one could smell a slaver on the high seas from miles away. Viewing those voyages from this comfortable and sanitary age, it seems impossible that anyone could have lived through it.

But there must have been a resistance of body and spirit, a cry of life that enabled those hapless Africans who survived to surmount the series of shocks that had begun with their capture and sale and were to continue with their enslavement in the strange new world.* There is a proverb of the Akan tribe of Ghana: "The spirit of man is without boundaries."

That remarkable resilience was never quite vanquished by the dehumanizing system and mythology set up by their masters that, according to historian John Henrik Clarke, "nearly always read the African out of human history."† Having been plucked from the ancient political and cultural hegemony of his tribe, "the African was transformed into something called a Negro," a lesser being who could always be replaced by another when he fell, and "the Catholic Church's justification for slavery was that the African was being brought under the guidance of Christendom, and that he would eventually receive its blessings."* The same reasoning had been applied to the nonreplenishable Indians who preceded him into bondage and a potential state of grace.

Under the system, African folkways and traditional means of communication were proscribed. However, slave owners in the islands and in some parts of South America inadvertently allowed a certain amount of individual expression to slip into the new life. Various tribal identifications were secretly carried through the middle passage and the transshipment camps of Curaçao and reached the plantation

Crumbling masonry walls and broken roof beams with the soft wind sighing through. The great house on Old Manor Plantation, Nevis.

*See Stanley Elkins, *Slavery, a Problem in American Institutional and Intellectual Life.*

†John Henrik Clarke, "Slave Revolt in the Caribbean," *Black World.*

*John Henrik Clarke, Ibid.

ground, which became, as the land had been back in Africa, the matrix of religious veneration.

Writing of folklore in Jamaica, Sylvia Wynter describes a "peopling of the [new] landscape with gods and spirits, with demons and duppies, with all the panoply of man's imagination . . . a cultural guerrilla resistance against the Market economy."* Although slaves were required to learn the master's language and, in some cases, did so eagerly, they also evolved a companion patois based on the required language but liberally sprinkled with Ibo, Dahomey, Yoruba, Ashanti and Akan words spoken pure or adapted to a kind of private tongue. In the English islands, words and pronunciations from the time of Cromwell, and earlier, are still heard. In the French islands, says Alfred Metraux, " 'Creole' [French patois] is not a kind of pidgin but the last-born of the Romance languages, derived from French in the same manner as French is derived from Latin."* What weren't in the island patois—which even a lordly planter could learn to

Island planters in the seventeenth century often built their homes like forts as protection against marauding Indians and runaway slaves (maroons). Few, however, were as elaborate as Colbeck Castle, believed to have been built by John Colbeck, one of Cromwell's soldiers.

†Sylvia Wynter, "Jonkonnu in Jamaica," *Jamaica Journal.*
*Alfred Metraux, *Haiti.*

"Approved models" of eighteenth century devices for the punishment of unruly slaves whose unruliness might have been anything from raising their voice to inciting an uprising.

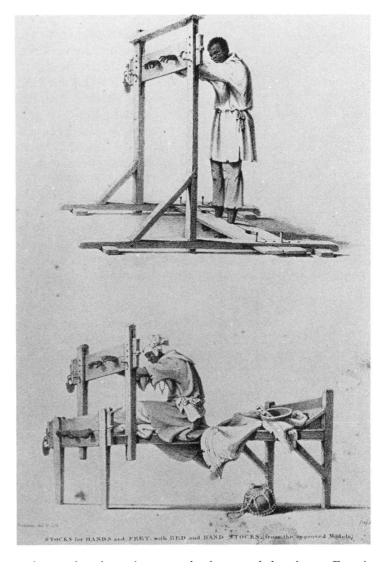

STOCKS for HANDS and FEET, with BED and HAND STOCKS (from the approved Models)

understand and speak—were the drum and the abeng. Exquisite refinements in drum techniques were developed: a female goatskin stretched across the drum base is subtly different from that of the male. The abeng, a cow horn, could send warning signals across great distances.

The arbitrary breaking up of families by slave ship operators and owners was partly calculated to break up such cultural continuity. In the Spanish islands the Church made efforts to protect the sanctity of marriage among the slaves. Elsewhere, many tales attest to husbands and wives being cruelly separated when auctioned off and nearly every slaver that put into port carried children whose parents had perished en route or had been sold off elsewhere.

Still, there were myriad instances of families managing to keep a unity, to which the sanction of formal rites was irrelevant. John Taylor, a seventeenth-century journalist, wrote of Jamaica that "when a planter hath purchased some 20, 30 or more Negro slaves, he first gives to each man a wife without which they will not be content or work. Then he gives to each man and his wife an half acre of land for them to plant for themselves . . . maize, potatoes, yam, etc.; which land they cleare (in their Leisure hours) and build them a wigwam on it, and then plant it as fast they can."* Taylor makes it all sound rather idyllic, but in a single quarter-page of the want-ad supplement of a typical issue of *The Royal Gazette*, an eighteenth-century Jamaican weekly, eight runaways were listed, and three auctions of male slaves were announced. No mention was made of wives or families.

On the smaller islands it was sometimes possible for a man to visit his woman and children on another plantation. A series of minuscule stone huts may still be seen near the salt pans of southern Bonaire. Barely high enough for a child to stand upright inside, they were used as sleeping quarters and a protection from the weather by male slaves mining the salt. Once a week the slaves were allowed to take an eight-hour, round-trip hike across the island to be with their families. This less-than-ideal situation bred more slaves for the future; it also tended to preserve fragments of ancestral cultures.

As plantations grew larger, they required more and more field hands. When forced to work and live together, people might begin as hostile strangers—second-generation slaves felt superior to those just off the boat—but because most came from familiar tribes in West Africa, the shared backgrounds eventually found expression in secret ritual (vaudou and myal), practical magic (obeah or "nigromancy"), or in music, dance and folk tales. A body of traditional wisdom developed and was passed through the generations vocally as everyday truth—"Rock stone in river bottom never know sun is hot"—and bush medicine—"leaves of three different kind of tree heal a wound." Anancy, the weak little spider born in Africa, had brought over its ability to outwit the lion. In song or story, "Busha" (overseer) and "Backra" (boss) could be ridiculed behind their backs.

Although such characteristic independence of expression survived into the mid-twentieth century, today's overlay of mainland movies, music and values may have done more to destroy it than did the repressions of the slave system. De-

---

John Taylor Manuscript (Port Royal: 1685).

Minuscule stone huts were used as sleeping quarters by male slaves working the salt pans of Bonaire. Once a week they were allowed to take a hike across the island to be with their families.

spite efforts of scholars and foundations to keep the culture alive, knowledge of the old music—for instance, the handmade instruments and cult or work songs—is dying with the older generation. The typical music that now entertains tourists in most of the West Indies is an ersatz version of Trinidad's calypso: a set of ribald lyrics stuffed willy-nilly into a set rhythmic frame that once served a practical purpose as an oral newsletter.

Their separate communication may have helped the Africans to preserve or transplant the pantheon of African gods, but everybody—slave or free man—was expected to conform to the white Christian Establishment then in force, whether it was Roman Catholic or Anglican, Lutheran or Dutch Reform Church. (There was also a surprising number of Maranos in the Dutch and English islands—Jews escaped from Spain and Portugal who could at last return to their Sephardic religious observations if the governor wasn't anti-Semitic. But although the Jews were involved with slavery like everyone else, they were in too precarious a social position to impose their beliefs on the Africans, even if they had wanted to.)

It wasn't until the Moravian, Wesleyan and Baptist missionaries began arriving in the early eighteenth century that

A series of prints showed the early
nineteenth century English public how
the sugar that sweetened their tea was
produced "out in the islands." Cane
stalks were planted in holes, chopped
with cutlasses at the harvest, carted
to the mill, boiled and crystalized,
and finally shipped off in hogsheads.

slave populations could begin to identify the Christian doctrine with themselves and their plight. These missionaries,
notably the Moravians in the Danish Virgin Islands and Jamaica, were teachers and artisans. Starting very small, they
instructed a few promising adult candidates for communion
in reading and a practical trade such as carpentry along with
the Gospel. Often they visited slave huts at night because it
was against company policy to allow gatherings of slaves for
any purpose, particularly after a devastating uprising that occurred on St. John in 1733. The planters mistrusted the missionaries, some of whom they threw into prison. "These were
perilous times for the planters, and they did not welcome efforts of the Brothers to instruct the slaves."* But the Danish
government was sympathetic, and in time, after it took over

*C.G.A. Oldendorp, an early Moravian missionary, quoted in Patricia
Shaubah Murphy, *The Moravian Mission to the African Slaves of the Danish West Indies.*

the company and purchased St. Croix from the French, the Moravians were also eventually able to form classes for the children as well as encourage their parents to develop skills that might eventually earn them their freedom.

The missionaries preached obedience, law and order and salvation after death, like the other denominations. In Jamaica they may have lost some credibility by having to depend on slave labor themselves to grow their food, but they did enable the black congregations to use their churches as places to express themselves. The church edifice wasn't Backra's—it was theirs, a clubhouse. In islands where this use of churches wasn't actually forbidden, it made the Establishment increasingly nervous, and with reason. Offshoot sects gradually sprang up around the missions and, led by self-proclaimed spiritual leaders who were slaves or so-called "free coloreds," they made liberal use of African tradition, animism and as much Christian doctrine and language as seemed to apply.

Later, the cults had a strong political influence and were at the heart of several insurrections. They also became the basis for the great religious revival movement that swept the West Indies in the mid-nineteenth century. Today the islands are still divided into Establishment churches and an astounding number of revivalist groups whose services are dominated by that strain of African spontaneity that has, in spite of all, refused to be snuffed, stamped or bred out. In many present or former British islands there are also Hindu, Moslem and Buddhist communities. Their members are descendants of indentured farm workers imported after the abolition of slavery in 1838, when the economic system centered around the plantation was fighting a losing battle.

THE SYSTEM OF SLAVERY

From the beginning that system set up a rigid dual-level society, with substrata in both levels. On top were the appointed government officials, the planters who often spent much of their time off-island, their managers (called "attorneys" in the English islands), the church dignitaries and the military. In the French islands members of the upper class were known as *grands blancs*. Merchants and traders might have formed a middle class, except that they, too, lived high above the bottom rung of the class ladder.

Wandering about in a social vacuum as time went by were the freed slaves and children of master and slave. In the French islands, Louis XIV's Black Code of 1685 decreed that a slave freed by a master or one who managed to purchase his own freedom would become a full citizen of France and even have the right to own slaves himself. These *affranchi* or *gens de couleur* gradually achieved some status as merchants and farmers and eventually even as planters and soldiers. In the English islands after emancipation in the nineteenth century a few of the "free-colored" became members of island assemblies.

However, during the heyday of the sugar plantations, they lived in perpetual fear of a catastrophe that would plummet them back into the dank hole of slavery. In St. Domingue the local *grands blancs* saw to it that anyone with a few milliliters of African blood was barred from public office or the professions. The women could not marry white men, although there was no proscription on sleeping with them and producing more *gens de couleur*. In St. Domingue, after a local law was passed in 1779, they even had to wear special, identifying clothes, observe a 9:00 P.M. curfew and sit in segregated seats in public places. As a result, they aspired to a position and culture continuously denied them and yet —like the "pure whites"—they hated and feared the great mass of blacks. Africa kept the slave population eternally replenished; by the end of the eighteenth century blacks outnumbered whites in all the islands—some by as much as seventeen to one. Fear permeated all strata above the lowest.

Slavery was not the only form of servitude in the islands, and the underdog was not always black or part black. Europe was still emerging from the old feudal pattern of principalities constantly at war amongst themselves; farmers and villagers were bound to fief holders to the extent that they were required to give military service, were traded off and actually sold. Rigid laws handed down from the Middle Ages prescribed punishments for anyone convicted or even accused of a minor malfeasance. When the New World expanded Europe's horizons, it also offered a convenient way to save jail money and populate the colonies: deport accused criminals, vagabonds, whores and loiterers to the plantations, docks and warehouses of the islands as indentured servants and laborers. Young indentured males who could read and write were sometimes used as plantation "bookkeepers"; they kept track of farm and factory supplies. A few escaped into buccaneering, as we have seen, but most indentured

Weathered circular stone windmills are still seen on hills throughout the islands. Only a few have sails still in place. This cane storage tower is on St. John in the Virgin Islands National Park.

whites remained on the bottom level. They were almost-slaves, whose lot, insisted Exquemeling, was in many ways worse than that of the blacks. Being white and having experienced indenture, Exquemeling was naturally biased, but other contemporary observers seem to bear him out. The indentured man was presumably able to buy his freedom after an agreed-upon period of service, but it was to the master's advantage to keep him in debt so that he would have to sign on again and again or be resold.

The low man on the totem pole actually had the upper hand from the beginning although he didn't possess the organization or weapons to use it until some hero occasionally arose to lead him. Slave masters were hostages to the necessities of the prevailing economy, and they knew it. In the English islands, the fear of slave revolt often forced planters to allow slaves the twelve days of Christmas as a time of carnival. Masked dancers called Jonkonnu or John Canoe (probably from *gens inconnu*) performed and begged money. Food and drink were supplied by masters to their lowliest slaves who became, for a brief time, elaborately costumed kings and queens, and sometimes even made themselves at home in the great house itself. Such freedom was brief, but there was often a subtle awareness of interdependence and mutual thralldom that led to affecting relationships between individuals and it most certainly was the psychology behind a series of slave uprisings that for more than two centuries were the prolonged and agonizing prelude to emancipation, almost invariably, leaders of revolts were trusted—and even loved—plantation headmen.

THE PLANTATION

The farms of the first island settlers in the sixteenth and early seventeenth centuries were anything but elaborate. For the most part these men were soldiers or adventurers, new at raising crops or cattle or keeping books that would satisfy the financiers back home. The owner's mansion—the "great house" that later came to symbolize luxurious upper-class plantation life—in the early days was simply a private stone fort with sleeping quarters or a glorified hut. The foundations were of local field stone, the house of wood. Or the owner resorted to his slaves wattle and daub—an island stick-and-mud plaster that may still be seen occasionally in rural cottages, especially in Haiti—and the roof might be thatched with coconut palm fronds. Spanish settlers tended to build more solidly than the early English and Dutch, but the on-

Sugar factory compounds usually consisted of a grinding mill, a boiling
house with a tall chimney, a curing
house, a distillery, and a cooperage.

slaught of other cultures, successive hurricanes, fires and wars
have almost eradicated their early buildings, except in Cuba,
Santo Domingo, Puerto Rico and Trinidad, where they had
more or less continuous tenure.

In the colonies that prospered, plantation as well as
town houses began to be more and more luxurious. In St.
Domingue, French colonists developed an immensely prosperous plantation system after the 1697 Treaty of Ryswyck
ceded the land officially to France. Profits from sugar and
cattle enriched the merchants and bankers of the mother
country; there were a thousand plantations in the fertile
northern plain that reportedly supplied as much as two-thirds
of France's foreign trade. The chief city of the Plaine du
Nord was Cap Français (also called Le Cap), a seaport with
such magnificent boulevards and mansions, cathedrals and

theatres that it became known as the Paris of the Antilles. By all reports, the great houses of the surrounding plantations were just as splendid; unfortunately, wars and time have destroyed all but a few of them.

Plantation great houses in the islands were devised to combat the year-round heat and humidity and to make the best use of prevailing trade winds that swept in from the northeast. Architectural details and decoration varied according to nationality, but the most usual shapes were rectangular or octagonal. Sometimes, a central block was the original building, and wings were added later. Cut stone was combined with wood or brick. (Segments of seventeenth-century yellow brick, brought to the West Indies as ballast in ships' bottoms, peer out of many rebuilt houses or forts standing today, particularly in the Dutch islands, which seem to have used it more frequently.)

The first floor was paved with tile or stone; it served as an above-ground storage cellar and coolant for the main floor above, which classically consisted of long, narrow corridors broken into chambers by arched and louvered interior

If the property had a stream, a huge water wheel supplied the power for the sugar factory. This one, on the Tryall estate in Jamaica, now supplies water for a golf course.

windows flanking a central doorway. If the island had enough termite-resistant hardwood, walls were paneled in it. On the big plantations, talented slaves would be taught the skills of joinery and fine woodcarving, and, as has been noted, sometimes they learned such arts from teaching missionaries.

Only a few exceptional practitioners in the islands are still able to fashion the huge four-poster bedsteads with their carved pineapple and leaf or "barley-sugar twist" designs, the gleaming mahogany doors and lintels and window sashes, the louvers that were sometimes set away from the outer wall to provide extra air circulation, the hurricane shutters and the massive but graceful curving staircases that became status symbols in the eighteenth century.* Patterns for the popular Georgian style of house, for Palladian window treatments, as well as for carved woodwork, roof trimming, and furniture, were imported from overseas and adapted by the island artisans. However, the planter and his family remained dependent on the old country for such niceties as wine glasses, fine china, crystal decanters, cutlery, brass locks, goose quills, penknives and chamber pots.

The main—or second—floor was entered from the carriage way by a central or twin flights of stone steps, and it was often surrounded by arched or louvered galleries. Floors were of mahogany or fruitwood kept polished by coconut husks (why has no one marketed this thoroughly tested product for today's floor-conscious householder?), and the use of rugs was minimal. Receiving rooms, the dining hall and perhaps one master bedchamber were on the main floor. Other bedrooms were in the wings or on the floor above.

Bedroom partitions didn't always reach to the ceiling, and this has been taken as a disregard for privacy, when it was more than likely another way of taking advantage of natural air conditioning. The most popular ceiling design was the inverted "tray." The roof above was pitched to form the four corners of the tray, and this allowed still more air to circulate; every element of the house's construction was aimed at cool comfort.

One feature common to all great houses deserving of the name was the dining hall, for there were no hotels and few inns, except in the towns. When planters or other *grands blancs* traveled about their islands, they depended on plantation hospitality for social diversion. If you went calling out-

*UNESCO conducts a program of instruction to assist artisans in learning some of these ancestral skills. A few island national trusts and historical foundations are attempting to pioneer similar programs.

side your own property, you might stay as long as two or three weeks at other people's great houses, no doubt comparing their grandeur with your own. Balls and garden parties were given, marriages were arranged—how else could prestigious families unite and keep the system going?—assignations were plotted, hunting parties organized, political decisions made and vast quantities of wine and food consumed.

So it is possibly surprising to discover how primitive the kitchen of the average great house was until one realizes that inconvenience wasn't the master's concern. In non-Spanish islands the kitchen compound was always separate from the main house, far enough away so that the heat and odors of the cooking wouldn't offend the master's nostrils; and there were many hands to transport the trays of food to the great house dining hall. There was a brick bake oven for breads and another for meats, a smokehouse, a "buttery" for storage of perishables and, sometimes, quarters for house servants. As for other amenities, by the mid-eighteenth century a few affluent and fastidious property owners had begun installing baths made of tin or zinc, but for everybody the outhouse was a long walk by lanternshine out beyond the provisions garden.

Also well away from the great house were the slave huts, occupied by couples and their children if the master was of a mind to permit nuclear families. Eighteenth-century prints show some of these huts set into grid-pattern communities or simply scattered at random where convenient. Indentured servants had accommodations nearby that were little better, if as good, and some estates maintained hospitals for their slaves. Being a sort of city-state, the property had to provide for death as well as taxes. Although some members of planter families were laid to rest in town churchyards, the gravestones and monuments there are more often of town people, Yankee ship captains, merchants and their children dead too soon, and their wives lost in childbirth. The principal plantation family tombs are still to be found on the old properties along with those of slaves and mistresses and children of the master's extramarital unions, albeit arranged for eternity according to rank.

Depending on the topography and climate of the island, exports from the plantations might include hides and tallow, dyewood, indigo, cocoa, cotton and spices, and the North American colonies were the English islands' principal market for these products. But it was the European demand for sugar that brought the prosperity that inspired the derisive description of a planter flaunting his new wealth on the continent: "rich as a Creole." Nevertheless, sugar profits built impressive town houses in London and Bath, in Paris, Nantes and Bordeaux. Edward Moulton-Barrett's house on Wimpole Street, where his daughter Elizabeth received Robert Browning, was probably financed by the Cinnamon Hill Estate in Jamaica. Barrett was born there, but returned to England and left the management of the family properties to his brother, Sam, who managed well.

Sugar could be grown in almost any type of soil, on hillsides as well as flat lands if there was enough rainfall or the means to irrigate. When the mid-eighteenth-century sugar boom came, planters with foresight either bought or wangled additional acreage and expanded, sometimes working as many as five separate estates at a time. In St. Kitts the saying went, "What I can see is mine and the rest belongs to my son."

Production of sugar demands that the processing of cane be accomplished as soon after harvesting as possible to retain the cane's high glucose content. This meant that the "factory" had to be near the fields. Ideally, it would also be close to running water but, failing that, at least in a spot where

The partially restored great house on the Dallas plantation in Jamaica. In the eighteenth century, Alexander Dallas migrated to the United States and became secretary of the treasury. George Mifflin Dallas, his son, was vice-president during the Polk administration, and the city in Texas was named for him.

prevailing winds would turn a mill. Sometimes grinding power was provided by mules or men; when it was the latter, a great many slaves were required. Harvesting and planting usually took place during late winter or early spring after the feathery stalks had matured and turned the empty fields into a dense, impenetrable-looking mass of green twice the height of a man. Old pictures show crude two-wheeled carts hauling away the disorderly cane shafts after they had been chopped down with machetes* by field hands, many of whom were women. Always on the watch over field hands, called the "great gang" was an overseer, usually astride a mule and probably armed. Replanting was done by "holeing" tops of harvested stalks into a series of framed squares.

Most of the time the cane had to be wheeled over primitive roads to the sugar works, but on one mid-eighteenth-century estate near Falmouth, Jamaica, a sophisticated transport system took advantage of contours of the land. An almost perpendicular, two-hundred-foot cut-stone chute ran from the fields to the factory, which had been built on a lower level. It had a flight of narrow stone steps on both sides where slaves stood to push stalks down the "shooter."

Factory compounds usually consisted of a grinding mill; a boiling house with a tall chimney; a curing house for the brownish raw sugar crystals and vats of molasses; a rum distillery; and a cooperage where hogsheads were built and equipment repaired. If the property had a stream, a huge

One of the most impressive of Barbados' many ruins is the massive great house at Farley Hill National Park. Rebuilt in 1861 for the use of the Duke of Edinburgh, a recent fire turned it into a ruin again.

*They were called "cutlasses" in the English islands.

Delicate iron work, carved wood, brick, and tiles add grace to a classic West Indian house with balconies, tray roof, and breezeways providing natural air conditioning. This one is at Moule, Guadeloupe.

water wheel supplied the power. Water was fed from an aqueduct made of faced stone* and usually arched. One way of locating the ruins of an old sugar estate today is to look for remnants of aqueducts. Another way of spotting the site of an old sugar works is to look for the ruins of weathered circular stone windmills with steps leading to the machinery room halfway up one side. Windmills are to be seen on hills and plateaus all through the islands; a few are in fair shape with sails still in place, especially in Barbados, where the National Trust has done restoration work on some of the old estates. (See also Great Houses, St. Croix, in this chapter.)

The growing cycle of sugar cane involves a full year, and where the soil is rich, a single planting may renew itself for several harvests before the quality decreases. This factor meant more profits with less manpower for a planter dependent on slave labor, but he had no field machinery and constant weeding of grass and leafy plants had to be done by hand. The fields were fertilized by farm-animal manure, which produced a rich crop of such weeds, and a second or third gang of field hands did this job. Also working outdoors were cartmen, drivers, mulemen, loaders and cooks, all under the eye of the headman, who was, in most cases, himself a slave.

When the cane arrived at the factory, another set of hands went to work feeding it into a machine that consisted

*"Faced" was an island word for stone blocks cut with a rough facing.

of three geared rollers, one of which turned the others. The juice was squeezed out into a sluice that took it into the boiling house. Here, in what could have served as a sauna (except that everybody was fully clothed, including the managers in their European morning coats and felt hats), the cane liquor was heated in huge copper bins. Boiling-house workers stoked the fires with bagasse—cane trash—and kept the liquid constantly stirred. As its water evaporated into clouds of steam, the liquid became crystallized, and while it was cooling, molasses was extracted and some of it was set aside for distillation into rum. Finally, when the muscovado —the rough-textured, brownish raw sugar—was ready for shipping, it was transported in kegs* to a nearby town dock or to a beach where the kegs were rolled into dinghies and ferried through the surf to a waiting ship. All of this additional activity required the services of carpenters, coopers, tinsmiths, masons, porters, saddlers, weavers, blacksmiths and bookkeepers.

Since life revolved around the king of crops, it should not be surprising that sugar-works buildings were often magnificent architectural achievements. Except for fortresses, a few public buildings and churches, more care was put into their design and construction than anything else in the islands. Even the treasured great house was less impressive or was sometimes simply a wing of the factory. The remains of these old castles of commerce, although in varying states of neglect and bereft of life, noise and urgent comings-and-goings, are still visually so evocative that it seems incredible that today's island governments or private individuals do not take more care to preserve them. The late architect-historian T.A.L. Concannon described such a ruin on the Kenilworth Plantation in the wooded hills of Jamaica's Hanover parish as "a striking and arresting building with its monumental flight of stone steps to first floor level, elliptical openings to wheel-shaft, and Palladian style range of three-light windows of the main upper wall. The connecting aqueduct, roof and interior timbers have gone, and limestone dressings to windows have in some areas badly eroded almost to the point of disintegration; but in general this superb structure has stood the test of time to emerge a silent but handsome witness to excellent craftsmanship, and [an] outstanding museum-piece in Jamaica's industrial history and a prime specimen of the country's architectural heritage."*

*Sugar kegs were always measured in the accounting as hogsheads, whereas rum was measured by the puncheon.

*T.A.L. Concannon, "Kenilworth Ruins," *Jamaica Journal*.

The care taken in the building of the Kenilworth works seems to have been typical throughout the islands: massive, half-circular stone steps, walls in dressed stone, sometimes a beautiful pink coral or combinations of brick and brain coral protected by tinted plaster, fine detail in the quoins and dressings, graceful window and door treatments. These sugar factories might well have been mansions; certainly their architecture had none of the dreariness associated with the word factory today. What went on inside was another matter.

Such mute shells, filled with the compost of past centuries and the beer cans, bottles and plastic junk of the present, are but one way to evoke those years. The slaves supposedly left little or nothing behind relating their part in the drama, but they built the factories and great houses and cobbled roads and stone fences, and these remnants are their legacy as surely as the children they begat. Other telltale bits of their lives are continually being found: Caches of blue glass—"barter beads" that served as money for those who had none—were discovered recently in a half-submerged ruin called Crook's Castle on St. Eustatius; pottery, hand thrown and decorated by slaves for their own use has been unearthed in Jamaica. Nor were such people anonymous. Burial stones,

Large sugar estates in the islands had their own hospitals for slaves, although doctors were scarce and sometimes traveled for miles from one plantation to another. This hospital at Orange Valley, Jamaica, was more impressive than the great house itself.

no mention of it in late seventeenth-century records, his "castle" is something of an architectural mystery.

Whatever the period of its construction, it is today a startling apparition: the shell of a huge H-shaped building of dressed limestone with reddish brindled brick quoins. The front, rear and both sides were terraced with balconies alternating with rooms, which at the corners formed towers. Two of these towers had rooms roofed over with brick tunnels and outside stair entrances, and were perhaps used as cells for any maroons who might be captured.

The kitchen, bake oven, reservoir and "bath" rooms, as well as the slave quarters, were all detached. Most of the wood is now gone, but the big main rooms were once paneled in hardwood. The mortar used for the bedding and pointing was probably a lime compound mixed with the customary molasses and goat hair. Not so customary was the installation of a fireplace in the main house, but then even in that warm climate, the castle must have been damp and chill. Colbeck may be visited today free of charge, but it is easy to get lost trying to find it, and there is no guide or interpretative information on the premises.

Raids on plantations and ambushes in the mountains were excellent training for the maroon ex-slaves in relearning how to think and act for themselves, although the cost in lives, property and violent reaction was high. But once they had tasted independence, they never gave it up. An exception was the Jamaican maroon chieftain Juan de Bolas, who, with his personal followers, eventually transferred his allegiance from the Spanish to the English after they offered him land and command of his own militia regiment. When he led an English attack on his former comrades, they used his famous tactics against him and cut him down on a mountain trail.

From that time, 1663, until 1739, when the first treaties in Jamaica were signed by representatives of the British Crown and two separate maroon groups, these wilderness freedom fighters lived hard and daring, adventurous lives completely different from the sad drudgery of the plantation slaves. They developed heroic leaders and a body of legend that must have kept their brothers and sisters in bondage in a state of some kind of hope. But when Cudjoe, leader of the Trelawny maroons, and Quao, of the Windward maroons in the Portland parish, were finally persuaded to sign agreements of independence with the British, one of the articles required them to assist in returning any runaway slaves they encountered. Although this part of the treaty still rankles, the people of today's maroon communities—mainly at Accompong and Mooretown—point out that in spite of their many accomplishments, the maroons had no choice but to sign. Carey Robinson writes: ". . . what the English had failed to do with sword and gun against a resourceful but illiterate people had now been achieved with pen and paper."*

Maroon-style rebellion in the islands was not primarily aimed at breaking up the institution of slavery. The runaways wanted to survive in any way they could once they had found the path to their own freedom. Their kind of violence was very different from that of plantation riots, although the results were the same: Cane fields, factories and great houses were burned, supplies and armaments looted, planters' families murdered. The 1733 riots in St. John, the Curaçao uprising of 1750 and the islandwide rebellion in Jamaica in 1760 led by a Koromantee called Tacky were secretly planned and ruthlessly carried out even though the participants must have known they would eventually be harshly punished and killed. In St. Domingue a series of conspiracies began as early as 1679 and continued erupting for more than a century. Secret planning was possible there because maroons could communicate through the drum language and forbidden ceremonies of *vaudou*. In 1758 a brilliant *houngan* (*vaudou* priest) named Mackandel conceived a plot for the slaves to poison their masters' drinking water, and he almost succeeded. In Jamaica an outlaw called Three-Finger Jack inspired rebellions.

However, Mackandel and Three-Finger Jack were the exceptions; the outbreaks were usually led by plantation headmen like Tacky who could read and write or had at least been given the responsibility of controlling large numbers of slaves. This partially explains the planters' mistrust of missionary activity that encouraged literacy.

WINDS OF REBELLION

But there was no way of stopping the ominous winds of rebellion blowing across the North American continent. It was a white wind, to be sure, and was generated by upper- and middle-class dissidents against British colonial policies. Trading between the mainland and the islands was lively, and the island plantocracy knew very well what was going on up there. Although as colonials they had their own complaints against the mother countries, in general they mistrusted changes in the status quo and feared—as did the planters of Virginia—that the spirit of rebellion would spread to the

*Carey Robinson, *The Fighting Maroons of Jamaica.*

church walls, island archives and last wills and testaments fill in a few gaps about human relationships between the classes that made their mark in history.

One of these wills pieces out the story of a planter father named John Tharp who sent his four sons to be educated in England, hoping they eventually would fulfill his visions of a sugar empire he had begun to establish near Falmouth in Jamaica. The sons were received into society and made the obligatory Grand Tour of the Continent. When they finally returned home, the family plantation must have seemed like the backwater of nowhere, the running of it a deadly dull procedure and the generation gap wide. Three of the young gentlemen made haste to return to civilization; the fourth, placed in charge of one of the father's several estates, devoted himself to the more interesting pursuits of gambling, shooting, drinking and taking unto himself the daughters of the land.

The elder Tharp disapproved of these ways of passing the time; yet he himself had practiced *droit du seigneur* and had sired an "outside family" of various color shadings. The eldest outside son eventually took over the running of the estates most efficiently, and when Tharp died, he and all the illegitimates were remembered in the will. But the bulk of the fortune was left to a legitimate grandson in England who turned out to be feebleminded.

Another story, found partly in court records and partly on tombstones, tells of a planter whose wife died. He couldn't legally marry his black mistress, but he freed her and her children and left his entire estate to her. She had to fight in the courts for years for the right to assume ownership and make a will of her own.

These stories were by no means isolated cases, yet the same planters who figured in them supported restrictive laws against the mulatto population they were helping to create. In St. Domingue especially, the *gens de couleur* might have sided with the whites and ultimately changed the course of the revolution if they had been treated with fairness.

But that is sheer speculation. In order to interpret what did happen, it is necessary to look back for a moment:

THE MAROONS

There was scarcely ever a time when slaves weren't in revolt somewhere in the islands. At first, it was a matter of runaways—women as well as men who simply could not endure bondage. Having no other recourse than attempted escape, they fled into the wilds and sooner or later began forming into bands for mutual protection. In some islands they grew bold enough to stage destructive raids on nearby plantations, both to get supplies and arms and to help other slaves escape. In the process, planter families were killed and their properties set afire.

The word maroon (in French, *marron*), which came to be applied to these guerrilla bands, may have been a contraction of the Spanish *cimarrón*, meaning wild and unruly. "Unruly" was almost always the way a slave undergoing cruel punishment was described. "Unruly" was his crime. The most notorious unruly Africans were the Koromantees, so-called because they had been assembled at the West African Koromantine shipping station operated by Dutch slavers. Christopher Codrington, a member of the plantation family that owned the entire island of Barbuda and much of St. Kitts and Barbados, and who was himself a governor of the Leeward Islands, apparently admired their courage in the face of nearly insurmountable difficulties, for he said, "No man deserved a Koromantee who would not treat him as a friend rather than a slave." Unfortunately, many did not deserve these proud men, and fear of uprisings tended to increase the cruelties inflicted on any slave who dared to exhibit any form of independence.

Maroon colonies developed in Dutch Guiana (now Surinam), St. Thomas, Hispaniola, St. Domingue, St. Vincent, Puerto Rico and Jamaica. In St. Domingue they were a constant menace from the time of the first settlements to the end of the eighteenth century, when they took an active part in the revolution. In Jamaica the movement began in the 1500's during the Spanish occupation, when runaways took to the mountains. But after the British moved onto the island in 1655, maroons actually helped their former masters organize guerrilla raids, striking down out of the bush on the new English forts and settlements. No wonder the walls of Jamaica's first plantation houses so often had slits for guns and cannon.

Two such private "forts" in areas vulnerable to maroon attacks were Stewart Castle in the parish of Trelawny and Colbeck Castle, an imposing pile at the edge of a present-day tobacco plantation near Old Harbour on the south coast.* The story goes that John Colbeck, who had been a member of the Penn-Venables invasion forces, was rewarded by the Lord Protector Cromwell with a land grant and remained to become a solid citizen and local politician. Because there is

*Both castles are now ruins under Jamaica National Trust jurisdiction.

slaves. The merchants and traders, on the other hand, tended to identify with their Boston and New York counterparts and be sympathetic to the American cause. But the English islands could not survive without American salt fish, meat, flour, livestock and plantation supplies. When word of rebellious acts on the part of English colonials in America came by way of merchant ships, it reverberated throughout the West Indies. Not only was business interrupted in both directions, but staples that fed the slave populations began to be cut off altogether. Historians George and Carolyn Tyson estimate that "by mid-1778, some three thousand slaves had starved to death in the Leeward Islands,"* particularly in Antigua, St. Kitts, Nevis and Montserrat. The Leewards governor worried that slave insurrection might result and reported that the taking of prize ships was often the only means of getting supplies.

It was not physical hunger alone that prompted a rash of slave outbreaks during the American Revolution, although that must have been the most urgent motive. In at least one island, planned uprisings occurred, say the Tysons, when "upon learning of American rebellion against British masters they resolved to imitate their example."*

Nor were the English colonies the only rebels. Grenada under the French had two uprisings in 1783, and Martinique saw another on the eve of the French Revolution, which sped republican firebrands across the Atlantic to inflame islanders of all shades and stations in life. Many *grands blancs* and traders remained royalists, but the prospect of freedom from the "exclusive"—a long-standing ruling that French colonies could trade only with France—was irresistible; the *gens de couleur* hoped they would at last receive legal standing; and blacks envisioned a new world without slavery. In 1794, emancipation actually did come briefly to the French-held islands before night closed in for them again.

The islanders were always about six months behind in getting news of events in Europe and, conversely, one of the chief island complaints has always been that the mother country doesn't keep up properly with what is going on in its colonies. In 1789 the planters of St. Domingue decided to take advantage of the new revolutionary regime in France by sending thirty-seven delegates to win the case for home rule. Instead, they were informed by the states general that the *gens de couleur* had been awarded their long-awaited legal

*George F. Tyson, Jr., and Carolyn Tyson, "Preliminary report on Manuscript Materials in British Archives Relative to the American Revolution in the West Indian Islands."

*Ibid.

rights. The mulattoes suspected correctly that the resident *grands blancs* were not about to countenance this, and, led by two young men named Ogé and Chayannes, staged a demonstration in Cap Français. It was stopped by the police, and Ogé and Chayannes were put to death in the public square by being broken on the wheel. In the so-called age of *liberté, egalité*, and *fraternité*, further seeds of class and color bitterness were being sown.

In August the most massive and terrifying slave uprising ever known in the islands erupted and spread throughout St. Domingue's rich northern plain, a volcano spewing blood and fire that razed hundreds of plantations, massacred planters and their families and realized the accumulated fears of centuries. Boukman, a plantation headman who was also active in *vaudou*, led the planning of this well-timed terror. Another headman-slave named Toussaint, a man deeply attached to his master and family, first made certain they were safe from violence and then joined the uprising, becoming its most brilliant and resourceful guerrilla chieftain.

Swiftly changing events in the course of the French revolution meant continual reversals of policy in France, which in turn created a chaotic series of changed loyalties in St. Domingue. At one moment the *petits blancs* (mostly dock workers, small shop-keepers or odd jobbers) and *gens de couleur* were fighting each other; at another, the latter were joining the blacks against the *grands blancs*. In 1792 republican France sent out new commissioners to control the situation, which had become complicated by Spanish assistance to the slave rebels in the central section. A strong royalist movement in the south provided the English—who were always waiting to pounce—a wedge for invasion. Their troops took Port-au-Prince for the royalist side in 1794.

It was at this time that Toussaint, later known as L'Ouverture, moved into the spotlight by bringing his well-trained black army to the aid of the French commissions and getting rid of the English. As a result, he was appointed lieutenant governor. Said to be ugly but possessing considerable charisma, this remarkable man is still a controversial figure because as soon as he achieved power, he began to set blacks against mulattoes, both groups against whites and invaders, while seemingly allying with all of them at one time or another. He ended by becoming a firmly paternalistic king of the island and simultaneously retained strong ties to France.

The slaves whose cause he had espoused were freed under his rule, but there was no land reform and they had to work the plantation as before. When all his exploits—the tangled years of violence, his pitting of side against side, diplomatic ploys and even the invasion of the Spanish side of Hispaniola to consolidate his position—at last brought him to the pinnacle, in the words of George Tyson, one of his biographers, he "resolutely set out to . . . convince France that only a black government could rule the colony profitably in accordance with the principles of the French Revolution. Concurrently, he sought to demonstrate that, contrary to planter propaganda, the Old Colonial system was not dependent on slavery."*

Toussaint's reign may not seem very revolutionary today, but that a country ruled by a black existed at all was regarded by establishments everywhere, particularly in the new United States, as a serious threat. The planter class in neighboring English Jamaica was particularly apprehensive because emigrés began arriving there from St. Domingue in large numbers—white planters with their slaves—and *gens de couleur*. All but the certified whites were suspected of inflammatory activities.

Toussaint's dictatorship was to last until 1802, when the United States under President Jefferson withdrew the support previously given St. Domingue by John Adams in a profitable trade deal, and Napoleon Bonaparte decided to launch an elaborate campaign to establish an empire in the Western Hemisphere. Napoleon sent out his brother-in-law, Victor Emmanuel Leclerc, in command of an invading force with instructions to get Toussaint out of St. Domingue. Soon after Leclerc arrived at Cap Français, Henri Christophe, Toussaint's general in the north, surrendered, leaving a scorched earth. Of two thousand houses in Cap Français, only fifty-nine remained. The troops in the south and in Santo Domingo gave up, and, a month later, with people of all classes going over to the French, Toussaint, along with his ruthless General Dessalines, had to surrender as well. Even his loyal blacks, the former slaves, had failed to support him. It was the final note for L'Ouverture. Through trickery he was pursuaded to sail to France, where he was taken to an alpine dungeon and there he died in the cold.

However, when it became known that the French government had decided to reinstate slavery, General Jean-Jacques Dessalines and the mulatto general Alexandre Pétion withdrew their support of the French and emerged as leaders of a new revolutionary movement. Leclerc's men, meanwhile, had been succumbing rapidly to the climate and yellow fever, and the disease claimed Leclerc as well in November 1802.

*George F. Tyson, Jr., ed., *Toussaint L'Ouverture*.

Although new troops were sent by France to assist General-Governor Rochambeau in fighting the resuscitated insurrection, a year of struggle followed, during which unprecedented atrocities were committed by both sides. In the summer the English again intervened, this time in the north. At Vertieres, near Cap Français, the French fought and lost their last battle for the colony of St. Domingue. But before they left forever, they destroyed most of the homes and plantations that had remained after all of those years of revolution and war.

Into this devastation Dessalines stepped on January 1, 1804, as first king of the independent nation he called Hayti after the old Indian name. He soon proclaimed himself emperor, but was assassinated in 1806, and the conflict between *les noirs* and *les gens de couleur*, which has not ceased in the hundred-seventy years since, was resumed by black General Henri Christophe and Pétion. Christophe took control of the northern provinces. Pétion, the south. Christophe's troubled reign as emperor of the north until 1820 has become legendary (see ch. 6), but the history of the West Indies' first republic has been scarcely less melodramatic. Continual thrusts for power, by ambitious politicians, occupation by the United States in 1915-1934, devastation of the land, illiteracy and a terrible, widespread poverty have been Haiti's tragic lot. Still, it struggles on and wears as proud a face as on the first day of its independence.

None of the other French West Indies colonies suffered

Chateau Murat, an elegant two-hundred-year-old carved stone mansion on tiny Marie Galante, was said to have had floors encrusted with gold louis d'ors. In the mid-1970s it was being meticulously restored—without the original floor covering.

St. Domingue's agony during the final years of the eighteenth century, but they had their share of trouble. Britain—as it had during the revolutionary confusion in St. Domingue—swooped down on other French islands whenever possible, counting on, and receiving, the support of royalist elements made up, of course, mostly of aristocrats fearing the Jacobin terror. The menace materialized in 1794 in the person of an old island hand named Victor Hugues, a *petit blanc* from St. Domingue and passionate supporter of the Terror who had contrived to get himself named Governor of Guadeloupe for the Republic of France in spite of the fact that the island was currently in British hands. In addition to his own shrewd ruthlessness, Hugues' weapons were a force of irregulars, a printing press for propaganda and a shiny new guillotine. Aided by an outbreak of fever among the British forces, he took Guadeloupe with comparative ease, destroyed the cathedral in Pointe-à-Pitre, set up his guillotine in the square and when enough heads had rolled, set himself up as dictator in the name of the Republic. The slaves were freed but forced to remain on the plantations under conditions similar to those Toussaint imposed in St. Domingue.

Next Hugues tried to pick off several other British enclaves, including Grenada, one of Britain's most important sugar islands. There he recruited the mulatto planter Julien Fédon to gather sympathizers with the revolution and organize a revolt against the British. Fédon's estate, Belvidere, may still be visited, and there are plaques in the Anglican church at St. George's commemorating his leadership in the rebellion. But during the year of Fédon's supremacy, more than half of the sugar estates were destroyed, with their great houses. Forty-four years later, the demise of sugar as a viable crop would be complete, due to the emancipation of the slaves. Today, Grenada is famous for its nutmeg and other spices.

Victor Hugues is little known in America, yet it was his fleet of corsairs, operating in the late 1790's out of Point-à-Pitre and Gustavia, harbor of Swedish St. Barth's, that preyed on U.S. ships, which had by then resumed trade relations with the British in the Caribbean. Among the cargoes were generous amounts of munitions. Hugues's forays were so successful that in 1798 the United States actually declared what was called the "Brigands' War" against the French in the Caribbean. It was brief, but it made the French government nervous; Hugues's tenure in Guadeloupe was terminated and he was eventually transferred to the South American colony of Cayenne.

During the final years of the eighteenth century and the

dawn of the nineteenth, Martinique suffered less disruption than Guadeloupe. The British invaded it in 1794, but it was their policy to encourage the status quo as long as that meant white plantocracy status for them. While they held Martinique, the island was allowed to retain its traditions and culture; it went right on growing sugar and its plantation workers remained slaves. It also escaped involvement when Napoleon decided to build his West Indian island bridge to Louisiana. One of his generals was sent to Guadeloupe, where slavery was reinstated. Another—Leclerc—went to St. Domingue, where the fear of the same thing happening was largely responsible for the violent black and mulatto reaction that culminated in independence. Thus it was that except for the Haitian third of Hispaniola, the slave system was once more in effect in all the islands in the Caribbean.

But protesting voices were heard both on the Continent and in England, where a strong abolitionist movement had sprung up during the first half of the eighteenth century, the groundwork laid by Quakers, who declared slavery to be inimical to Christian morality. Author Thomas Clarksen and an eloquent lobbyist with excellent social and political connections named William Wilberforce aimed for emancipation but for the time being were at least determined to halt the slave trade. Pamphlets detailing the horrors of the middle passage and cruel treatment on plantations succeeded in rousing the British public, but the cause was weakened by the increase in slave uprisings; planters, who also had a strong lobby, were able to point to the violence as a national danger.

The success of the American Revolution and the chaotic events in France that led to the rise of Napoleon delayed official consideration of the problem in England. In the French colonies, as we have seen, the prospect for emancipation depended on who happened to be in power at home. The slaves themselves kept hoping and acting on rumor. A major uprising took place in Curaçao as a direct result of what was heard about the French Revolution and the brief emancipatory rulings in the French islands.

Oddly, it turned out to be Denmark—which had as firm a plantation system as any of the others—that first abolished the slave trade to its islands in 1802. (The United States had placed restrictions on bringing slaves to the mainland in 1794.) Britain followed suit in 1808 and the French agreed to conform after 1819. The new rulings meant that colossal indemnities had to be paid to Spanish and Portuguese slave traders for their losses, and these men made out exceptionally well. A period of smuggling and piracy began, slavers illicitly bringing in their merchandise to the islands while local authorities looked the other way. Many of the official "observers"—government cruisers in charge of preventing slave ships from entering the West Indies—cut themselves in on the profits with all the zest for defying an unpopular law that prevailed a century later in America during Prohibition. For slavery itself had not been abolished and the planters had to maintain their labor forces somehow.

Reforms that had brought about the transporting of slaves from Africa in a somewhat more humane manner were now forgotten. Smugglers had no interest in anything but their profits. The increase in absentee ownership of the plantations meant worse treatment of the slaves by managers who as often as not were cheating their employers. A new rash of rebellions began breaking out in Jamaica and other English islands, fed by rumors that abolition had been declared in the mother country but was being withheld by local officials.

But by 1825 the abolitionists in England had renewed their lobbying, adding the relatively new public relations technique of saturating the public with propaganda broadsides. Probably their cleverest maneuver was to agree with their adversaries, the absentee plantation owners and bankers, that a period of "apprenticeship" would be necessary for successful transition to freedom. The prevailing planter argument was that the average slave was naturally lazy and too ignorant to grasp the responsibilities of supporting himself. Despite the tendency to sentimentalize and dramatize their case in propaganda leaflets, the abolitionists saw that generations of dependency could not be suddenly ended without some form of preparation. Wherever missionary activity had been allowed—or, as in the Danish islands, actually encouraged—some of that transition had already taken place, although it was a drop in an ocean. In England it was at last decided in 1834 that after seven years of apprenticeship, all slaves would be freed and planters awarded giant sums of consolation money.

Antigua was selected as a kind of guinea pig. The slaves of that island were given instant freedom, and instead of the expected pandemonium, the changeover was so peaceable that the British emancipation program went ahead. By 1838 all British island colonies were declaring the slaves free. This immediately brought on more problems, since islands under other governments still had slavery and the English planters were now facing unfair competition.

Another kind of competition confronted the French islands: The sugar beet had been introduced into mainland France, where producers were getting price supports, and depression hit planters and slaves alike. A traveling salesman in porcelain products named Victor Schoelcher was so distressed by conditions he saw during his West Indies sojourn in 1829 that he spent the next nineteen years working and writing in the hope of achieving emancipation in the French islands. He was finally named under-secretary of the colonies in 1848 and enjoyed the reward of his labors when he was able to proclaim freedom for the slaves. In Martinique there is a town bearing his name, and in Fort-de-France, a library, which can only be described as architecturally bizarre. Built for the Paris Exposition of 1889, it was transported in pieces across the Atlantic and still stands in all its rococo cast-iron glory, with its towers and grilles and majolica tiles.

Unfortunately, Schoelcher's original manuscripts are not in the library's files—they were destroyed by fire just as the library was about to open—but on his monument are inscribed his "inflammatory" words: "When we committed ourselves to the army of abolitionists, we knew very well that the battle would be hard and that we should face defeats; but we always were convinced that the final victory, whether we should see it or not, would belong to those who have faith in justice, in the right; in liberty and equality. This is as certain for us as the fact that tomorrow follows today."

Immediately before Schoelcher's pronouncement in the French islands, an entirely different drama reached its climax in the Danish Virgin Islands, starring yet another white hero whose role was a tragic one. Peter von Scholten, son of a Virgin Islands governor and apparently a man of deep sensitivity to island problems, had himself been named governor and later, governor general of St. Croix, St. Thomas and St. John after they had jointly become a Danish Crown colony. Von Scholten had good connections at court and among the planters, but he sympathized with the Moravians' efforts at education and did all he could to encourage the building of schools and churches. He must have been very skilled at shuttle diplomacy.

When he was made governor general, he shared the splendors of a hilltop great house above Christiansted called Bülowsminde with his mistress, a former slave named Anna Elizabeth Ulricka Heegaard. After a long look at island life, his wife had sailed with their children back to Denmark for an indefinite stay.

Gossip persists that the lovely Anna Heegaard was in close touch with dissident slave leaders, principally the former Bajan headman Moses Gottlieb, a.k.a. "Bodhoe" or "General Bordeaux," who was organizing an islandwide revolt against a twenty-year apprenticeship-before-emancipation ordered by the Danish king. Anna was said to have influenced von Scholten in the rebels' favor, but because of his record of enlightenment throughout his tenure, the influence may have flowed both ways. For when, on the morning of July 2, 1848, a great gathering of people from plantations around Frederiksted came to lay siege to the town, the mood was that of peaceful disobedience rather than violent revolt.

Most of the planters, who believed themselves threatened, brought their families to the harbor and sent them aboard anchored ships to safety. By the next day some eight thousand slaves had gathered in the town. General Bordeaux set a noon deadline for meeting their demand of immediate freedom. Why von Scholten was not notified in Christiansted or why he delayed getting across the island—a two-hour carriage ride—until about half an hour before the deadline, now advanced to 4:00 P.M., is not known, but when he did arrive, he managed first to calm the mob. Then he went to Fort Frederik to do the same with an assemblage of the military and leading planters. He emerged from this stormy meeting minutes before four o'clock, and, drawing on an obvious talent for high drama, mounted the ramparts of Fort Frederik to proclaim to the crowd below without assistance of bullhorn or microphone: "All unfree in the Danish West Indies are from today emancipated. The estate Negroes retain for three months the use of the houses and provisions grounds of which they have hitherto been possessed. Labor is in future to be paid for by agreement but allowance is to cease. The maintenance of the old and infirm, who are not able to work, is until further determination to be furnished by the late owners."

The whoops and huzzahs that greeted von Scholten's pronouncement unfortunately couldn't be heard on the Christiansted side of the island, and before he could get back there, the militia had already shot into a gathered crowd which had been behaving more threateningly than the one at Frederiksted. Violence ensued, with burnings, looting and killings, but when the governor-general was finally heeded, the riot turned into a celebration.

The Danish Establishment responded by recalling von Scholten to stand trial in Copenhagen, where he was convicted for his unauthorized action. Yet the government eventually backed him up and the slaves were indeed freed. Vindication must have afforded him some wry satisfaction although he was never to see his beloved islands—or his Anna—again. Bülowsminde, a series of ruined stone arches suggesting classic breezeways and cool graciousness, still commands the hilltop.

When the Dutch islands at last announced emancipation in 1863, the West Indies became virtually free of slavery, since Spain had, in a sense, liberated its islands through the back door, without making a formal announcement about it until 1873. Now that a century has passed since emancipation, it would be a joy to announce that it brought peace and prosperity to both the occupants of the great house on the hill and the newly created peasants in the valley. But there had been no real apprenticeship or preparation for independence, and the plantation owners were as dependent as ever on a work force they could afford. Sugar prices fluctuated wildly and the cost of producing it varied. In some islands, particularly Trinidad and Jamaica, indentured laborers had to be imported from China, India and the middle East—in some others, from Malta. Free Africans were also brought in to supplant those who "declined to work," as it was then phrased. It was a protracted götterdämmerung for the sugar economy and there was no rainbow bridge across which the gods could gracefully retire.

Some islands turned to other crops, such as cotton, coffee, tobacco, bananas and coconuts, and where sugar was still grown, the tendency was to consolidate: One large sugar factory would serve a number of estates and small individual farmers. This pattern holds today, and it is one of the reasons why so many of the old houses and factories have been abandoned to the subtropical wilds, mercilessly reclaiming their own.

Martinique claims that La Pagerie, across the bay from Fort-de-France, was the birthplace of Marie Josephine, who became Empress of France. St. Lucia also claims the honor of having been her birthplace.

The post-emancipation nineteenth and early twentieth centuries also saw continued social injustice and unrest; white, brown and black attitudes were too deep-seated to change in spite of a rapidly changing outside world. Some British islands actually moved backward, losing their local assemblies and becoming Crown colonies. A general migration to the towns and cities began, and agricultural work came to be considered a mark of the old subjugation.

With the arrival of the automobile, a new expression of status became achievable, and the traffic snarls endemic in all island towns today are the result: It is considered undignified to walk, even for a few blocks. Too many people once had no choice but to walk, however far they were going. (Former residents returning to the village of Loíza Aldea in Puerto Rico for the festival of Santiago Apostal have turned the traditional sacred walk with the image of the saint into one long start-stop procession of horn-honking cars bought with middle-class earnings in San Juan.) Like walking, agriculture is disdained, in islands where green belongs to the landscape and great smoking industrial chimneys do not. Vast numbers of people crowd into tin-roofed hovels and noisome slums where there is little chance for employment rather than remain on the farms that would keep their islands from having to import expensive foodstuffs. Employers in remaining sugar estates find it difficult to persuade people to cut cane. The wrongs of centuries are still being paid for.

A SAMPLER OF GREAT HOUSES AND PLANTATIONS

The following pages are intended to whet the appetite for discovery of estates—in ruins or preserved—that remain as a heritage of the islands. Because so many are unidentified and neglected, a complete guide must remain to be assembled by some adventurous enthusiast of the future—who, by the way, had better hurry before the more obscure ones are entirely swallowed by tropical growth or modern development.

Antigua

Clarence House was built in 1787 on a hill above English Harbour for Prince William Henry, Duke of Clarence, later to become William IV. While he was stationed at Antigua he became friendly with Horatio Nelson and was best man at Nelson's wedding in Nevis.

The elegant mansion has been well kept and is now the

country house of Antigua's governor, but visitors may go through when he is not in residence. Of typical one-story stone construction, cooled by a raised basement and louvered outer galleries, it has high, tray ceilings, gleaming native hardwood floors and appropriate antique furnishings, a fine example of graceful building to suit the climate.

Barbados

Numerous restored as well as handsome new plantation houses are scattered throughout Barbados. The National Trust takes an active interest in the cultural heritage of this agricultural island, which is one of the few in the Caribbean to offer informal tours of its stately homes. (St. Croix is another.) Visits to these private residences may be made during the winter "season"—January to March.

In St. James parish on the mid-northwestern side is *Porters*, parts of which are believed to be of seventeenth-century origin, with later additions. The plantation and great house were owned for more than two hundred years by the prominent Alleyne family. The present owner has made modern additions.

Holders 'House, also in St. James, is another seventeenth-century structure recently restored. The owner has discovered foundations and the arched basement of the original "buttery"—traditional island word for the place to store yams. A Holder family graveyard is on the grounds.

On property spilling over into the parishes of St. George, St. John and St. Philip in the southeastern section, is *Byde Mill*, an eighteenth-century plantation with modern additions. Of especial interest are the old mill wall and garden.

Nearby on Highway 4 in St. George is *Woodland*, a working plantation with a great house of undetermined date.

Mullins Mill, in St. Peter, was included in a 1717 map of the island, and the house built around it dates from 1831, following a devastating hurricane. The restoration by its owners includes the kitchen and bake ovens, the boiling house and old servants' quarters, which is now a garden house overlooking the Caribbean. Furnishings are period antiques.

Bay Mansion, Bay Street, near Bridgetown, St. Michael, is an authentic haunted house, the resident ghost since 1840 being Sir John Beckles. His sisters are buried on the grounds. Built at the turn of the eighteenth-century by the venerable Beckles family, Bajans since 1650, it was vast, with receiving and dining halls, thirteen bedrooms and a gazebo with a fountain. The great house is filled with heirlooms: furniture, glass, silver, china and needlework.

Two other well-preserved great houses are *Nicholas Abbey* and *Drax Hall*. (There is a plantation by the same name in St. Ann's Bay, Jamaica, which contains a polo field.) The Barbados National Trust is restoring the *Morgan-Lewis* sugar grinding windmill and hopes to acquire the rest of the plantation ruins for preservation. Another of the Trust's landmarks is *Sam Lord's Castle*, a hotel using the great house for its public rooms, and a much-publicized visitor attraction.

On high, wooded ground overlooking the rugged, Cornishlike east coast is *Farley Hill*, now a national park. The great house is a massive two-story stone structure with arched windows and was rebuilt in 1861 for the use of the Duke of Edinburgh when he paid Barbados a visit. It was recently partially destroyed by fire but remains one of the most impressive of the island's ruins. It is set in a public park, oddly, in a depression between hills so that the house itself does not command a view except of the grounds, which are attractively landscaped.

Near the east coast in St. George parish is *Codrington College*, a handsome group of restored buildings approached by a long avenue lined with royal palms. Christopher Codrington of the famous early planter family retired here after having succeeded his father as governor of the Leeward Islands. He lived on the estate from 1703 until his death in 1710 and willed the property as a college. Opened in 1745, it is the oldest English institution of learning in the Western Hemisphere.

Curaçao

Cattle and salt were the chief products of the ABC islands in the early times, aside from such profitable trading activities as *zeeroving* and slave transport. The Curaçao Foundation for Preserving Ancient Monuments has seen to the salvation of many great houses. Although not precisely ancient, the houses are certainly old and beautiful.

The *Civil Service Registration* office, prosaic as it may sound, is a restored, pre-1740 mansion which combines several typical Dutch West Indian elements. Originally a three-story rectangular building with a dormer-windowed tile roof, later additions feature an arched colonnade around the main floor over the raised ground floor. One of the rooms is furnished with antiques.

Stream View, a late eighteenth-century mansion, is near a filled section of St. Anna Bay. Octagonal, with steps leading to the projected main story, it is privately owned and has been restored.

Jan Kock, great house for a salt mining estate, was built about 1750 on foundations then a century old. Its main story is close to ground level, and its dormers are set in a double-level roof. In the basement the owner has installed a wine bar and he sometimes entertains visitors with local music.

Brievengat (1750) and *Ascension* (1700) have been restored by the Foundation; *Casa Venezolana* (1750) and *Stroomzigt* (1780) are privately owned and restored.

The Curaçao Museum at Otrabanda dates from the mid-nineteenth-century and was originally a quarantine station.

Grenada

Belvidere was the estate of the spearhead of the 1795 rebellion, Julien Fédon, deemed monster by the English and hero by the French. Ruins of a great house presumed to be his are near the rebel military camp on Morne Fédon in St. John parish; the road leading to the site begins on the Atlantic side near the airport and continues across the mountains past the spice and banana plantations that have replaced sugar, to Gouyave on the north leeward coast. Tradition has it that the first nutmeg of Grenada was grown on the Belvidere estate. If true, it was long after Fédon had disappeared into the bush—and into legend.

Sans Souci in the parish of St. Andrew is an old sugar estate known locally as the birthplace of Henri Christophe, although historians have him coming from St. Kitts. In any case, he named his palace in northern Haiti Sans Souci, supposedly in memory of this estate.

Near *Mount Horne* in north central St. Andrew are the ruins of a sugar estate with a rosy-brick arched aqueduct and gigantic water wheel. Planter owner George Rose was among the English taken prisoner here by Fédon in the 1795 rebellion and executed on the spot.

Tufton Hall is on the northwest coast in the parish of St. Mark near the seashore town of Victoria. The area is high and wildly fertile. Pink stone ruins and an arched footbridge, as well as a supposedly salubrious hot-and-cold mineral spring, grace the property, which is said to contain the tallest bananas in Grenada because the groves are so high above sea level.

La Fortune estate near Sauteurs* in St. Patrick parish

*See the story of the Carib's Leap near Sauteurs in ch. 2.

has an old canal built in the mid-eighteenth-century. *Mt. Rich Estate* in central St. Patrick has a lovely great house with stained glass windows and spacious receiving rooms. On the property are petroglyphs popularly thought to be of Carib origin, but recent studies may identify them as religious symbols of earlier people. Like many estates, this one has its own private graveyard.

Bellevue and *Capitol (formerly Penang) estates are near* Soubise on the mid-Atlantic coast. The Capitol Estate was also supposedly the first in Grenada to grow nutmeg.

Guadeloupe

The sugar estates of Guadeloupe were on Grande Terre for obvious reasons. Basse Terre is too hilly and rugged to support any bulk cash crop but bananas. The remains of one old sugar mill are near *Gosier* on the south coast of Grande Terre, where an elegant inn, *Auberge de la Vieille Tour*, not long ago was host to a meeting of the American and French presidents.

Haiti

A few relics of the colonial period, when the plantations of St. Domingue supported the merchants and investors of France so handsomely, are still scattered about the countryside. But travel in any sense of carefree exploration is not easy in today's Haiti. Back roads are difficult, flying from place to place isn't the answer and the country buses—colorful as they may be—are only for the most adventurous. One couple recently rode horseback from Port-au-Prince to Cap Haitien in a matter of several weeks, but found little time to search for anything like abandoned great houses or sugar-mill ruins. And it is virtually impossible to get over to Ile de la Tortue without special permission and arrangements by the government. The offshore island is inhabited and there is a Roman Catholic establishment there, but no visitor amenities or means of access except by fishing boats.

Several years ago a big investment combine from Texas announced that a huge complex was being planned for this island of Arawaks, buccaneers and other lost souls, but nothing has come of it. Indian artifacts are picked up and sold at random to those who do get there, and the pleasure palace of the fun-loving Pauline Bonaparte Leclerc* was so thorough-

*When General Leclerc was sent by Napoleon to St. Domingue in 1802 he brought along his wife—Napoleon's sister. She lost no time in establishing residences in Cap Français, Port-au-Prince and Ile de la Tortue.

ly looted by a group of French "archaeologists" that virtually nothing is left of her sojourn there in the years when her husband was pursuing Toussaint L'Ouverture.

On Haiti's northern plain and in the hills south of Cap Haitien, a few old plantations survive. *Vaudravil*, fronting the road east of Le Cap is one, and between *Belin* and *Limbé* is a famous sugar refinery that devised a clever system of circulating heat around the kilns. At *Camp Louise* there are covered water mills in good condition, with underground conduits that carried water from the river. In the same area animal mills were also used. The oxen were placed on a level above the vats under a conical roof and turned the grinder round and round.

On the *Grande Rivière du Nord*, which flows toward the Atlantic near Cap Haitien, huge dikes were built to shorten the river and direct it to the coast. The giant "sandbox" trees planted centuries ago to hold the dikes, are still standing.

Unlike any other country in the Caribbean in so many other ways, Haiti unfortunately shares with them all the need for a thorough cataloguing of its treasures. There is a grand challenge here to students and doctoral candidates for original research. Although serious work has been done through the years by private individuals, for the casual, interested visitor only momentary, tantalizing glimpses of its heritage are possible because except for the most famous landmarks, few have been preserved or interpreted.

Jamaica

The good doctor of Worthy Park, Dr. John Quier, lived a long (1739-1822) and useful life. His career was distinguished for medical innovations as well as for the use of purges, blisters and bloodletting that were the violent remedies of the time. He charged a fee of 6 shillings, 8 pence per patient or—one should say—per head, for he was hired by his fellow planters to keep their slaves healthy, or at least try to prevent their dying off.

His prescription for staying off the sick list in the tropics was to "choose a dry, healthy location; practice temperance, drinking a little wine but selecting a diet more vegetable than animal, including fresh fruit; rise early, take a moderate amount of exercise and avoid the night-time damp; bathe frequently and change clothes according to time of day and season; maintain a cheerful disposition."* It would seem that the only recommendation the slaves he treated could possibly

*Michael Craton, "Dr. John Quier," *Jamaica Journal*.

have followed was the one about rising early.

Smallpox and measles were twin scourges, especially among the slaves, and Doctor John is said to have been a pioneer in the West Indies in diagnosis of both and in inoculating patients for smallpox. As time went by he also began to gain a familiarity with bush medicine and may even have resorted to some of the traditional African practices. Living at a time when medicine was only beginning to come out of the dark ages, he was apparently a kindly, if not completely enlightened man. He recommended such new practices for the slaves as a two-week lying-in period for women in childbirth and opiates to kill pain, allowed his black assistants to use their own healing or soothing methods and attempted to improve the diet of the workers in general.

Quier himself owned a plantation at Lluidas Vale near the vast sugar acreage at *Worthy Park*, which has been in continuous operation since the 1700's. The old slave hospital of mortared field stone, with an arched entrance on the ground floor and the customary twin steps to the main floor entrance, is still to be seen there in the overseer's yard. The good doctor, who was a bachelor, had a number of slaves to work his own lands and keep him comfortable; his family tree shows reputed sons and daughters of four different mistresses, who along with their children, were all generously remembered in his will.

A few years ago, as one drove east along the winding coastal road of north Jamaica, a ghost would suddenly appear on the green hillside. It was the ghost of a huge great house, its window and door apertures staring like sightless eyes, its roof bashed in, its walls crumbling. The stuff of legend, the story of Annee Palmer, White Witch of *Rose Hall*, became a bit more elaborately gruesome with each telling by the old caretaker, who expected a small tip for taking visitors around (always in the daytime—no one would go there at night).

Today Rose Hall is restored to a better condition than it ever enjoyed when it was a great house for the Rose Hall and Palmyra sugar estates. Massive and imposing, with every stone and tile in place, it gleams white in the sunshine. Carved woodwork in its high-ceilinged rooms is copied from the original. Elaborate silk wall coverings—not authentic—and period antiques or meticulous reproductions fill the rooms. The grand staircase is supposed to be exactly as it was when Annee or the previous mistress of the estate, Rosa Palmer, descended it to greet visitors. The grounds are landscaped and manicured, swans swim in the garden pool

Whim Great House, pride of the St. Croix Landmarks Society, dominates an eighteenth century plantation with restored mills and outbuildings. The single-story mansion was built in 1796 by Christopher McEvoy, an eccentric Dane much given to whims.

and tourists come by the hundreds each day to shiver at the tale costumed hostess-guides tell of Annee and the husbands and lovers she was said to have murdered.* But the story they tell today is no longer easy to believe and the ghostly quality of the place is gone.

The case of Rose Hall suggests the question: Is it better to preserve a ruin as it stands or is restoring it—perhaps too perfectly—really doing it a service? The question has to be posed and solved in each specific case. When private money becomes available to make a restoration, at least the site is saved from complete disintegration. However, island national trusts and historical societies, chronically short of funds, might consider the less expensive expedient of preserving their national treasures as ruins, which are often breathtakingly beautiful and evocative reminders of a period equally ruined and lost.

*Their version of the story is based on a 1929 novel by Herbert G. de Lisser and has not been authenticated. Indeed, there is some doubt that Annee ever lived there at all.

Orange Valley, a 2,300-acre plantation, has an H-shaped great house with loop holes for defense on all sides. It is still being used as a residence, but the remains of the factory complex are partially in ruins. Lying in the parish of St. Ann on the north coast between Brown's Town and Discovery Bay, it has a boiling house, to which a nineteenth-century steam boiler has been added, and a stone slave hospital with interesting iron window frames that is beautiful enough to have been a mansion. To visit, inquire at Estate Community Center.

Patrick Tennison, the owner of *Good Hope,* a vast working plantation has lovingly restored the classic great house and written a book on its history.* Once joined to Potosi Estate in the parish of Trelawny, the property may be explored on horseback. Along the wooded trails visitors will come upon ruined walls, arches, water wheels and that ingenious chute which carried cane to the mill and was known as the sugar shooter. Of special architectural interest are the dressed-stone counting house and the old coach house of Good Hope, headquarters for the rental of horses. Inquire at the Jamaica Tourist Board in Montego Bay.

The story of *Hampstead* and *Retreat* estates in Trelawny parish could provide the plot for a best-selling gothic novel. They are two of three plantations once owned by Jane Stone, a lady of color who died at the age of eighty in 1774. She had been the beloved of planter Jonathan Barnet, a man of parts and great courage, not to mention impatience. During the 1720's he grew exceedingly weary of continuous and vicious pirate raids on the estates of the north coast and mounted his own search-and-destroy mission against the notorious pirate "Calico Jack" Rackham, so-called because of his loud sartorial habits. The pursuit route was westward by sea past Lucea's Fort Charlotte and Green Island Harbour to Bloody Bay at the head of Negril Beach, where he found Rackham's ship at anchor. Boarding the pirate vessel, Barnet and his volunteers fought Rackham's men and women (two of his crew were Ann Bonney and Mary Reid) with such fury that he captured the lot. Rackham and his surviving crew were later gibbeted at the islet outside Kingston Harbor known as Rackham's Cay, but Ann and Mary escaped execution by "pleading their bellies." They did not say whether Calico Jack was the sire of both expected babies, if indeed they were pregnant at all.

*This great house was the eighteenth-century home of John Tharp whose four sons dashed his hopes of establishing a sugar dynasty. (See earlier in this chapter.) Tharp also had a town house in nearby Falmouth.

After his triumph over Rackham, Barnet returned to the arms of Jane Stone. His wife was dead, and although he could not marry Jane, he cared for her enough to make her his business partner in a profitable real estate deal which involved subdividing part of his Catherine Hall estate (now the downtown section of Montego Bay). He also gave her a town house and willed her and their three children the Catherine Hall Property. After his death in 1744, Jane managed with great diligence, making enough money to purchase for herself the Retreat and Hampstead plantations.

According to historian-author Ray Fremmer, "Plans for the mill buildings were drawn by English architects, and they resembled mansions more than factories. All the roofs were slate. All the windows were iron, cast in England in every variation of form: square, oval, round, Roman-arched and some were the largest ever shipped to Jamaica. The glass . . . was aqua-colored bullion or crown glass, hand blown. Cast iron bars for the lower windows were fluted and embellished with acanthus leaves. All face stones, arch stones and lintels in both the mills and great houses were sawed, not rough hewn.

"The engineering design of the grinding mill at Retreat was more complex than any other mill in Jamaica. Using an undershot water wheel to turn a cog gear attached to a 24-foot round wooden shaft, the cane was ground two floors above the level of the wheel's axle. The floors were paved with flagstone shipped out from England as ballast. . . . Despite the ravages of time, these mills deep in the woodlands, even in ruins, still show the strength and artistry of their original construction."*

At Hampstead, the great house is now restored and privately owned. It may be possible, by contacting the Jamaica Historical Society, to view the ruins of the factory, millpond, water tank and cattle mill.

Some houses and mill ruins not previously mentioned are now listed according to the parish in which they are located, starting on the northwest coast and moving clockwise around the island.*

ST. JAMES (Montego Bay area)
   Sign Great House. Restored as public rooms of a hotel.
   Fairfield. A hotel and tennis club. Built in 1776.
   Richmond Hill. A hotel.

*Ask the Jamaica Tourist Board to put you in touch with the Jamaica Historical Society for guidance in visiting sites not usually open to the public.

*Ray Fremmer, "Jonathan Barnet—Pirate Huner," *The Gleaner.*

TRELAWNY (east of Montego Bay)

Claremont Estate. Ruined walls, old graveyard.

George's Valley. Ruins.

Green Park. An eighteenth-century house with adjacent sugar mill, undergoing restoration by American Ray Fremmer, who has a fascinating collection of great house antiques. Write for an appointment to Mr. Fremmer at Green Park, Trelawny Parish, Jamaica, W.I.

Stewart Castle. A ruin maintained by Jamaica National Trust.

Kent. Ruins.

Windsor. A government youth club is situated here.

ST. ANN (Ocho Rios area)

Bryan Castle. Private; visit by request.

Llandovery. Plantation, open to visitors.

Unity. A great house that may be rented.

Minard. Great house.

Runaway Spice Plantation and *Caves.* Regular tours.

Eaton Hall. Restored as a hotel.

Annandale. Great house near Lydford, south of Ocho Rios.

Edinburgh Castle. Another of Jamaica's legendary "haunted" houses, as well it might be, for its owner used to lure travelers to the place and then toss them down a shaft, which may still be seen.

Seville. A private estate, but it may be visited. Here were uncovered foundations of the earliest Spanish settlement.

ST. MARY

Grays Inn. Private producing estate.

Prospect. Conducted Estate Tours twice daily.

Llanrumney. Henry Morgan's old property. Private.

Brimmer Hall. Conducted Plantation Tours three times daily.

ST. THOMAS (southeast Jamaica)

Stokes Hall. Seventeenth-century ruin; one of Jamaica's first sugar plantations. Maintained by National Trust.

Ladyfield. Ruin.

ST. ANDREW (Kingston area)

Bellevue. University hostel and Catholic seminary.

Mount Atlas. Ruin.

Halberstadt. Ruin.

Mona. Hotel.

ST. CATHERINE (west of Kingston)
Green Castle. Ruin, maintained by National Trust.
Rodney's House. Ruin.

MANCHESTER (in the central plateau)
Derry. Ruin.
Marlborough. Classic Georgian great house. Privately owned, but may be seen by appointment.
Albion. Ruin.

ST. ELIZABETH (west of Manchester)
Appleton. Modern working rum factory.
New Forest. Ruin.
Fulford. Great house ruin.

WESTMORELAND (southwest)
Auckendown Castle. Ruin. South coast road.
Bluefields. On the south coast; now a guest house. Spanish settled here in early 1500's.
Hendon House. Hotel in Savanna-La-Mar.
Paradise. Cattle ranch and plantation; restored great house. Check with Tourist Board in advance.
Frome. Modern working sugar estate.

HANOVER PARISH (west of St. James)
Friendship. Pimento plantation; tours and lunch available.
Kenilworth. Sugar mill ruins, government youth camp.
Abingdon. Near Negril beach. Guest house.
Blue Hole. Private estate, but visitors may watch polo on historic grounds Sunday afternoons.
Tryall golf course. A huge working water wheel.

Marie Galante

On this sixty-one-square-mile, gourd-shaped island southeast of Basse Terre, Guadeloupe, sugar and cotton are still king and queen, although the abolition of slavery in 1848 caused many of the old planter families to give up and go back to France. Among these was the Murat family, whose sugar holdings and great house were among the most impressive in the entire Caribbean. *Chateau Murat*, the two-hundred-year-old carved stone mansion built by planter Dominique Emmanual Murat rivaled Jamaica's Rose Hall in size and elegance. Of rectangular design with a solid facade, it had an arched portico ribbed by columns with ionic capitals and a three-sided flight of stone steps leading to the entrance. The house faced formal gardens, and legend has it that M. Murat had the original floors encrusted with gold louis d'ors.

The property, including the ruins of the elaborate factory, has been meticulously restored under the direction of architect Mme. Regine Dumesnil, who contrived to so interest local craftsmen that they boned up on early stone and woodworking techniques. Eventually, it is hoped that the great house and sugar mill will be opened as a hotel.

Martinique

The design of *La Pagerie*, a sugar plantation near Trois-Islets on the southern shore of Fort-de-France Bay, was similar to many another in the eighteenth century. This one is noteworthy because it was supposedly the birthplace of Marie Joséphine Rose Tascher de la Pagerie, who voyaged to France in 1779 for her wedding to the Marquis de Beauharnais, bore him a daughter and saw him guillotined during the French Revolution. In 1796 she married an ambitious Corsican who made her Empress of France and Queen of Italy and whose grandson would eventually become Napoleon III. Only one stone building remains of Joséphine's childhood home. It has been restored as a museum filled with mementos of her life.

Leyritz Plantation on the northeastern shore near Basse-Pointe dates from the early 1700's when it was built by a cavalry officer, Michel de Leyritz, who was apparently sick of war and also a bit homesick for his native Bordeaux. The estate, with the Atlantic ocean pounding on the east coast and the Pelée mountain brooding in the west, covers 250 acres of sugar land. Like so many others, the plantation had an elaborate sugar mill, distillery, guardroom, storehouse, a private chapel and houses for the slaves. The fairly small great house echoed Bordeaux in its design. Its front facade was cooled by a wide gallery and its interior had open, high-ceilinged rooms.

The kitchen was separate from the main house, which began to deteriorate after 1827, when de Leyritz's descendants abandoned it for a more "civilized" life in France. The present owners have restored the great house, granary, chapel and factory and turned the complex into a luxurious country inn complete with a small theater and museum. Some of the original slave houses have been converted into guest cottages. The surrounding acres, incidentally, are still a working plantation.

Nevis

The idea of restoring old estate houses and converting them into attractive hotels and inns seems to have occurred more to the businessmen of Nevis than to hoteliers in other islands. Four of the tiny island's sugar plantations are now receiving paying guests: *Old Manor, Golden Rock, Nisbet Plantation* and *Montpelier.*

Montpelier was the scene of the Horatio Nelson-Frances Nisbet wedding reception, and much attention is still paid to this almost two-hundred-year-old social event (1787) without too much mention of the fact that his marriage to the widow didn't work out. The estate itself has been carefully handled by its present owners.

The *Nisbet* plantation, sixty-four acres planted in coconuts situated at Beachlands on the north shore, belonged to the family of Fanny Nisbet Nelson's first husband. *Golden Rock* was a hillside sugar estate with typically spectacular views. Restorations have been made on the old buildings, and the hotel itself is cottage-style.

Nevis's other well-publicized historic site is the birthplace of Alexander Hamilton, which consists now of a few pieces of the foundation and the traditional twin stone steps leading to the main floor entrance. No attempt has been made to restore it, but it is kept in fair condition. The site was dedicated in 1957 by the Alexander Hamilton Bicentennial Commission.

St. Lucia

Père Labat, who reported on just about everything he observed during his year's stay in the West Indies, claimed that St. Lucia was uninhabited at the beginning of the eighteenth century. There were scattered groups of French colonists and numerous Caribs living there, however, and by 1744 the French government was helping planters to establish estates, mostly in the southwestern volcanic district. The island's oldest town, Soufrière, was the center, and the remains of six sugar estates are still visible, though they are mostly in ruined condition. *Malmaison* was the estate of the Tascher de la Pagerie family, parents of the girl who was to become the Empress Joséphine. *Diamond*, with its pre-1745 windmill, *Anse Mamin, Palmiste, Rabot* and *Union Vale* all have ruins of interest. Most were destroyed during the French Revolution-inspired disturbances in 1795. An eighteenth-century stable on the Union Vale estate is still well-kept, and it also has ruins of a water mill and factory.

Around *Micoud* on the south windward coast, the *Beauchamps, Fond* and *Troumassee* estates all had sugar mills which are in a state of ruin now. Supposedly, pirates hid in the house on the *Mahaut* property and then burned it, taking their treasures with them. To the south at Vieux Fort, where an American airfield was established during World War II, is *Giraudy House*, which the Americans used and is still in fair condition. Nearby are the ruins of *Savannes*, with a dock where the sugar used to be rolled in barrels onto the sloops that took it to France or England, depending on which country was in control.

Joséphine's actual birthplace in 1763 is considered to have been at Dauphin on the *Morne Paix Bouche* estate. Martinique claims her because she was baptized there, but St. Lucia says she spent the first eight years of her life on one of her father's several properties and this one was where he lived most of the time. The house is now in ruins and many of the old stones have been carried off by modern builders. *Marquis*, another estate near Dauphin on the northeastern coast, has ruins of the estate church, overseer's house, slave quarters and the sugar factory. It was the home of one of St. Lucia's governors. Near the town itself behind the Grand Anse, a major find of Amerindian zemis and a skeleton dated about 600 A.D. was made and may be seen at the museum at Morne Fortuné.

The *Mamicou* estate on the midwestern coast at Praslin has recollections of two eighteenth-century wars. In 1770 it was owned by the Chevalier de Micoud, who so desperately fought the English invaders in 1778 (see ch. 6), and in 1795 it was the scene of a battle leading to the so-called Brigands War. A large part of the old estate buildings remain: the stone and wood estate house, the sugar factory, the mill, a rum distillery, a bakery, slave quarters, a hospital and a dungeon.

South of Gros Piton, St. Lucia's most famous volcanic wonder, a number of sugar estates thrived in the eighteenth century, especially around the southwest coast between *Choiseul* and *Laborie*. Most notable was the *River Doree* acreage belonging to the Alexander-Lloyd family. A road lined with royal palm leads one to the ruins of the mansion, church and rectory, a school, and outbuildings of the factory —structures that date from 1770 to 1850. Several windmills in a fair state of preservation are also in this area. Around Castries and to the north reaching to Gros Islet (now Rodney Bay), there were as many as twelve sugar estates. One of the oldest is probably the one that belonged to Commandant de Longueville, who was in office beginning about 1748. The present-day "Cap House" was built over the foundations of his mansion, and the outbuildings include an overseer's house, slave quarters and the ruins of an old jail cell. At *Grand Rivière* one of the original cattle-powered sugar cane crushers is still being used to manufacture molasses.

To make finding these landmarks easy, *St. Lucia Historic Sites*, a new book with an excellent map, has been published by St. Lucia Archaeological and Historical Society (P.O. Box 525, Castries). It covers the treasures of the island in every category, from the wilds and the Indians to the many kinds of constructions men have built since the coming of the first Europeans.

St. Kitts

Fountain Estate, on a steep hilltop north of Basseterre, was originally the grandiose chateau of the Chevalier Phillipe de Longvilliers De Poincey,* who was governor of the French West Indies for twenty-one years during the seventeenth century. Foundations and cellars of the 1640 mansion —postcards on sale in Basseterre have a reproduction of an old print showing what it looked like then—are the basis of the present great house, which in itself is quite beautiful.

Early-style small red brick went into the construction of the outer wall and an inner chamber which was a gun room. A secret passageway was supposed to have run between the house and St. Peter's church more than a mile away. The chateau may be visited by permission of the present owners. From their garden, the ruins of a sugar mill and boiling house are visible.

The Glen is a two-story great house ruin at Monkey Hill below Fountain Estate with a view of Basseterre. It is overgrown and neglected but very picturesque. Almost nothing is known of its history except that at the turn of the century it was used as a dance hall.

Stapleton is a working sugar estate with ruins of earlier buildings on the grounds. *Greenhill* is in bad condition and the walls that survive are overgrown. *New Guinea*, at the foot of Brimstone Hill, was once the lime works that supplied materials to the fortress. Access is by permission only. *Gibson's Pasture*, overlooking Dieppe Bay on the northwest coast, was probably a sugar mill and fort combined. Since

*The poinciana, or flamboyant flowering tree, was named for His Excellency.

the site faces St. Barths, the theory that it was used as a battery against Victor Hugues's pirates based in Gustavia, seems logical. Two cannon have fallen onto the reef below.

Fairview, an inn with cottage rooms, has been built around the eighteenth-century great house, which has been attractively restored. The property has beautiful gardens and a panoramic view of the sea and of Nevis.

St. Vincent

Witty and indefatigable while shifting hats as zoologist, archaeologist and historian, St. Vincent's Dr. Earle Kirby is a man for all seasons. His 1973 report* on the island's old sugar mills reveals his tirelessness but only traces of his sense of humor. What remains of some 182 different estate works and 13 water canals he explored personally is not a laughing matter, since most are either neglected ruins or have been subsequently built upon or destroyed altogether.

Remarkable for their intricately engineered solution to the energy problem, a majority of the old mills used water power—hence the canals. One of these, stemming from the Rabacca River which winds back and forth toward the windward coast to supply four different mills situated miles apart, is described as "the giant of them all!" The aqueduct is still visible at *Orange Hill*, and at *Government House*, Kingstown, an old aquatint shows the "chain spout" by which the canal crossed the Rabacca at one point.

Some of the works were powered by windmills; *Harmony Hall* in St. George parish is one of the few still in existence. Others used animal, and later, steam power. The water-powered works still reasonably intact are at *Arnos Vale*, near the airport (dating from 1791 and now housing a cigarette factory) and at *Collins* in St. George. With modifications, a number of the old mills are being used as other types of factory, especially for arrowroot. The river-streaked fertile Mesopotamia Valley is a good place to start on any hunt for plantation ruins, but to avoid frustration, check in first with the St. Vincent Archaeological and Historical Society.

U.S. Virgin Islands

ST. JOHN

Annaberg, Cinnamon Bay, Reef Bay are sites of early sugar estate factories which underwent reconstruction during the nineteenth century. Built of hand-formed local yellow and

---

*I.A. Earle Kirby, *The Sugar Mills of St. Vincent*.

Danish red brick, ballast rock and brain coral, and mortared with local materials (including molasses and goat hairs), the walls present a rough, free-form appearance. Some of them were given protective coats of plaster and painted red. Where native termite-resistant hardwoods were used for lintels and door or window frames, pieces of wood can still be seen, but the softer wood beams are long gone. These are among the most beautiful estate ruins in the islands.

The U.S. National Park Service conducts "living history" demonstrations at the Annaberg estate, which has a magnificent windmill and boiling house, and field-stone walls. All over St. John are remnants of original roads of bluish slate-like paving installed by the Danes.

The *Reef Bay* great house and sugar factory ruins were originally on two estates; the great house was built on a hill northwest of the big triangular bay. The estates are now part of the Virgin Islands National Park. Property surrounding the house was called Par Force for many years and had its own factory until it was consolidated with the Reef Bay plantation, where the ruins of the later factory are located near the shore. Although architectural changes have been made in both building complexes, it is believed that the great house must have been built in its original form before 1780.

The house, its outbuildings and the factory are of local stone with bricks used in the cornering arches and trim. All buildings were stuccoed and painted.* Rectangular and with galleries at each end, the house has a formal entrance portico on the second floor with twin stairs. Pillars with doric capitals support the roof, and a cistern enclosed by a dry wall is attached to the left side of the house; such cisterns are still a necessity in the dry islands. The Par Force great house is an excellent illustration of the classic small estate-house design, with the kitchen outside the gate, the servant quarters beyond, near the garden, and the stable and outhouse built into the hillside at the back.

Made of similar construction materials, the factory had a curing house, boiling house and a still; the attached steam machinery was added in 1860. Originally, it was powered by horses, and the horse mill foundations, with a grinding platform and animal pen, are in a circular area.

ST. CROIX

Near Frederiksted on Mahogany Road is *Prosperity* plantation, which still has a great house and manager's resi-

---

*See Frederick K. Gjessing, *Observations on the Architecture of Reef Bay Estate.*

dence. *Jolly Hill, Orange Grove* and *Two Friends* plantations are in ruins and hidden by dense vegetation. *Morning Star* plantation is near Fredensfield.

Little Princess is a plantation harking back to St. Croix's first governor, who owned it during the early eighteenth century. Its present owners have restored the ruins and willed the property to the Nature Conservancy.

Mount Victory ruins, a classic example of sugar estate construction, are near the Creque Dam Road. Most of the buildings are down in the valley in a cluster, with the windmill on a hill above and the aqueduct leading down along the slope. The two-story factory buildings at the bottom are well-constructed souvenirs of plantation life.

Also on the Creque Dam Road are the ruins of *Annaly*, once a very large sugar plantation. Its factory has a windmill dated 1803, but since the complex has been in more-or-less continuous use for other things than sugar manufacture, it is much altered. Another mill tower in the vicinity is called *Bodkin* and bears the date 1808.

Possibly the most famous of all great houses is *Whim*, which has been restored by the Landmarks Society and is considered the showplace of St. Croix. Located off Centerline Road east of Frederiksted, it is a large complex of the sugar estate once known as *John's Rest*. How it acquired the name Whim is anyone's guess, but it may have something to do with the peccadillos of its late-eighteenth-century legendary owner. Christopher MacEvoy, Jr., a Dane despite his Scottish name, was given to such eccentricities as showing up in Copenhagen driven by white horses allowed only to the king.

The estate house is comparatively small and, unlike the usual great house, its one floor is set on a basement instead of being raised over a ground-level floor. To obtain light and air, a moat was built around the oval-shaped building with its matching oval roof. The house also has a remarkable number of windows, arched and flanked by shutters; being close to the ground, they give the appearance of doorways so that the house seems more like a pavilion than a home. It was built about 1794 of cut stone and coral with walls three feet thick and ceilings sixteen and a half feet high. There are three large rooms, a gallery and a small wing, which was apparently added after the house was built. The careful restoration has included furnishing the mansion with antiques of the period.

As always, the cook-house is a separate building, which has now been incorporated into a museum displaying the artifacts of sugar production, a pot-still for making rum, iron-work and military implements, engravings and a color diorama. Perhaps the most interesting article is the tombstone of Anna Heegaard, described by the museum people as the "consort" of Governor-General von Scholten.

Other buildings on the property are a watchhouse, the ruins of the sugar boiling factory, a mule mill, a steam chimney and a windmill with its sails and grinding machinery fully restored. The islands once contained upwards of 115 of these classic stone mills, each representing a producing estate.

The St. Croix Landmarks Society sponsors a number of events at Whim, such as concerts and art exhibits, and the museum is open six days a week. During January, February and March, tours of estate houses on the island are available to visitors, with the proceeds benefiting the Society's restorations.

5

Bastions, Parapets, and Citadels

SPANISH: El Morro and Other Fortresses of Puerto Rico

Overlooking the harbor of San Juan, Puerto Rico, is a rugged cliff: *El Morro* is the Spanish term. Far to the northwest at Havana is an even more famous El Morro. The Spanish conquistadores built upon them both, fortresses that are unmatched in the Caribbean islands except for La Citadelle in Haiti and the British-built Brimstone Hill in St. Kitts.

The two El Morros—or Morro castles—are medieval-looking stone structures, ponderous and impregnable. At least they were in the days of unsophisticated armaments aboard sailing vessels. Both forts guarded important harbors and were vital to the Spanish in their attempt to retain the supremacy that they had established in the New World at the beginning of the sixteenth century.

As the gold deposits in the rivers of the Greater Antilles soon began to give out, the conquistadores went searching elsewhere, all through the mainland of Central and South America. Their discoveries there, the crushing of the Indians, the establishment of gold and silver mines, cities and plantations set off a tremendous explosion, the repercussions of which were felt throughout the islands, and of course, Europe. Many colonists and soldiers in Puerto Rico, Hispaniola, Cuba and Jamaica tried to desert in order to reach Peru and seek the fabled riches of El Dorado, the lake of gold and the man who bathed in gold.

Cuba's port of Havana stood at the entrance of the Straits of Florida, a principal going-home route for the treasure ships that had commenced their twice-yearly voyages from Mexico, Panama and the north coast of South America. Convoy fleets laden with gold, silver, pearls and miscellaneous loot would rendezvous at Havana before setting sail for the long way home across the Atlantic. Fully as important if less spectacular, San Juan Harbor served as gateway for Spain's supply ships west and south bound for the increasing number of colonies.

As long as the other European countries observed the papal bull of 1493 that imposed the Spanish Line,* the *flotas* were safe from attack. But those other countries were looking on with envy at Spain's New World riches, and Francis I of France was not the only one to wonder aloud where there was any divine writ that could cede an entire hemisphere to Spain and Portugal. (The latter country had received a big chunk of Brazil.)

By 1521 French pirates with royal commissions up their lacy sleeves began sailing into the forbidden waters, and that started it. Puerto Rico, first point of attack, was defenseless —both against pirate and Carib raids—and after many appeals to the Spanish Crown, in 1529 the colonists were authorized to start building a fort.

Juan Ponce de León was the original governor, and he seems to have been feckless in many things he did here and elsewhere. In this case he built his palace in unstrategic and unhealthy Caparra south of San Juan Harbor and insisted on living there. At last he was forced to move the capital to the present site of Old San Juan, an island that forms an arm of the bay.

Ponce's successor didn't seem to have much of an eye for selecting locations either. The new fort began to rise on the inner shore of the bay, where it was inneffectual in warding off enemy ships; they could sail right around it, and did. One prosperous citizen, worried about the proper defense of his goods, proclaimed the fort to have been "built by blind men." He and others in the town urged that cannon be placed on the cliff that stood at the head of the harbor; currents are such there that any sail attempting to pass is left vulnerable to attack from the heights. They were finally heeded, with batteries logically placed at last, San Felipe del Morro eventually became a mighty fortress.

The original one that had been built in the wrong place stood for about eighty-five years until some Dutch raiders virtually destroyed it. A new building went up on the old

*The Spanish Line gave Spain everything west of 47° longitude. (See also ch. 1, p. 00.)

foundations and became the governor's residence. Restored today, it is known as La Fortaleza and lays claim to being the Caribbean's oldest such official residence in continuous use.

It was 1584 before the castle of El Morro was a reality, and it took two more centuries of additions for it to look as it does today, a sleeping giant.

In four years the remarkable reign of Elizabeth I would launch England into its centuries of sea power. Over in the Channel the invincible Spanish Armada would be proved vincible, with much of the credit due to the feared Francis Drake, whose series of devastating raids had long been harrying and terrifying Caribbean islands. Then in 1595, after a number of assaults by other English vessels on Puerto Rican defenses, Drake and his uncle Sir John Hawkins began an official out-and-out attack on all the Spanish islands.

One of Drake's most potent weapons was his trick of striking without warning. But for once one of his potential victims had received secret intelligence from Spain that the English were on their way across the Atlantic. Governor Diego Menendez de Valdés of Puerto Rico had ample time to prepare the island's defense. Those were indeed unhurried days.

Meanwhile, Drake and Hawkins received some intelligence themselves, informing them that a ship from the

It took two centuries to build the giant fortress, El Morro, that guarded the city of San Juan Bautista in the years when Puerto Rico was Spain's gateway to what she considered her private preserve—the Caribbean.

Christmas, as well as sugar harvest time, was celebrated in the islands by characters such as Jaw-Bone (or House John) in roving troupes of dancers called Jonkonnu. The dances may still be seen today in Jamaica and the Bahamas. This lithograph was "drawn after nature and on stone" by the Jamaican artist, Isaac Mendes Belisario, in 1837. INSTITUTE OF JAMAICA

In a quite different style from his Jaw-Bone drawing, Belisario portrayed a cocoa factory (top) and a Kelly's Sugar Factory (bottom), both at St. Cathrine, Jamaica, in the 1830s. INSTITUTE OF JAMAICA

These two Jamaica scenes—a view of Kingston and Port Royal (top) and of leisurely traffic on a bog walk in the hills (bottom)—were engraved by James Hakewill, probably in the 1820s. WEST INDIA REFERENCE LIBRARY

The Spanish always managed to build beauty into their fortifications. The "castle" rising above El Morro affords a sweeping view of San Juan harbor as well as the northern and eastern approaches to Puerto Rico.

The world slipped into the seventeenth century with a weakened Spain that went on neglecting its gateway colony. Elizabeth was dead and the Dutch star was rising in rebellion against a long subjugation to Spain. In 1625, when Juan de Haro was governor of Puerto Rico, a Dutch fleet under the command of Boudewijn Henrikszoon appeared before the battlements of El Morro. It isn't known why de Haro thought the Dutch would attack at the same spot Cumberland had, but he wasn't taking any chances and ordered everybody to the beach. So the Puerto Rican troops were awaiting Hendrikszoon's men at Condado while back in Old San Juan the Dutch were swarming ashore from ships that now lay in the bay. The Puerto Ricans had to hole up in El Morro again, but they were prepared to endure a siege and the governor refused all offers from Hendrikszoon to give up.

The Dutch finally set fire to the city, which so infuriated the Puerto Ricans that they launched an attack of their own. It began to appear that the invaders' ships would be caught in the harbor, so they left their vantage point on shore, boarded their galleons and retreated beyond the range of El Morro's cannon. Soon after this it was decided that El Morro wasn't enough defense, and a wall began to rise around the city, strengthened at one point by San Cristobal fortress, which was ultimately completed 147 years later.

San Juan's great fortresses played their part both in

raids and defense against the great influx of English, Dutch, French and Danish pirates and privateers during the century. At last Spain relaxed its own restrictions against privateering and thus allowed its colonists to begin preying on other nations' ships. San Juan harbor became a busy port once again, a place to store treasure and booty, repair ships and offer sustenance and entertainment to friendly sailors.

The *Castillo de San Felipe del Morro* of today is separated from the old city by a nine-hole golf course and is maintained by the U.S. National Park Service. Looking virtually as it did on its completion in 1776, there is little evidence of the haphazard additions and changes one would expect to find in a complex that was centuries abuilding. In the shape of a lopsided diamond lurching 140 feet above the sea, the four-level giant menaces potential enemies as if it were still armed, yet with a certain grace.

The Spanish always managed to build beauty into their fortifications by the judicious use of arches and courtyards and clean sweeps of balanced space. Even the dungeons where political prisoners of the Autonomé Party* were incarcerated have arched ceilings and a pleasant view of the sea.

At the entrance are a dry moat and a drawbridge. On the main level, museum displays now occupy the arched chambers. An interesting triangular stairway with sprung and cantilevered arches connected the main level with the middle deck, while a huge artillery ramp bordered by stone steps allowed quick transport of armaments down to the *Santa Barbara Bastion*, so named because Barbara was patroness of gunners. A castle rising above the gun emplacements of the top level affords a sweeping view of the entire harbor as well as the northern and eastern approaches.

El Morro's last military role was played out during the Spanish-American War, when its batteries answered an attack by Adm. William Sampson. In October 1898 the United States took official possession and, after four centuries of Spanish domain in Puerto Rico, established Fort Brooke* at El Morro's gates. Visitors may wander through it at will all day long (8:00 A.M. to 5:00 P.M.) and avail themselves of guided National Park Service tours at 9:30 and 11:00 A.M.; 2:00 and 3:30 P.M. for a nominal charge.

Fort San Cristobal lies half a mile east of El Morro on

*The Autonomé Party, which rebelled against Spanish rule in 1887, was led by Baldorioty de Castro, for whom a boulevard in Santurce is named.

*Fort Brooke is named for Major General John R. Brooke, first "peacetime" American military governor of Puerto Rico. He served from October 18 to December 6, 1898.

Avenida Muñoz Rivera leading into the Plaza de Colon, central square of the old city. It was a stronghold in the wall which is still very much in evidence around the outer reaches, and was designed to ward off land attacks such as that of the Earl of Cumberland. In 1765 the original batteries were strengthened and improved by a Spanish engineer named Tomas O'Daly. (His Irish surname was no odder than that of the field marshal who hired him: Alejandro O'Reilly.)

The strengthening of the redoubt took seven years and the workmen used their picks on the live rock of the promontory to obtain its stones. The Plaza de Armas is encircled by gun rooms; the main gun-deck is approached by tunnels and on the top level a gun platform extends 150 feet above the sea. In its prime the fort had defense works extending from the ocean to the bay. San Cristobal is also a National Park Service landmark with the same visiting and tour hours as El Morro.

Fort de San Gerónimo del Boquerón, sitting with anachronistic dignity on a rock in the Condado Lagoon between the Caribe Hilton Hotel and the resort beehive that is the Condado district of Santurce, was begun during the second half of the sixteenth century. It played its part in the defense against El Draqui in 1595 and also figured in an English invasion attempt in 1797. The Institute of Puerto Rican Culture achieved a minor triumph in 1957 by talking the

Eighteenth century English fortifications on St. Lucia's Morne Fortuné (Good Luck Hill) have been partially restored and adapted for modern use as classrooms and museums. The contemporary building at right blends well with the venerable structures around it.

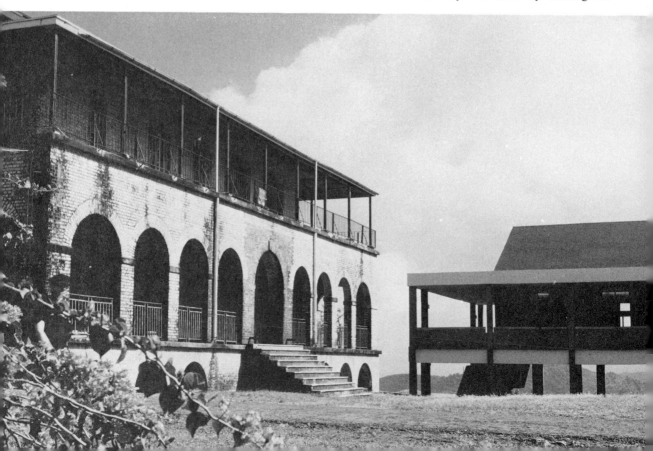

management of the Hilton Hotel out of razing the ruins and using the site for a restaurant. It has restored San Gerónimo and installed a museum that presents the military history of Puerto Rico, with exhibits of all the different attacks the island has survived from Carib times to the American occupation of 1898. Typical arms, uniforms and insignia and other mementos of the sixteenth through the nineteenth century are on display here in surroundings more like a cloister than a fort. San Gerónimo is not under the aegis of the National Park Service, which does have jurisdiction over *El Canuelo*, a small fort in San Juan harbor, the majority of the *Old City Wall*, and *Casa Blanca*, restored home of the Ponce de León family.

Over in Vieques (Vee-ay-kess), an island off the southeastern coast of Puerto Rico, the *Fort of Isabella II* has been meticulously restored, originally with the idea of turning it into part of a giant resort. But the presence of the United States Marines on the island prevented civilian access by air and the ferry ride from Fajardo is so lengthy and rough that the idea was abandoned. Vieques is well worth a visit, however, by anyone not in a hurry and interested in an unspoiled town and old estates.

DUTCH, ENGLISH, FRENCH

It would be easy to believe the old West Indian yarn about the enterprising salesman who traveled through the Caribbean during the seventeenth and eighteenth centuries with a sample case full of arches and returned home with it empty. Arches and guns and powder magazines appeared on every strategic hill. War was the norm in Europe and its black light was reflected in the colonies; they were the spoils of war.

The action kept shifting back and forth from one fort to another, and one of the most dramatic sequences of events occurred during the tense years of the North American colonies' revolt against England. It linked the major fortifications of St. Lucia, Martinique, Antigua, St. Kitts and St. Eustatius and produced side effects in Jamaica, Cuba and Yorktown, Virginia.

Involved were: the British, French and Spanish Caribbean fleets; one Dutch, two British and one French island governors; three admirals, five generals; and uncounted officers, dragoons, sailors and foot soldiers, not to mention citizenry, slaves and other unfortunates in St. Lucia, St. Eustatius and St. Kitts who were tossed about like the proverbial swallow in a badminton game.

A Caribbean Drama in Four Acts

The curtain went up in 1776 at Fort Oranje on the Dutch island of St. Eustatius. Act II shifted down the island line to Morne Fortuné, a big military base on St. Lucia, and to Fort St. Louis, Martinique, with offstage action up at Yorktown and an interlude back at St. Eustatius. Act III was set at Brimstone Hill fortress, St. Kitts, with a scene at English Harbour military and naval base, Antigua. Act IV took everybody back to St. Lucia and Martinique, then on to a thrilling chase sequence in the channel between Dominica and Guadeloupe culminating in a whirlwind finish.

ACT I

On November 16, 1776, the lookout at Fort Oranje in Dutch St. Eustatius spotted a brig of war of the American Continental Navy approaching in the roadstead. Statia was ringed with fortifications, some almost within spitting distance of English-held St. Kitts's northwestern shore. Fort Oranje, on the southwest coast, had been important for some years. The island it guarded had been openly trading with the American rebels, transshipping supplies from their European allies via the vessels that sailed in and out of spacious Oranje Bay almost daily. It was no secret that arms and ammunition were included in the bills of lading.

Statia had little agriculture. It grew tobacco, some sugar and provisions. Its real wealth lay along the black sand beach in the many brick warehouses that stored much needed commodities destined for the thirteen rebellious American colonies. Perched on the cliffs above was Fort Oranje.

There was a large Jewish community in St. Eustatius as well as a number of traders from Rhode Island. Business was so booming throughout the period that the tiny island was affectionately nicknamed "The Golden Rock." It is also important to the story to mention that merchants in St. Kitts—and their parent companies in England—had sizable investments on Statia, a fiscal reality that didn't sit well with the British War Office.

Fort Oranje had been built in 1636 by the Dutch on foundations of a 1629 French installation. The venerable compound—still used as a center of island government—was constructed around an open plaza facing the roadstead at which sixteen iron cannon were aimed.

Brimstone Hill, St. Kitts—a great expanse of walls, arches, towers, and paved areas, an abandoned Camelot. The fortress saw action only once, when the French in 1782 successfully beseiged it.

The Dutch governor, Johannes de Graaff, had been in communication with the American rebels, and it is believed he was well aware of their July Declaration of Independence.* On that November day as the American ship *Andrew Doria* dipped its flag (still the Great Union flag) in salute, the Officer of the Day at Fort Oranje dipped the Dutch flag in reply. The American captain, Isaiah Robinson, then ordered a thirteen-gun salute. The Dutch O.D., Abraham Ravené hesitated at this point. Should the gun salute be returned? Holland was neutral, so far, in the conflict between England and its thirteen colonies.

Since Fort Oranje was but a few steps away from the governor's mansion, Ravené hurried over and begged de Graaff's advice. He was given a go-ahead, and an eleven-gun salute was thus fired in honor of the Americans.

It wasn't exactly the shot heard round the world, but it was the first salute by a foreign power to an armed vessel of the Continental Navy, and it acknowledged for the first time the sovereignty of the United States of America.

The repercussions in that sea of fortified islands were distinctly felt, especially among the merchants and military men of St. Kitts. When the news reached London, there was great indignation. Some midnight oil was burned in White-

*In St. Kitts sympathizers had been drinking toasts to George Washington and his cause since August.

hall and a protest was lodged with the Dutch government, which made a show of reprimanding de Graaff but continued him in his post as Statia's governor. So the island went right on assisting the Americans and the St. Kitts merchants continued to reap profits from their investments.

Then in 1778 France and the United States signed a treaty. War broke out between England and France, and their respective armed forces spent the rest of the century fighting—first, over the United States—and then trying to gain dominance in the Caribbean by taking island colonies away from each other. The first island they battled over was strategic St. Lucia.

ACT II

Shaped like a pineapple or a hand grenade and lying a few miles south of Martinique, St. Lucia was called the Helen of the West because its possession was disputed by the English and the French almost continually from the day of the first English landing in 1605 until Great Britain won it at last in 1814. Beautiful and fiery (it has had its share of volcanic outbursts, with a soufrière and two bulletlike "pitons" remaining as evidence), it is blessed with fertile valleys and rounded hills, many of which are called Morne-this or Morne-that. Whenever the French reigned in St. Lucia, they managed to give everything French names, which have been kept, even throughout British occupation.

The capital and main port midway along the leeward coast is Castries, named for Charles Eugene Gabriel de la Croix, Marquis de Castries, Maréchal de France.* St. Lucia's original fortifications were at Vigie, a strategic point north of Castries, but the French decided that Morne Fortuné (Good Luck Hill) overlooking the port, was a better location, so they removed the Vigie works and reassembled them with some additions on the big morne. By the crucial year 1778 the French had been in residence for fifteen years,† but the deputy governor, the Chevalier de Micoud, had only a small force at Morne Fortuné. Realizing this, Adm. George Brydges Rodney, who was England's chief strategist in the West Indies began urging that the war office approve a British assault on St. Lucia.

His arguments must have been persuasive, for Sir Henry Clinton up in New York was ordered to send reinforcements to the West Indies Command at the Antigua Station to assist

*The British tended to give their island capitals names like Kingstown, Georgetown, Spanish Town, Road Town.
†The Treaty of Paris in 1763 had awarded St. Lucia to France.

The chain of islets in the channel between Dominica and Guadeloupe called Les Saintes lent their name to the most famous naval battle ever fought in the West Indies. British Admiral Rodney's 1782 victory over French Admiral de Grasse established England's supremacy in Caribbean waters and somewhat compensated for the loss of the North American colonies.

Admiral Barrington's forces there. They added up to about five thousand men and twelve transports when the English fleet sailed for St. Lucia.

The French defenders, with only two companies of militia made up of local volunteers and a few seasoned officers, were soon evicted from Morne Fortuné and barely managed to hang on by their fingernails at another hill seven miles away. Micoud tried sending a small boat through the English lines to beg for help across the channel at Fort-de-France, Martinique. Admiral Count D'Estaing was over there with a complement of nine thousand men, preparing a raid on St. Vincent and Grenada. Micoud's boat made the rough crossing, but D'Estaing, for some reason, failed to act. When he finally did come to Micoud's rescue, the English were prepared for him and the rescue attempt failed. He then tried an assault on the Vigie Peninsula and the ensuing battle went on for ten days. D'Estaing finally withdrew, leaving the Chevalier de Micoud to surrender to the English, who began fortifying Morne Fortuné to their own specifications.

The English now held the Eastern Caribbean islands

that boxed in Martinique and Guadeloupe, and they had their eyes on the Dutch islands of St. Maarten, Saba and St. Eustatius as well. When war was declared against Holland in 1780, Rodney was ordered to take these three islands—especially, the latter, which was being so helpful to the Americans.

It was now 1781 and two new characters appeared on-stage: the talented French admiral le Comte de Grasse (not to be confused with Statia's Governor de Graaff) and the general le Marquis de Bouillé.

With a large fleet, de Grasse was headed for Martinique, and Rodney had an ideal opportunity to intercept him. Although he was occupied with carrying out his orders on the Dutch islands, it should have been easy for him to subdue all three and turn his attention to the menace of the French fleet. Letters written at the time show that he greatly resented St. Eustatius, calling it a "nest of vipers,"* and the loot he found there was apparently too much for him to resist. The French went unchallenged.

On Statia, Governor de Graaff wasn't even aware that Holland and England were at war, when Rodney and his fleet moved in, decapitated all the houses and warehouses, took over the governor's mansion for himself and allegedly treated the inhabitants inhumanely—especially the Jewish merchants. During his occupation the Dutch flag was left flying over Fort Oranje and the unsuspecting ships thus lured into the harbor were immediately taken as prizes. Rodney's profit from his sojourn on Statia was later estimated in excess of four million pounds; the island never recovered economically.

This second episode on Statia, accomplished without gunfire, had a far stronger ripple effect than the first. Not only were the St. Kitts merchants furious, but their London counterparts had also lost considerable sums and the scandal forced Rodney home to face charges.

That was in February 1781. In May—during Rodney's absence from the Caribbean—de Grasse tried to retake Morne Fortuné in St. Lucia with the help of General de Bouillé. They got into Gros Islet, a bay on the northwest coast protected by a big hump of land known as Pigeon Island with fortifications at the summit. Aided by an informal fleet of citizen sailors, the English defenders drove de Grasse off, saving St. Lucia without knowing it for the last act of the drama.

*"Had it not been for this infamous island," he wrote Rear-Adm. Sir Peter Parker, "the American rebellion could not possibly have subsisted." To his wife Rodney noted in a letter, "This rock has done England more harm than all the arms of her most potent enemies."

De Grasse, apparently undismayed by his defeat, offered to go to the rescue of the Americans in Virginia. George Washington replied by immediately bringing sixteen thousand American and French Troops to Yorktown, where de Grasse anchored at the mouth of the York River, preventing Cornwallis and his eight thousand men from escaping by sea. Cornwallis's surrender on October 19 rang the changes for the Americans and the Revolutionary War was all but over. Many historians have charged Rodney with ultimate responsibility for this decisive turn of events, saying that he could have prevented de Grasse's arrival at Yorktown if he hadn't been so preoccupied with looting St. Eustatius. Although it is ultimately a matter of opinion, there certainly is no disputing the fact that during Rodney's absence de Grasse was the busiest admiral in the Western Hemisphere.

ACT III

Taking advantage of England's loss of the thirteen colonies, de Grasse now turned his attention to St. Kitts. Not in the line of passage from the Old World to the Caribbean, St. Kitts sits at about the neck of the long, curving spine of the Lesser Antilles, dominated by a huge volcanic crater appropriately named Mount Misery. Because it was so successful in growing sugar and sending out colonists to take up life in other islands, it was named Mother Colony of the Caribbean.

After the Caribs had been disposed of by French and English settlers who shared its limited acreage, their countries began fighting in the usual way over its ownership. The first guns were placed by the French at the foot of a giant northwest coastal outcropping covering thirty acres. The Caribs were said to have believed that in time past remembering Brimstone Hill was the cork plugging up Mount Misery's molten fury, and one day was spewed out to the edge of the sea. It was such a logical place for a fortress that it is strange real construction didn't begin at the summit until 1736, when the English, put forty-nine guns there. Almost a hundred years went by before it was entirely finished. Designed so that enemy forces could be blasted out of commission at almost any point on the way up, Brimstone Hill is an incredible complex of bastions, tunnels, walls, keeps, turrets, powder magazines, parade grounds and barracks. Inevitably it was described as the Gibraltar of the West Indies—yet the one real battle it experienced had a surprising outcome.

The battle began in late January 1782, led by the same two who had attacked St. Lucia the year before, Admiral de Grasse and General de Bouillé, this time with the French Caribbean fleet and eight thousand troops. St. Kitts's English

Fort Oranje, St. Eustatius, looks much the same today as it did when the Dutch-held island was vilified as a "nest of vipers" by Admiral Rodney because of its role in supplying arms and supplies to the American rebels. The first foreign salute to an American naval vessel was given here on November 16, 1776.

Leewards Governor General Shirley had less than one thousand men to defend the Brimstone Hill garrison, but being outnumbered wasn't his only problem. About half of them were comprised of the local citizenry, who were still seething over Rodney's sack of Statia, and they apparently refused to help hoist the necessary ordnance up the hill. (Why it had been left down below is not clear, but it might have been because the fort wasn't completed at the time of the siege.) De Bouillé was able to turn the British's own sixteen-pound cannon and fifteen-inch mortars against them and keep up the onslaught for an entire month. With de Grasse's fleet lined up in Basseterre's roadstead, the defenders' prospects looked dim indeed.

By now Rodney was on his way back to the islands, and orders were dispatched to Adm. Sir Samuel Hood at English Harbour, Antigua, to sail to the rescue with his fleet of twenty-two ships. Hood mustered a sizable company of soldiers and put them ashore at Frigate Bay, on the opposite side of St. Kitts. But as he approached the French fleet, two of his ships collided, a mishap that enabled de Grasse to take a new position away from shore. (This proved a mistake, as it turned out, for Hood then found an opportunity to move into the area where de Grasse had been, cutting off the French fleet's land base.) In the following battle that lasted all afternoon, evening and through late afternoon the next day, Hood was clearly in the lead. When de Grasse finally withdrew, his ships were full of holes and his dead numbered 1000, while Hood's fleet sustained 73 dead and 244 wounded. Considering what conditions were for wounded men on board those crowded ships after a battle, it is a miracle any of them survived.

During this grim sea encounter, Hood's soldiers were advancing from Frigate Bay across the island and managed to attack de Bouillé's forces from the rear. But Hood's victory was too little and too late. The French land forces finally breached the northwestern redoubt and Brimstone Hill was lost. Brigadier General Fraser surrendered, but de Bouillé, gallant eighteenth-century gentleman, paid tribute to the defenders' courage by allowing them to leave the hill with "drums beating, colours flying." Commander-in-Chief Shirley returned to Antigua and Fraser was allowed to "continue in the service of his country."*

With the French flag now waving atop Brimstone Hill, Admiral de Grasse sailed back to Martinique, where, unaware that the curtain had gone up on Act IV, he began preparations for the moment when he could rendezvous with the Spanish fleet out of Havana and have a try at the grand prize, Jamaica.

By mid-February, Rodney, on his return from England, had gotten as far as Barbados, about 150 miles southeast of Martinique. Receiving intelligence of de Grasse's intent, the sixty-year-old admiral, suffering from the gout but now knighted and freed from charges of having raped St. Eustatius, sailed immediately for St. Lucia so he could keep watch on the movements of the French fleet across the channel.

ACT IV

The same Pigeon Island fortress that had seen de Grasse's defeat the year before was now a prime lookout for Rodney. He anchored his fleet in Gros Islet Bay and ascended the hill to keep tabs on the French at Fort-de-France. From the walls atop Pigeon Island hill a broad view of the channel and Martinique was possible on a clear day, which must have been the weather condition in early April when the English lookouts saw several of de Grasse's ships on the move. It was the signal for the beginning of one of the most innovative, celebrated and politically important sea battles ever fought in the West Indies.

*Both quotes are from the Articles of Capitulation.

Only a month before, in March, the story goes that the French became bored waiting for the proper moment to proceed to Hispaniola for their rendezvous with the Spanish fleet, and when some fresh supply ships arrived from France, de Grasse decided to suspend the cat-and-mouse waiting game for a night. He sent out invitations to a ball, to the English officers on St. Lucia as well as his own. Unable to dance because of a flare-up of his gout, Rodney declined, but the others went, and the unaccustomed luxury of an elegant French buffet must have seemed like manna to soldiers and sailors living a spartan existence on hilltop barracks and uncomfortable ships.

The ball was a smashing success, but after it was over, everybody returned to watching and being watched: de Grasse anchored off Fort-de-France and Rodney perched on Pigeon Island. Then on April 8, when de Grasse's fleet was spotted on the move, Rodney took off in hot pursuit with thirty-six Sail of the Line. De Grasse sailed a northwesterly course toward the channel that divides Dominica and Guadeloupe. Because his fleet was anticipating a major siege of Jamaica, his ships were weighted with cargo. Rodney's frigates were lighter and faster, and in the urgency of the chase, eight of them became separated from the van. De Grasse paused to attack these, but didn't move in for the kill because he wanted to take advantage of the trade winds to get his entire fleet through the channel. He would have gotten through, except for a serious collision between two of his ships. Rodney pressed his advantage, and early next morning the formal battle—later named after the chain of rocky cays in the channel called Les Saintes—began.

The orderly progress in a line of the thirty-five English and thirty-three French ships passing each other was like the slow steps of a minuet at court. Just when they had completely passed each other, the wind switched from easterly to southerly, and to Rodney's great good fortune, a large gap in the French line opened where he could observe it. Reportedly it was Fleet Capt. Charles Douglas who saw the advantage first, but it must have been Rodney who gave the command for his flagship to breach the gap with six ships following. To the horror of de Grasse, the French fleet was soon split into three sections, its flagship *Ville de Paris* fatally separated. The great battle ended when Rodney's men captured the flagship and five others.

Rodney's strategy in breaking the line has been called the forerunner of a similar ploy used by Nelson in the Battle of Trafalgar. For the English in the last two decades of the eighteenth-century it established their sea supremacy in the

The St. Lucia Archaeological and Historical Society has established an excellent small museum in the old officers' quarters of Morne Fortuné, its displays going back to archaic Indian periods. The society has also published a guide to historic sites throughout the much fought-over island.

Caribbean, saved Jamaica from invasion and especially saved face for the loss of thirteen colonies on the North American mainland.

Fort Oranje, St. Eustatius

Although it is little more than a fragment of lava thrust up from the vast sea bottom, St. Eustatius at one time had seventeen forts and batteries strung around its rocky shoreline. The entire eastern half of the island is a steep incline leading to an extinct volcanic crater with a rain forest inside called "The Quill." On the southeast coast a rugged natural fort made of forbidding rock faces known as Whitewall is separated from the old battery of *Fort De Windt* by steep canyons. Across the channel St. Kitts's Mount Misery dominates the southeast skyline. Until a recent road was put through from Statia's one town, Oranjestad, few but goats knew this high place where cannon once pointed at Brimstone Hill. (Not that they could ever have reached their mark.) The cannon, rusting and forgotten, still lie there and the old breastworks are crumbling down the cliffside.

Fort Oranje is on the southwestern coast overlooking a line of sheer cliffs and the roadstead that once accommodated as many as two hundred sailing ships when business was good.

An eighteenth-century plan drawing shows Fort Oranje as having within its limited space a commander's house (Quarters of Abraham Ravené, who performed that salute to the American flag), a town hall, prison cells and provost quarters, barracks, a cistern and powder magazine and gun emplacements overlooking the roadstead. The fort probably looks very little different today except that government offices, a post office and a large monument commemorating the First Salute dominate the premises.

On the beach below are the ruins of the warehouses that once stored valuable supplies, at least three forts and powder houses, cisterns, officers' quarters and other installations that can no longer be identified. The rocks and masonry are sunk in an overgrowth of trees and bush. Tides have washed over them and landslides from the cliffs above have shot boulders down to bury still more. A contemporary print of the scene

The Prince of Wales Bastion at the summit of St. Kitts' Brimstone Hill has been restored with great care as a national treasure. It was spared in a recent earthquake that damaged other parts of the giant fortress—a strong argument for proper preservation or restoration of historic sites in the Caribbean.

looking toward the town and fort from the roadstead shows one fort that either existed only in the artist's imagination or was really there but is no longer identifiable: a square castle on a sandy cay off the Lower Town shore. A recent exploration made informally by Robert Marx uncovered remains of such a fort under the base of a new pier that was begun with funds from the European Common Market. The pier is located at the southern end of the bay, just about where the print shows the fort to have been. Buried under the waters of the bay are yet more traces of buildings, as well as the sea wall that once protected the shore from erosion.

Access to the sites of coastal forts—or what is left of them—is limited to the road out of Oranjestad south to *Fort Nassau* and on to Fort De Windt. Moving northeast across the island, the road goes behind the mountain only to a point where St. Kitts becomes visible. Wilderness takes over from there, and anyone interested in finding a lost *Fort Correcoure* or *Lisburn's Battery* had better walk or ride a local donkey. The northern section of Statia is a jumble of rocks and wild places harboring one historic fort and caves once used by pre-Columbian Indians. This is one of the many islands within easy access to North Americans that offers a challenge for primary exploration.

Morne Fortuné, Pigeon Island, St. Lucia

After the Battle of Les Saintes came the Treaty of Versailles in 1783 and, as so often happened, what mortars and shells had decided, diplomatic horse trading reversed. Back to France went St. Lucia. But it wasn't destined to enjoy much peace for the next thirty-one years. As Eric Branford of the St. Lucia Historical Society remarks, "Every morning we'd wake up wondering whether to sing the 'Marseillaise' or 'God Save the King.' Mostly, we just sang our own song— under our breath."

So the great fortress atop *Morne Fortuné* went on changing hands and flags. After 1789 the impact of the French Revolution began hitting the island hard. The *Tricolore* was hoisted above Morne Fortuné in 1791; a time of anarchy followed with a brief Republican government during which slavery was abolished. Then the English took St. Lucia in 1794, only to lose it again to Republican sympathizers inspired by the famous revolutionary Victor Hugues in Guadeloupe. In 1796 Lt. Gen. Sir Ralph Abercrombie and Sir Hugh Christian made an assault on a Morne Fortuné, newly strengthened by the French Republicans. Although the English took the fortress, they didn't gain the island, and guerrilla warfare went on. When they finally managed to get control and pacify the dissidents, along came another treaty —at Amiens in 1802—restoring St. Lucia to France. There was to be one more bloody battle at Morne Fortuné, in June 1803; the English stormed the stronghold and won. If Horatio Nelson had fought Villeneuve in the West Indies instead of chasing him across the Atlantic and vanquishing him at Trafalgar, St. Lucia would again have suffered bloodshed. The Treaty of Paris in 1814 gave the island to Britain, which held it until St. Lucia got its own constitution and became a West Indies Associated State of the United Kingdom.

For many years Morne Fortuné was allowed to deteriorate. The early French fortifications have never been looked after, and they are still in poor shape. The English buildings have fared better in recent years, and the vast hilltop site is now an attractive place to visit and explore, although modern automobiles parked before old yellow brick facades tend to obstruct the mind's eye; imagining troops of redcoats storming the heights with bayonets isn't easy under the circumstances.

Near the entrance a well-preserved building that was once used as officers' quarters is now the museum of the St. Lucia Archaeological and Historical Society. Small but well organized, its displays go back to archaic Indian periods. Across the way the stone walls of the noncommissioned officers' barracks face the parade grounds. If and when funds permit, the Society hopes to make use of these buildings for an expanded museum.

The reason for all the parked cars is that most of the restored buildings have been preserved outside as they originally were, while the interiors have been adapted for schoolrooms and laboratories. Today's St. Lucians are studying there, and a branch of the University of the West Indies is in one of the buildings. A Physical Planning School, a Rockefeller Foundation Laboratory and some government offices are using others. An American bank has assisted in landscaping a large and impressive monument, the site of which offers a fine view of the lands below and the islands beyond. Here one begins to understand why the belligerents were constantly trying to storm the place. Anyone with enough purchase money who wishes to make the vision permanent may build a home at the Sentinel Hill.

That mythical traveling salesman of arches did very well at Morne Fortuné. The buildings, generally rectangular, have two stories, with arched galleries on the lower floor and slim posts supporting the familiar pitched roofs that extend to the edge of the galleries. In some cases, buildings are connected by masonry arches.

Morne Fortuné's historic partner, *Pigeon Island*—or, to be more comprehensive, the bay of *Gros Islet*—is another story. It juts out at almost the northwestern tip of the island and was of more realistic value in defending St. Lucia than Morne Fortuné or even Vigie, which guarded Castries harbor.

The first battery at Gros Islet was built in 1778, and was greatly strengthened under Rodney's direction between 1780 and 1782. Ancillary works were put in, such as lime kilns, whale-oil processing plants, and on the tall, peaked island itself there were four twenty-four-pound cannons, two mortars, a powder magazine, a bunker and a water catchment.

Today the beach and lagoon areas that ring what is now called Rodney Bay have received man-made help that may have destructive ecological effects. A causeway that covered a reef, landfills and a 450-acre "residential and leisure community" with shopping centers and hotels have disturbed, perhaps permanently, the fish-spawning areas. A proposal is before the government to turn the entire Pigeon Island section into a national park that would include an underwater preserve.

At the south base of Pigeon Island are a sea-eroded cemetery dating from 1781, cannon from a battery of 1762 and also the ruins of a hospital near the powder magazine of Fort Rodney which is still in use as a water-storage tank. Today in the lower sections one finds romantic-looking houses; they turn out to have been isolation wards for St. Lucians thought to have yellow fever. The military works are in a badly ruined condition. A steep and difficult climb to the top—not a jaunt for anyone with a heart condition—reveals that famous view of the Martinique channel. But a few walls and gun emplacements are all that are left up there, and Rodney must have had a strong lens in his spyglass to have seen de Grasse's ships from so far away. Except for the modern developments on the bay side, this is a place where reliving the centuries is easy, as one considers how a single sentry's view from here could have affected hundreds, and often, thousands of lives.

Brimstone Hill, St. Kitts

On October 8, 1974, an earthquake registering seven on the Richter scale, rumbled through a number of islands in the northeastern Caribbean. Antigua and St. Kitts were hardest hit, although some damage was reported on neighboring Nevis, St. Eustatius, St. Maarten and other islands. (The Seventh Day Adventist meetinghouse in Oranjestad, St. Eustatius, was the only church there completely spared, resulting in a number of conversions, it is said.)

The Honorable D.L. Matheson, a St. Kitts resident who has been the leading spirit in the restoration of *Brimstone Hill Fortress* and president of the society responsible for the recent work on Prince of Wales Bastion, reported that the quake damaged the citadel, parts of the soldiers' barracks which have so far not been restored, the retaining wall supporting the parade level and the wall along the road to Fort Charlotte and the artillery officers' and infantry officers' quarters. Matheson said that those sections of the latter building which had been renovated in honor of a visit by Prince Charles of England were not cracked in the earthquake, leading him to believe that proper restoration may do more than save the fortress from normal disintegration.

We tend to think that time stops when a building or city —or fortress—reaches the landmark stage and becomes a "historic" ruin. Certainly in the Caribbean, nature and man are continuing to help time kill the mementos of the past. The recent damage at Brimstone Hill is especially distressing because so much meticulous effort and hard-to-come-by funds have been expended to restore it, to transform it from an overgrown pile of decaying masonry to a living national park.

Two hurricanes in the nineteenth century had led to its abandonment as a fortress, and during the following years it was shamelessly vandalized and neglected. In the late 1960's and early seventies, through the combined efforts of the Caribbean Conservation Association, Island Resources Foundation and the Society for the Restoration of Brimstone Hill, the Prince of Wales Bastion began to be revived. Standing on the Citadel today, it is easy to conjure images of the dramas that went on here, particularly during the great siege by de Bouillé's six thousand troops while de Grasse's fleet in the roadstead beyond was engaged in a dance of death with Admiral Hood's ships. However, Brimstone Hill is envisioned as more than a monument to past bloodshed. Recreational and crafts centers are planned, and it is hoped that the site will become a valuable place for the people of St. Kitts as well as for tourists.

To reach Brimstone Hill from Basseterre, capital city and harbor of St. Kitts, one follows the route that must first have been taken by Sir Thomas Warner and his settlers in 1623 when they decided to colonize Sandy Point on the northwestern coast. One of the chief gun emplacements on the Citadel of Brimstone Hill faces Sandy Point and was cracked in the recent earthquake.

The fortress looks very different from Morne Fortuné, which is yellowish and seemingly far younger. Brimstone is predominantly gray and white, a great expanse of walls, towers and paved areas, an abandoned Camelot. Beyond and above the eight-hundred-foot wall from the Magazine Bastion on the northwest to Orillion Bastion at the southwest point are the restored Prince of Wales Bastion, Fort George, Fort Charlotte, an officers' mess and barracks, a parade ground, artillery officers' quarters and soldiers' barracks, all connected with roads and walls of stone and brick. (The arch salesman passed this way, too.)

An incredible variety of installations for military living once functioned here: a hospital, which will eventually house a museum, ordnance stores, cook houses, a "mental" house, a cemetery and a sophisticated cistern system that provided fresh water by collecting rain in the Citadel courtyard and draining it down to cisterns on lower levels. It is possible that the great siege might have been shorter if the defenders hadn't had these life-giving resources.

Looking down from the hill now, it does seem odd that the English could have been taken by any amount of troops storming the green slopes, for they could spot anybody com-

English Harbour, Antigua, was Britain's major military and naval base in the Eastern Caribbean (Jamaica's Port Royal dominated western waters). Restored as a marina and visitor attraction, it is the Caribbean's finest example of proper use of an historic site.

ing from any direction. The view beyond the coastline seems to stretch out endlessly; actually it is about seventy miles. Dramatic, rocky Saba is on the horizon to the northwest, with Statia's "quill" looming close in the same line of vision. To the southeast is sister island Nevis and then Montserrat. To the north are the low, peaked silhouettes of St. Barth's and its cays, and in the far distance, the voluptuous hills of St. Maarten. But the siege of Brimstone Hill was won by constant battering from the French guns immediately below. The final assault on the heights came only when the English were exhausted.

Quite naturally, Brimstone Hill wasn't St. Kitt's only fortified protection. At Sandy Point, the walls and foundations of the old French *Charles Fort* remain except for the sea wall. A powder magazine inside is in good condition. However, the site is currently in use as a leper colony; they don't expect many visitors. In the bay are said to be some drowned French works—*Fort Lewis*—similar to those structures under the waters of Statia's Oranje Bay and Jamestown Bay in Nevis.

On land, other forts, all in various degrees of deterioration and twentieth-century litter, are the French-built *Fort Smith* of the sugar depot (the island has an old narrow-gauge railroad for the transport of sugar to the docks); *Fort Tyson* overlooking Frigate Bay, which Hood's soldiers from English Harbour stormed in the hope of rescuing Brimstone Hill; *Fort Thomas* on the grounds of a big chain hotel in Basseterre; *Stone Fort, Fig Tree Fort* and *Fort Ashby*, all of which are evidence of deliberate or careless neglect by residents and government. Perhaps the restoration of Brimstone Hill will serve as an inspiration to do something about the less glamorous sites that represent lost moments in this stately island's past.

Fort St. Louis and Diamond Rock, Martinique

When Pierre Belain d'Esnambuc, who had managed for a time to share St. Kitts with the Englishman Thomas Warner, arrived in Martinique in 1635, he had already bought it, along with St. Lucia, Grenada and the Grenadines. His patron back in France was Cardinal Richelieu, whose long-term goal was to supplant the Spanish in the islands and meanwhile to vie with the English for those islands the Spanish apparently didn't want.

Relations between the French settlers and the Caribs in Martinique seem to have been more friendly than they were elsewhere. The Caribs kept to themselves on the windward side of the island, and the French, under the governorship of Jacques Dyel du Parquet, d'Esnambuc's nephew, established plantations and settlements along the west coast, particularly around St. Pierre and Fort Royal, which later became Fort-de-France, the capital.

The French farmed and also took advantage of offshore ventures provided by foreign shipping. French corsairs had become notorious by the end of the seventeenth century. With the increasing menace of retaliation by freebooters from England and the Netherlands and the uncertainty of Carib intentions, it was natural that defenses were the first order of public building. Du Parquet began constructing *Fort St. Louis* on a rocky spur jutting out over the bay of Fort Royal in 1640. After his death, in 1658, the succeeding governors, de Baas and Blenac, continued strengthening the fort. The Dutch attacked it in 1674, and, by then, the Caribs were no longer docile and were organizing raids against the plantations. Eventually the increasingly militant French pushed them out of their traditional area around Sainte-Marie, and defenses were built all over the island.

By the beginning of the eighteenth century, Fort St. Louis needed further strengthening, and Sébastien Le Prestre de Vauban, Royal military architect to Louis XIV is reputed to have designed the new version of the giant brickwork pile. It had all the appurtenances of a medieval castle: underground passages, esplanades, casements and a moat. Nevertheless, the English managed to take it three times: in 1673, 1794 and again in 1809. But it was a thorn in the side of the English during the constant battles over nearby St. Lucia, and it served de Grasse well on the eve of the Battle of the Saintes.

The old moat, which was a navigable canal, has been filled in and changed and is now the Boulevard of the Chevalier de Ste.-Marthe. The grand old castle set in wooded grounds, with giant cannon still pointing at forgotten enemies, may be visited by permission of the military authorities. But it seems to be less interesting to tourists than the high, pointed rock off the southern tip of the west coast known as *Pointe du Diamant* (Diamond Rock), which had a curious moment of military glory and is the only rock in the world officially registered as a ship.

In 1804, when England and France were again squaring off—this time the protagonist was Napoleon, who dreamt of including Britain in his empire—Sir Samuel Hood was in command of the St. Lucia Naval Station. From Pigeon Island, where Rodney had spied on de Grasse's fleet in Martinique, it was possible to see Le Diamant. French ships were

Guadeloupe's Fort Fleur d'Epée, like most defense works in the Caribbean, commands the finest possible view of the sea and the surrounding island. Plans are underway to use the original steps as a setting for concerts and folklore shows.

sneaking through the channel between the rock and the mainland a thousand yards away to find safe harbor at Fort Royal. Hood conceived a daring plan to prevent this. Sailing his flagship over to the rock, he ordered his sailors to climb to the peak, loop a hawser over the top and haul several cannon up the side. They were to remain there like lookouts in a rigging, aiming at any French ship that tried to pass. The contingent of 120 remained up there for eighteen months, effectively preventing the passage of any more French. So successful were they that their aerie was officially commissioned H.M.S. *Diamond Rock*.

Admiral Villeneuve, who was in Martinique under Napoleon's orders, decided that the impertinent presence of the English "ship" was not to be suffered any longer and sent a small fleet of sixteen vessels to get rid of the menace. Before it was all over, the men of H.M.S. *Diamond Rock* had sunk three French gunboats and wounded at least seventy men. Their feat is still acknowledged today with an official salute by any passing English ship.

English Harbour, Antigua

In 1782 when Hood received orders to sail to the rescue of besieged Brimstone Hill Fortress, his fleet was at *English*

Harbour, Antigua, about fifty miles to the southeast of St. Kitts.

The first European settlers on the island had come from St. Kitts in 1632, but a combination of Carib raids and the perpetual warfare of the European nations kept this rather flat, dry island—ringed with white sand beaches unappreciated in those days—from becoming much of a success as a colony for either side.

Then in the early eighteenth century the British government decided to keep a year-round fleet in residence in the Caribbean—one at Port Royal, Jamaica, and one at English Harbour, Antigua. This was possible for the English because they could obtain supplies for their military and naval forces from their north American as well as their Caribbean colonies. French practice was to send fleets out to the colonies when the hurricane season was safely over in late autumn, and return them home in summer, when storms were threatening. Most of their supplies had to come from France, which was a disadvantage, but their ships were on the whole larger and swifter and their crews and soldiers had not been debilitated by long tours of duty—a year to eighteen months —in an enervating climate as were the British.

Antigua's south coast provided a made-to-order anchorage for the English fleets. It was spacious, with just enough flat land at the foot of the protective hills for military installations and a carenage. The harbor opening was so narrow, it could almost literally be locked up at night. On the hills above, a string of fortifications was later built, begun in 1781 just before the siege of Brimstone Hill; these are known as *Shirley Heights*, after the Caribbean commander-in-chief, Governor Shirley. Falmouth Harbour next door to the installations at English Harbour had its own fort atop *Monk's Hill*, giving the area further protection.

Thus, in 1725 English Harbour became the key English naval base. Ships were careened and troops quartered there, but although its location was ideal strategically, the military rank and file complained bitterly of the unsanitary conditions under which they had to live.

The complex, which included a dockyard with capstans and other equipment for careening vessels, was later named for twenty-five-year-old Horatio Nelson, who served his second Caribbean tour of duty there as a captain and then commander between 1784 and 1787, long before his triumph at Trafalgar and his wooing of the fascinating Lady Hamilton. In the last year of his service at English Harbour, the handsome and admittedly lonely bachelor sailed over to Nevis, where he wed the widow Nisbet, the Duke of Clarence serving as his best man. Whether he grumbled about living conditions at English Harbour after that is not known.

After an earthquake in 1843, Nelson's Dockyard was gradually allowed to fall into ruin until 1951, when the Society of the Friends of English Harbour was organized by Sir Kenneth Blackburne, then governor of the Leeward Islands. Money and time were volunteered by local residents, as well as concerned people in England, beginning with the queen and Princess Margaret. Original plans of the buildings were researched, and as the restoration began, the volunteer and local professional craftsmen had to learn eighteenth-century building techniques. The same procedure had to be followed in Brimstone Hill, and similar problems were encountered in reproducing materials, methods of joining and particularly in obtaining authentic hardware. Quite often, the hardware would have to be made from scratch by a skilled artisan in a faraway place like New Jersey.

Today anyone plying Caribbean waters is likely to know *Nelson's Dockyard* as a destination, safe harbor, repair base or winter anchorage. The use to which the English Harbour restoration has been so imaginatively adapted could be an example to all islanders who don't know what to do about their old ruins except to bulldoze them under or build something modern over them.

In their restored state, many of the buildings are designed to be used as they were originally, such as the carenage, the master shipwright's house and galley, paint and rigging rooms, the blacksmith's shop and a saw pit. Other buildings necessary in the eighteenth-century, such as a guardhouse for the recalcitrant, have been transformed for modern use. The admiral's residence is now an atmospheric inn and restaurant and the officers' quarters a yacht club. One of the most instructive and vivid museum displays in the West Indies is in the admiral's headquarters; it details history from early Indian periods through the times of British sea supremacy to the 1890's, when English Harbour lost its official reason for being.

The Shirley Heights fortifications, on a two-hundred-foot cliff overlooking the entire scene, haven't been restored at all, and the arched walls are in a sorry, picturesque, ruined condition. The brickwork is decayed and broken, and little remains of the original installations except a blockhouse and a cemetery with a memorial to the 54th Regiment. The view is glorious. Other forts on Antigua badly in need of proper attention, either for preservation as ruins or restoration, are Monk's Hill and *Fort James* and *Fort Barrington*, across the island at the capital, St. John's. Perched on a point of land at the entrance to St. John's Harbour, Fort James dates back to 1704 when the laying of the cornerstone was celebrated with Masonic rites. The fort, named for James II, guarded the town and the northwest coast.

Jamaica's Many Forts

With all the sea battles, landings, assaults, sieges and retreats the French, English, Dutch and occasionally the Danish and Spanish engaged in during the late seventeenth and throughout the eighteenth century in their deadly chess game for profit and supremacy, it would seem surprising that Jamaica didn't participate in more of the turmoil. Jamaica was Britain's queen colony, the venue of immense investments.

About the size of the North American colony of Connecticut, it had the topography of a small continent, was endowed with a great variety of natural resources and positioned so as to be a convenient trading center. Some of its commerce was legal and some—as we have seen—less legal; in both fields of endeavor it was a point in the triangle linking the West Indies, New England and the mother country.

Yet the "Jamaica station" boasted no vast forts, no immense accommodations for thousands of troops and huge armament stores such as were built on the much smaller islands of St. Kitts, St. Lucia, Antigua and Martinique. Modest defenses were placed at strategic points overlooking Jamaica's many bays, but the 200' x 125' Fort Charlotte on the northwest coast seems to have been one of the larger fortresses. Its mounting of twenty-two to twenty-five guns in its heyday suggests a continuing fear of Spanish invasion from Cuba, if not from pirates.

In truth, the Eastern Caribbean islands proved to be Jamaica's real fortifications. The European nation that held the whip hand there, where the wind carried sail through the Antillean barrier, also had access to Jamaica in the west. Columbus, naturally, was the first European to reach Jamaica, on two different occasions—becoming stranded on the second landing at St. Ann's Bay on the north coast near today's town of Ocho Rios. (The Spanish called it Las Choreras—"the spouts"—for its many waterfalls.) After beaching his caravels and camping out for an entire year he was rescued in 1503 through the bravery of one of his men, Diego Mendez. To get help, Mendez took his canoe against the prevailing trade winds through the treacherous Windward Passage to the colony at Isabela on Hispaniola's north coast. That channel is a vortex of winds and currents and it is a miracle that on the second try, Mendez made it.

Four years later Don Christobal's son Diego dispatched a group of colonists from the Hispaniola settlement to the same site in Jamaica and Sevilla Nueva was founded in the swampy coast of St. Ann's Bay, which they called Santa Gloria. Historian C.S. Cotter, who spent thirty-five years searching and digging for known remains of Sevilla Nueva's castle, well, church and sugar mill, has noted that in 1509 "Hundreds of caravels arrived bringing cows, pigs, horses, sheep, fowl, fruit, plants and seeds. Roads were outlined through the island and the settlements of Melilla (Port Maria) and Cristiana (Bluefields) began."*

Intermittent digging has been going on at Sevilla Nueva since 1937 by several teams (some of them amateur groups), and in 1970, the Jamaica National Trust Commission announced that this was perhaps the most important archaeological site in Jamaica and that a professional survey indicated a great potential for further archaeological and perhaps restorative efforts. As of this writing, the remains of Sevilla Nueva still lie under many feet of plantation humus and coconut forest. Stubbornly patient, Cotter was able to locate the site of one fortification, at the governor's house, or "castle." He says he removed a thousand tons of "overburden" and many Indian and Spanish sherds. He also found a gun emplacement connected to the fort by a six-foot trench. "The main armament appears to have been on the top of the building which was terraced 24 feet above ground level [and was] directed towards the vulnerable southern approach."* Its plan was identical to that of a fort-castle found in Hispaniola from the same period.

The little city's armaments weren't needed as protection against the Arawaks and didn't do any good in saving the inhabitants from fever. About 1532 they decided to move south to the drier but fertile St. Catherine plain beside the Rio Cobre in south central Jamaica. This much-written-about capital, not far from present-day Kingston, was called Villa de la Vega (City of the Plain), and later, Santiago de la Vega (St. James of the Plain); still later, to the English, it was Spanish Town. But almost nothing has been documented on other settlements around the island. Cristiana (or Oristan and, later, Bluefields) was a place on the western section of the south coast where some crumbled walls still exist. In 1505 a shipload of famished Spaniards arrived there, hopelessly lost and looking for Hispaniola. During their stay ashore they dealt with the Arawaks in the accustomed man-

*C.S. Cotter, *Sevilla Nueva, The Story of an Excavation.*
*Ibid.

The architecture of Fort Frederik shows the Danish influence on West Indian building styles. Begun in 1752 in Frederiksted, one of St. Croix's two "planned" communities, it has survived a tidal wave and two centuries of fires, slave riots, and hurricanes.

ner; obtaining provisions and directions from them and then betraying their trust. Some of the Spaniards, who must have been acutely ravenous, betrayed the Indians' trust to the ultimate by dining on them.

The group moved on and obviously wasn't the one that built the Bluefields walls. According to the present owner of the property, the masonry was part of a fort dating from 1509, which seems to tie in with the fanning out of settlers from Sevilla Nueva. Historian H.P. Jacobs speculates that Oristan may have been the oldest regular European settlement in the New World, but Santo Domingo and other towns in Hispaniola, if not Sevilla Nueva, predate it. Whatever was built on that hillside is lost to history, and no official preservation effort has been made. A dedicated ruin-buff might obtain permission to view the site by writing to Bluefields Estate, Westmoreland Parish, Jamaica, West Indies.

C.S. Cotter believes that the move to Santiago de la Vega may have been inspired as much by the gold rush to South America as by susceptibility to swamp fever. The south coast was closer to the ships that could carry them to El Dorado. But some of the settlers must have withstood temptation, for after 1534 they settled down to 120 years of relatively peaceful plantation life, especially at White Marl, where the large Arawak village could have conveniently provided them with a work force within walking distance. Slaves were also brought in from Africa, and it is interesting that some of these—turned guerrillas—later decided the fate of the Spaniards in Jamaica.

Current excavations in Old King's House* and elsewhere in Spanish Town, under an archaeological program of the Institute of Jamaica, have established no fortifications from the early days. There were churches, an abbey, a hall of the audiencia and probably some taverns—certainly a jail. *Passage Fort* at the harbor mouth of the Rio Cobre was the city's major protection and its access from the sea. Under the King's House was an underground tunnel, possibly a cistern but reputedly reaching as far as Passage Fort. Perhaps further excavations will solve the mystery, but if it was constructed as an escape hatch, it didn't serve its purpose when the English turned up en masse at Passage Fort and demanded that the Spanish governor, Juan Ramirez Arillano, surrender unconditionally.

A clumsy mishap in Santo Domingo brought English Adm. William Penn and Gen. Robert Venables to the gates of Santiago de la Vega. The year was 1655, the time of Oliver Cromwell's "Western design" to capture Spain's possessions in the Caribbean. His admiral and general had been ordered to take Hispaniola but they failed miserably and decided to try saving face—and perhaps even their necks—by assaulting vulnerable Jamaica instead. The initial conquest turned out to be almost as easy as they expected, and their surrender terms were so harsh that after Ramirez signed the articles of capitulation, a number of his compatriots took to the hills and spent the next five years harassing the English settlers with a series of guerrilla raids that almost succeeded. Their leader became the last Spanish governor—one might call him a governor in exile in his own territory. In his surprise raids, Cristobal Arnaldo Ysassi stole cattle and provisions and ambushed the increasingly discouraged British soldiers, who didn't like the country anyway. Ysassi was greatly aided by escaped slaves who had become maroons in the wilderness and knew every pathway through the mountains.

Until 1660 the black hill people, under the leadership of a fierce fellow named Juan de Bolas, helped the Spanish resist being pushed further and further toward the north coast. But a decisive battle fought at Rio Nuevo, a half-moon-shaped bay between Ocho Rios and Oracabessa, along with the defection of Juan de Bolas to the English and a curious lack of cooperation by the governor of Cuba only ninety miles to the

*A museum with displays of archaeological finds from the Spanish Town dig was opened in October, 1975. It is located at Old King's House near the Jamaica Folk Museum.

north, forced Ysassi to capitulate at last. The Fort of the
Conception at Rio Nuevo, where the bloody last stand took
place, is no more. It was on a hill at the western edge of the
bay near a string of wooded cliffs. Under Col. Edward D'Oyley, the British landed on the western side and worked their
way inland to take the Spanish defenders from the south. On
May 3, 1560, Ysassi and a few followers finally were able to
make their way to Cuba in hand-made canoes while the English were still searching for him, unaware that they were
now in full possession of Jamaica. An attractive memorial
has been placed on the site of the old Rio Nuevo fort, an
easy drive from any of the mid-north coast resorts.

Penn (father of the father of Pennsylvania) and Venables
were followed to Jamaica by successions of English settlers,
and the need for shoreline protection became evident. Some
of the early planters built their own houses like forts (see
ch. 5), with gun embrasures enabling them to snipe at
marauding Spanish or the escaped slaves who continued to
form into guerrilla bands in the hills.

Official forts eventually dotted the south coast's huge
triangular harbor, which is seventh largest in the world. At
its extreme western point near the Great Salt Pond was *Fort
Clarence*; then came *Fort Augusta*, built when Passage Fort
became silted with river mud; *Rockfort* and *Fort Nugent*
were set at the eastern arm. At the tip of the long sandspit
called Palisadoes which forms the southern arm of the triangle, the English chose Point Caguay, a Spanish careening
base, for the location of five separate forts. One of these was
Fort Cromwell, later renamed *Fort Charles*.

Although the harbor was spacious enough to accommodate several fleets, few ship's captains cared to chance
being bottled up in there and preferred anchorage around
Point Caguay. A town sprang up alongside the forts; it was a
natural for trade and reveling after long nights at sea. In
chapter 4, Port Royal, the famous city built on the sands of
Point Caguay, was given its due. The 1692 earthquake and
tidal wave that erased most of the city and all but one of the
forts left parts of Fort Charles standing, and the fort was
rebuilt in 1699. Imaginatively shaped, a section of it resembles a ship's quarterdeck, and imbedded in the masonry is a
plaque commemorating young Nelson's tour of duty there in
1779. (He got around almost as much as did Admiral Rodney, it seemed.) The quarterdeck at one time was surrounded
by water. Since then a series of earthquakes, hurricanes and
high tides has so changed the land structure that one now
looks out from the catwalk to a parched piece of overgrown
sandspit. The effect is the same as if Tosca, leaping over the

parapet at Castel San Angelo, had landed on a highway instead of into the Tiber.

With its venerable red brick and its menacing cannon peering through the embrasures, Fort Charles invokes romantic fantasies of eighteenth-century life, or would, if a white stucco structure had not been recently superimposed onto the lower level for the comfort of tourists. There is nothing wrong with providing for the comfort of tourists, but the structure could have been constructed of matching brick. Modernization at Antigua's English Harbour and St. Lucia's Morne Fortuné has been carried out to harmonize with the old buildings. At Fort Charles an archaeological excavation has uncovered remains of the original, pre-earthquake foundations. It would be interesting to know why such meticulous care has been expended on one part of the fort while another is insulted.

Regular guided tours of the fort may be taken, and since the parade ground of the Jamaica constabulary training school is next door, visitors may be fortunate enough to watch the proud precision drill of uniformed young men in sun helmets and shorts.

The coastal road which closely follows the shoreline of Jamaica, with the exception of certain inland detours in the south, also links Jamaica's forts. Moving counterclockwise from Kingston, the road comes to a large housing project called Harbour View. What is left of Fort Nugent on the hill above is a Martello Tower guarding the eastern end of the Palisadoes. The fort was originally built by a Spanish agent for a slave trading company whose name, El Capitano, Don Santiago del Castillo de Barcelona, was changed to Sir James Castile when he became a British subject. He tried to get reimbursed for his expenditures but the House of Assembly paid him only 500 pounds, and the government took the property over as well. It became Fort Nugent during the Napoleonic Wars, when it was further strengthened and the Martello Tower built by Governor Nugent, whose Lady was a tireless diarist and has left vivid descriptions of Jamaican life and times in the early 1800's. The word "Martello" stemmed from a cape in Corsica, Napoleon's birthplace; such towers were built to ward off the Corsican or his far-flung forces. A martello is circular, with a square penthouse and gun embrasures. Fort Nugent, although rebuilt a number of times up through World War I, succumbed at last to the bulldozers of the housing project.

The road east reaches Port Morant, a harbor much used today by sugar and produce freighters; in the days of sail, prevailing trade winds caused it to be the first Jamaican attack point. Fortified in 1675 at Battery Point, *Fort William* was abandoned in the mid-1700's to the appetite of the sea in favor of a battery near the town and *Fort Lindsay* on the opposite side of the bay. Today, the battery is lost and Fort Lindsay just barely visible in the bush, with one twenty-four-pound gun still mounted and others partly buried. About 150' x 150', with a thick wall facing the bay, it could accommodate nine cannons, and it is believed that the site once had many more buildings than would appear now. As from most forts, the view is magnificent.

At Port Antonio on the north coast near the eastern tip, a modern elementary school has been built on the grounds of the Titchfield estate across the harbor from Navy Island. Remains of the fort, including the powder magazine, are in the schoolyard.

Taking the north coast road west from Port Antonio to Port Maria, one sees a stretch of new highway curving around the wooded promontory that figured in the famous 1760 slave uprising, Tacky's Rebellion. At first the heights contained an officers' house, barracks and kitchen. By 1800, there were eleven buildings, including a powder magazine. Today, a battery and the brick pitched-roofed powder magazine are about all that are recognizable of *Fort Haldane*, but it has an even more breathtaking view than that from Fort Lindsay.

Pie-shaped *Fort Dundas* at Rio Bueno is also half lost in a school grounds. It was apparently planned by a local builder, and its curving gun wall with square abutments at each end measured about 160 feet. Standing at the harbor head, it replaced an old battery on the opposite side which is now completely lost.

All of the forts and batteries along the north coast of Jamaica saw service at one time or another as protection against pirates. *Fort Frederick*, overlooking the inner harbor —or River Bay—area of Montego Bay was no exception. Second only to Kingston Harbour as a shipping terminal, the bay was nicknamed "Manteca" (lard) by the Spanish, a reference to the export of lard taken from wild hogs abounding in the hills to the south. After 1739, when the British Crown signed treaties with the hill-country Maroons, Montego Bay began to open up for trade in sugar and rum. Yet Fort Frederick (or Fort Montego or Fort George; it bore each name at one time or another) was the only real fortification in the area. The gun embrasures stretched only about a hundred feet, and the barracks and hospital area behind were not much longer. In 1764 it was reported that the fort "is garrisoned by a detachment of His Majesty's regular troops, and mounts two 24-pounders and eight 18-pounders.''*

The report failed to mention that the gun carriages were rusty, setting off a comedy of errors that wasn't very funny to the gunner who was celebrating the surrender of Havana in 1760 when the whole thing blew up in his face. Nor was the fort commander amused in 1795 when his men dispensed "several volleys of grape shot" at the English schooner *Mercury*, mistaking it in the gathering dusk for a French privateer.*

Today the ruins guarding the road uphill to the Upper Deck Hotel and the Montego Bay Racquet Club, as well as Gloucester Avenue and a long string of Montego Bay resort hotels below, are virtually ignored by the waves of vacationers who pass it daily.

Fort Charlotte, on the west prong of the harbor that houses the lovely town of Lucea, probably receives more attention; for one thing it is in an excellent state of preservation and, for another, is a classically designed fort some 150 feet on each arched sea wall side of its triangular layout. It was probably built before 1752 of stone and yellow brick that are still in good condition. Its old circular magazine didn't function very well, so a new one was built on the land side to the north of the gate.

Three additional guns were added to the standing twenty-two during the Napoleonic Wars. These may still be seen in their mountings; two are in good condition, one damaged by salt spray. The fort is open to visitors without charge. A plaque at the entrance explains that the fort was named for King George III's queen, and quite probably it was the queen of Jamaica's defenses—during the eighteenth century, at any rate.

All along the west coast is a series of coves with no heights suitable for fortresses. Only when one reaches Savanna-la-Mar on the throat of the big southwestern head of Jamaica does there seem to be a place for a fort. This neglected town is not far from the original site of the Spanish landing at Bluefields. From the very beginning of its building the sea kept working away at it and its magazine was described as "bad." Today sugar loading occupies most of the area and a swimming pool is situated in the fort. This strange, lost little fortification may have been more important to the planters of the region as a protection against guerrilla raids from the inland maroons than from seagoing pirates.

*Dr. D.J. Buisseret, *Fortifications of Jamaica* (1764).

†Ibid.

Defenses of Montserrat

Montserrat lies at the southern apex of a triangle formed by St. Kitts and Nevis to the northwest and Antigua on the northeast and was therefore of strategic value to the English. Like St. Lucia, which is about three times its size, it was in perpetual uncertainty as to its identity. And, as in most of its sister Eastern Caribbean islands, the changing tactics of the Carib inhabitants* kept the settlers busy building fortifications.

The original colonists, who were English, arrived in 1632. The first fort at Dagenham Beach is now lost beneath a pair of bulk oil stations. In 1664 Gov. Anthony Briskett, Jr., built a fort which was supposed to be impregnable. Three years later it fell to the French, and its remains are now a prison, but the magazine, dating from 1664, survives. The French invaders, aided by Caribs and some Irish indentured

As the trail winds around the wooded north Haitian hillside, Henri Christophe's Citadelle with its shiplike prow suddenly appears, sprawling over eighty thousand square meters, three thousand feet above the sea.

*In 1975, Montserrat issued a set of postage stamps depicting Carib ceremonial houses, weapons, canoes and jewelry.

servants, chased Briskett, his family and two hundred settlers up to a small mountain redoubt called The Garden, where they were taken captive. It is said that the losers were shipped off to other islands clad in nothing but their shirts. What the ladies were wearing is not known.

The British soon took Montserrat back again, and the new governor, Sir William Stapleton, began building defense works at *Plymouth, Carr's Bay, Old Road* (then called Stapletouwne), *Bransby Point*, Gun Hill at *Streatham* and Cove Castle at *Semper's Cove.* A law was passed that if an enemy was sighted, guns would be fired from the Plymouth Fort to warn the nearest plantations, which were in turn to warn other plantations by the blowing of a conch shell. Like volunteer firemen, everyone was to repair to the nearest fortress in battle-ready condition.

The French staged another invasion in 1712, landing at Carr's Bay and moving south in force. At *Runaway Ghaut*, Capt. George Wyke with a contingent of sixty defenders, held the pass against the superior numbers of French until the families and slaves of the surrounding plantations could reach the mountains and safety. *Reid's Point Fort* was built immediately afterward.

Other eighteenth-century defenses were placed at *Kinsdale*, on an old estate that is now a private home, and on the top of a cliff above the banana pier. The latter, *Fort Barrington*, has a local legend attached to it about a gunner who was trying to fire the usual 8:00 P.M. curfew shot but found that

The Citadelle, memorial to Haiti's bloody and continuous search for leadership at a time when it was the only independent country in the Caribbean. Thousands died in its construction early in the nineteenth century, and it proved virtually worthless as a defense.

the cannon refused to go off. He looked into the barrel to see what was wrong and was instantly hurled into the hereafter. The curfew was discontinued.

Fort St. George, in the hills northwest of the soufrière, was built in 1782 as a hurried defense when the French turned up in force again. This time they occupied Montserrat for ten years, building their own style of defense works and well-constructed access roads. Among the ruins to be seen today are the magazine and a long house of stone and outbuildings which were probably a barracks. Pieces of the old roads and an interesting graveyard are also in the vicinity.

Montserrat has begun tabulating its historic places, and at this writing, the National Trust is about to publish a record of what still exists. Interested visitors to this beautiful and relatively undiscovered island should find the guide of great value.

DANISH:
Christiansfort, St. Thomas

In 1881, an editor of the *St. Thomas Almanack and Commercial Advertiser*, signing himself Jno. Lightbourne, published a history of *Christiansfort*, St. Thomas's most important building. The text had been given to him in Danish by a Lutheran minister, Rev. Emil Lose, who had written several histories of the island and his church's role there. For many years the Lutheran church had been one of the chief buildings in the fort complex, which was located in St. Thomas' only town, Charlotte Amalie. It also contained the governor's residence as well as the town hall at one time or another. Today the fort is still part of St. Thomas's daily life: the municipal court, the police station and the jail are situated in the Christiansfort, the basic structure of which has survived almost three hundred years of hurricanes, fires, attacks by the British, by pirates and other forceful events such as earthquakes. Even Halley's comet was sighted from the tower on Christmas night, 1758.

The first governor of St. Thomas, Erik Smidt, representing the Danish West India Company, planned a fort on Lucchetti's Hill (site of the Bluebeard's Castle Hotel), but apparently never built it. His successor, Governor Iverson, began construction of Christiansfort, using one or more slaves as master masons, sometime after 1672 and ordered all citizens of the island to "assemble to Service on Sundays in the Fort by beat of drum."* Backsliders had to pay a fine

*Jno. Lightbourne, *The Story of Fort Christian*.

of twenty-five pounds of tobacco. One of the leading property owners of the time was also ordered to change the location of his great house because it was located on what is now *Government Hill*; anybody who visited him could look right down into the fort.

Apparently the governor had cause for his fears; an intruder named Ole Smed wriggled his way through the beams one night for some unknown purpose and, when caught, was ordered to leave the same way and pay for his crime with two hundred pounds of sugar. Money was less useful in island transactions than commodities. The cost of building the fort was estimated at forty-two thousand pounds of sugar. The fort and its complement of officers and men was vital to the planters, who by 1680 had developed 50 estates around the island with a population of 156 whites and 175 slaves. However, Governor Iverson was criticized by the Company for not forcing the planters to volunteer their slaves in building fortifications, as was the practice in other islands.

Iverson's replacement, Nicholas Esmit, was soon deposed by his brother Adolf, the same Adolf Esmit who became notorious for his protection of pirates. Some of the amenities and improvements he made in the fort were no doubt for the comfort of his clandestine visitors, since one of the complaints by neighboring English against him was that he entertained the master of the pirate *La Trompeuse* in an apartment in the fort. Esmit himself described his additions as "four good rooms and an office against the western Curtain, each of the rooms having two doors and a lock and floored with Dutch fire bricks. The large room was tapestried with gilt leather, the ceiling painted red and the beams white, while the second room was hung with leather on which were painted biblio-historical pictures."* Among other additions was a "Cavalier" accommodating two large cannons, a lantern for lighting up the fort and the harbor and "a perfect passage from the north west to the north east bastions so that there was a walk along the entire fort inside the wall."* The enterprising governor also built a water battery on the beach between the southeast and the southwest bastions and made certain that all fifty guns of the fort were in shooting condition. It was a perfect setup for fending off the Nevis and St. Kitts English, who were accused by Esmit of trying to make repeated invasions of the Danish islands and stealing cattle and slaves.

*Ibid.
†Ibid.

It seems the English were not solely preoccupied with getting rid of pirates. Esmit's successor, Gov. Gabriel Milan, complained that his English neighbors had set a bad example of stealing slaves and that now the Spanish were doing it too. Milan made snide comments about Esmit's handsome fort, however, saying among other things that it was dangerous to walk on the walls in the wind at night and that it was an unhealthy place to live. He, too, made numerous additions, but he was soon deposed and replaced by Esmit, whose wife had been successful in clearing his name at the Danish court. The fort now became increasingly elaborate—Esmit made several mentions of "tapestries of gilt leather" but apparently he saw to it that the defenses, gates and guard houses were strengthened as well—with its own cotton gin, oven, physician's room, cistern and a curious addition called a *demilune* outside the main gate. This half-moon-shaped structure was found many years later in a pile of rubble.

In 1690, just after Esmit disappeared from the scene forever, a major earthquake cracked the wall of the Company storehouse; it was the same tremor that shuddered its way down the archipelago, swamping shoreline buildings in Nevis and St. Eustatius, among others. The only other earthquake of equal intensity in St. Thomas occurred in November 1867. The colonists were more afraid of British, French and Spanish invasions than they were of earthquakes, though, and early in the eighteenth century fortifications were put up on Lucchetti's Hill (*Frederiksfort*), and on *Maroon Hill*. Inhabitants manned the forts and provided slaves to make building repairs. The water battery was provided with moats and tests were made to determine how far the cannon would shoot over the harbor. Presumably other precautions were taken against a threat that the planters had all begun to fear, slave insurrections, particularly around estate Tuto, where there were no white managers. But again human enemies didn't cause the destruction. The hurricane of July, 1696, did major damage to the fortifications, and, according to Mr. Lightbourne, "the healthiness of the place [was] so impaired that the garrison by February of 1697, was reduced to one lieutenant, one ensign, one drummer and five privates, while a month later, of all the officials, the bookkeeper was the only one left alive."* In 1702 Gov. Claus Hansen complained that he hadn't been well since his arrival at the fort, so conditions apparently hadn't been improved.

In the early part of the eighteenth century there were repeated raids by pirates, threats from maroons and more

*Ibid.

fears of invasion. On one occasion, divine services at the fort were suspended because somebody spotted a suspicious canoe loitering off the eastern shore and the worshipers all rushed over to see what was going on. Until 1706 Lutheran observance had been held in the fort's armory. The wooden church edifice built that year was situated against the eastern curtain and was 49′ x 25′. The dampness of the fort walls was perhaps not considered a menace to men of God, for the Lutheran clergymen were given apartments near the church while the governor moved into town. Nevertheless, the Reverend Mr. Riise soon died and the Reverend Mr. Brandt followed the governor's example.

The dampness was damaging not only to health but to gunpowder and many complained that the fort was positively inadequate. Repeated repairs and changes were made during the next century and a half, with delays caused by the changeover from Company to Crown government in the Virgin Islands. Finally a little Lutheran church was built at 41 Norregade in Charlotte Amalie, but a hurricane blew its roof off the moment it was finished and everybody had to report to the fort again for Sunday services. This went on until a new Lutheran church in town was built in 1793. The fort remained much the same in plan until the earthquake of 1867; seven years later, it received a complete reworking. Iverson's old watchtower, vaults and passages between the Queen's and Prince's bastions on the north were replaced by a ravelin—a detached building projecting from the main wall—and corps de garde room. A ravelin surrounded the old demilune; placement of the new tower was different and interior rooms were much changed. In October 1875, its face permanently lifted, the venerable fort became the St. Thomas Police Station.

Today it also houses the Virgin Islands Museum. Barring further unexpected changes by man or nature, Christiansfort will eventually be entirely given over to the history and culture of the islands.

HAITIAN: La Citadelle

Described and photographed countless times, a candidate for eighth wonder of the world, the Citadelle is as curiously divorced from the mainstream of Haitian history as its location was irrelevant to the country's defense needs. Like the man who commanded it to be built at the cost of many thousands of lives—but probably nowhere near the twenty thousand cited by the accepted legend—it stands haughtily on its mountaintop as if to say, "I know what I know, and such wisdom is born only in solitude, in rarefied air."

Henri Christophe, Toussaint's black general who burned Cap Français rather than deliver a prosperous town to Napoleon's forces under Leclerc but who later defected to the French in one of the moves that led to Toussaint's immolation, was never a slave himself, according to the accepted version of his history. Born free on St. Kitts and said to have participated in the Battle of Savannah during the American Revolution, he was unlettered but vastly admired both English and French culture. After Dessalines's assassination in 1806, Christophe was in line to become president of the Republic of Haiti. Cap Français (which he renamed Cap Henri), was still the country's political and cultural center; the northern plains with their great plantations were the chief source of Haiti's economic potential. When Christophe discovered he was being discriminated against by the educated mulattoes in the government, and that he would have little power as president, he revenged himself by seizing the northern section, while Petión, who was elected to succeed him, was left with Port-au-Prince and the less important south. Crowning himself king of the northern domain, Christophe immediately set out to prove that a man who cannot read may yet command the creation of masterpieces and cause his people to be unprecedentedly productive.

For the first goal he imported talented engineers and designers; the second meant strict work rules for the masses of people which kept them in a bondage little different from the burdens of their former slavery. In the early days of his reign his image was that of an all-knowing father, and he achieved the kind of improvements always attributed to such dictators: universal education, road building, a balanced budget, encouragement of the arts, building of monuments and striking of coins. A palace elite developed around his queen and princess daughters; the palace itself was a magnificent pile of arched galleries, giant staircases and regal halls designed in the Louis XV style, with tapestries lining the walls and gleaming mahogany woodwork and paneling. This was *Sans Souci*, which with its outbuildings, lorded it over the humble village of Milot like a castle in a feudal fairy tale.

If Christophe could have known that he was to inspire novels and plays and learned literary dissections of his life and character, he would have been pleased to be the center of such attention if not by the way he was depicted. He appears to have been a living proof of the cliché that absolute power corrupts absolutely, and his *Citadelle* was a monument to that power.

The trail begins at Milot above the Sans Souci palace and winds continuously upward around the wooded massif that culminates after a two-hour climb on foot, donkey or horseback at a pleateau above which the fortress with its shiplike prow suddenly appears. It sprawls over eighty thousand square meters, three thousand feet above the sea. The stones and the gun carriages, the hundreds of cannon and thousands of cannonballs weighing twenty-five to fifty pounds, the mahogany for gates and window frames, the tapestries and the furnishings all were carried up this rocky trail by hand over a period of sixteen years. The incredible height and thickness of the walls, the myriad rooms, the gun emplacements, each with a separate chamber for the cannon in its mahogany carriage, the brick factory, storage vaults, dungeons, cisterns, galleries, apartments framed with huge doors and gates—all are a memorial to the men who died during construction as well as to the genius of the French and English engineers Christophe brought there to realize his dream. He refused to see that it was almost worthless as a defense. And who was to tell the king that he had on no clothes?

A story is related that on Ascension Day, August 15, 1820, Christophe refused to go to church, saying "If Our Lady wishes to celebrate the holiday, let her follow me." This hubris was exceedingly disturbing to the Bishop of Limonade Cathedral, who, when the king next attended a mass, thought he saw a vengeful ghost and hesitated during the singing of the credo. Going into a fit of rage, Christophe suddenly suffered a stroke. Although a doctor bled him, as was usual then, he remained paralyzed on the left side. Dramatic as always, he issued an edict that all animals which made any kind of noise be removed from the neighborhood of the sick bed. He lay in his palace for three months, calling in witch doctors and receiving massages and linaments to relieve the condition. The fear that he would lose his power must have maddened him, for he had himself dressed in his all-white uniform and put up on his horse to review his troops at Sans Souci, to prove that he was still king. And there, in front of them all, the great Henri I slipped from the saddle and fell to the ground.

It was the end of loyalty, the end of everything. The bullet with which Henri Christophe shot himself is said to have been silver, but whatever it was made of, it did the job and his queen reportedly managed, with the aid of one loyal retainer, to drag him up that terrible trail to the Citadelle, where his tomb is today. Passengers on the cruise ships making weekly calls at Cap Haitien usually elect to take a bus over to Milot for a look at the Sans Souci Palace, but few attempt the tortuous, bumpy ride up the Citadelle trail. Resident Haitians have wattle-and-daub cottages at all levels of the mountainside. Their adeptness at negotiating the rocks in bare feet can be abashing to a visitor riding a tiny, breathless horse, especially when some nimble small boy appears on a rock above playing "Haiti Cherie" on his bamboo flute. Rumors persist that a jeep tour is being developed to make the Citadelle more accessible to tourists, but this would put out of business the horse guides, who have a poor but well-established monopoly. On a Sunday about fifteen or twenty people make it to the top, and the vision there is worth every bumpy step.

6

The Town by the Bay

If it appears from the foregoing that island life in centuries past was located entirely on the sea or in forts or plantations, it may be because there were few real cities functioning as magnets in the way that great metropolises do today. Santo Domingo. Havana and, later, Kingston and perhaps Port-au-Prince might have qualified, but although San Juan, Port Royal, St. Pierre, Fort-de-France, Willemstad and Charlotte Amalie were called cities, they were mostly contained within limited spaces, which were sometimes walled, without the space for expansion that mainland Boston, New York and Philadelphia had.

Towns were built wherever there was a natural harbor; they lived on shipping and freebooting. As in Port Royal, the dock area was the average town's heartbeat. Activity centered around the sometimes elaborate customs and warehouse buildings, and merchandise and provisions were sold from anchored sloops or by hucksters and country people peddling on the streets. Small shopkeepers, particularly free-colored women, ran grog houses and dry goods stores and brothels which doubled as rooming houses. There was a central slave market and a horse trading market; there were turtle crawls and taverns. The French towns nearly always had a theater. Planters maintained town houses, and if the "city" happened to be the capital, there were government buildings clustered around the main square. Appointed officials usually lived on some hill above the common hurly-burly.

In Willemstad, Curaçao; Oranjestad, St. Eustatius, Port Royal and Kingston, Jamaica and Charlotte Amalie, St. Thomas there were at various times sizable Jewish populations actively engaged in trading. These towns had synagogues; impressive cathedrals and churches were built in every place of any size, and in the British islands, parishes were political as well as Church of England domains. If the town's location was strategic, of course there was a fort and, depending on available space, a parade ground.

The general street pattern was that of the High Street in English islands, Rue de la Quaie in the French, running parallel to the wharves. If the town was hilly the main street ran at right angles down to the sea. Commercial buildings had covered walkways, their roofs extending from the main floor of the building over the sidewalk and shielding pedestrians, customers and hucksters on the ground level from the noonday *mal de soleil*. In Kingstown, St. Vincent, the overhang is on one side of the street only, so that sentries in the fort above could see when the governor—or a possible enemy—was arriving in the harbor.

Houses and commercial buildings were of wood or brick or a combination of both. The usual shape was rectangular or octagonal, and the roof was pitched to create the familiar tray ceiling. A porch along the street facade formed the overhang, and windows were louvered. Shutters closing over the louvers protected the building if the owner was afraid of night vapors or when there was danger of a hurricane.

Today what one sees is what is left of yellow, pink, red brick and white plaster towns, mostly dating from the nine-

Town life on Harbour Street, Kingston, Jamaica, in 1824. Engraving by James Hakewill.

Much of the harbor area of Pointe-à-Pitre on Grande Terre, Guadeloupe, remains as picturesque as it was in the days of Victor Hugues, when he set up his famous guillotine in the Place de la Victoire in 1794.

teenth or early twentieth century. If parts of the older structures remain, they have probably been overlaid several times by successions of residents, and the modern additions of "zinc"-tin-roofs for the original slate, shingle or tile haven't helped retain a house's character. There probably isn't a town anywhere in the islands that hasn't been seriously attacked at least once by a disaster such as a fire, an invasion, a hurricane, earthquake or volcanic eruptions—or all of these. Now twentieth-century Miami Beach modern is making inroads to finish the job of destruction. Old San Juan, clustered around El Morro, is probably the only town whose urban character has been adequately maintained. The Puerto Rican Institute of Culture awards tax relief to property owners who restore their buildings according to specifications which extend to hardware, type of tiles, woodwork and other authentic details. (See the section on Puerto Rico at the end of this chapter.) The result of this effort is pleasure for the visitor and a living city, culturally diverse and with interesting new tendrils growing out of the old roots.

Across the bridge in Santurce and the surrounding communities it is another story. For some 25 to 30 years these sections have been enduring all the familiar growing pains of a modern mainland metropolis. Incidentally, the residents of La Perla, a shantytown clinging to the rocky edges of Old San Juan's ocean side, have resisted relocation to more hygienic housing and consider themselves an integral part of the central city.

Part of the difficulty of keeping a West Indian town from losing its character, as has already happened in downtown Kingston and in Georgetown, Grand Cayman, is attributable to the rush to build commercially in the image of multinational big business. Jamaica, which counts tourism as its second largest income earner (after bauxite), has torn down the wonderful old Victoria crafts market, destroyed all the rococo pink warehouses and what was left of the lovely, rickety, Somerset-Maugham-style Myrtle Bank Hotel along with its royal palms, in favor of a waterfront full of glass towers with iffy elevators and frigid air-conditioning that is a necessary protection against the perpetual curtain of smog overhead. The urban planners, anticipating international trade, forgot national character, and the old buildings could have been adapted to today's uses. Now everyone is wondering why money-spending tourists don't favor the downtown area anymore.

Tiny Grand Cayman, flattered by the influx of foreign investors, has hurried to spread out the red carpet for them with tacky new construction irrelevant to this delightful island's real ambiance. In neither the Caymans nor in Jamaica does it seem to have occurred to those in charge that it is possible, and indeed profitable, to combine the old with the new.

Nearly every town in the Caribbean islands may be considered endangered in the same way. Beside Old San Juan only Santo Domingo (Dominican Republic), Christiansted and Frederiksted (St. Croix) and Willemstad (Curaçao) have recognized that a neighborhood should be considered as a unit and as important as a single building. The large number of visually rewarding towns and villages losing something of themselves every day constitutes as great a problem as the lack of funds and expertise, and the people's general ignorance of the situation they face.

In the following pages, architectural reminders of the past in historic island towns are explored in the hope that they will be illumined, both for those who live there, and for those who visit.

Antigua

Old ST. JOHN is swiftly disappearing into a mélange of cinder blocks, tooting horns and rush-hour traffic standstills. But a walking tour is still worthwhile to see the eighteenth- and nineteenth-century wooden buildings, of interest if only because wood like that, in its slim-columned rendering, would be hard to find on the island today. A few structures are in ornamental stone; the *Parham Church*, the *Courthouse* in the downtown area and *St. John's Cathedral*, with its dominating twin towers on the hill above, are prime examples. Built of stone but completely wood paneled inside, the cathedral has been meticulously restored through public contributions after having been repeatedly damaged by hurricanes and fires. Now the 1974 earthquake has wounded it again.

Some efforts have been made to retain the atmosphere of the old town in the tourist shopping centers, and hardworking locals are trying to get a National Trust off the ground. The Mill Reef Foundation is also assisting with funds for a projected museum.

Aruba

Tourism and oil refining are Aruba's two products. ORANJESTAD once had all the picturesque Dutch colonial qualities of Bonaire's Kralendijk but the duty-free shops echoing the bargain malls of Willemstad have crowded out some of the earlier charm. Older buildings are a mixture of Dutch and Spanish influences with a palette of colors that equals those of Curaçao. A local joke has it that every year the Maduro Company gets in a new paint color and sells it throughout the Dutch islands. Each householder automatically orders enough to paint one wall; next year when another color arrives, another wall gets that.

Of landmark buildings there are few: Public offices on the waterfront, some town houses, an old lighthouse, a revived windmill converted into a restaurant and the ruins of the gold mills to the southeast of Oranjestad at *Balashi* are the most interesting.

Barbados

Pink coral stone has been used in many of the buildings of BRIDGETOWN, which despite its founding in 1628 is mostly a city of Victorian vintage, since fires and hurricanes have done as much damage here as invasions have elsewhere. All

The spirit of Henri Christophe is very much alive in the northern city of Cap Haitian. At nearby Milot, his incredible palace, Sans Souci, is a ghostly re-minder of princesses, court balls, and theatrical performances. The Bust of Comedy ironically commands the ruined courtyard.

but a few of the seventeenth- and eighteenth-century build-ings are gone, although *St. Ann's Fort*, with its clock-towered guardhouse, was built in 1702.

It is a town for poking about. Start at *Trafalgar Square*, which honors Lord Nelson and whose central monument dates from 1813. Shopping streets—some restored—and resi-dential districts have retained much of their attractiveness despite disproportionate new building. A curiosity is *Wash-ington House*, so-called because George visited his brother Lawrence here when he was nineteen, on his only trip outside mainland America. (His reward was a bout with smallpox.) Near the water are a number of *government buildings*—rebuilt after a fire in 1860—whose most interesting feature is a series of stained glass windows in the east wing. One of the older structures, *St. Michael's Cathedral* was built in 1665, and again in 1789 after a particularly ugly hurricane leveled it. *St. Patrick's* is more recent; it suffered from a fire, while *Government* (or "Pilgrim") *House*, official residence of the governor-general, was damaged in the 1831 hurricane.

On the perimeter of Bridgetown are the old *Queen's*

Park, once the residence of the general commanding British West Indies troops; the *Garrison Savannah*, a park that was once the parade ground for the garrison and is now used for sports events and recreation; and the *Barbados Museum*, which has a fine collection of antiques and historical records.

Northward along the leeward coast is *Holetown*, where the first settlers landed in 1627; it is said to have been named by homesick English sailors after the "hole" in the Thames. The early *James Fort* is now the site of the Holetown Police station. Nearby is *St. James* Anglican church, which still has a bell inscribed, "God Bless King William—1696."

Still farther north is SPEIGHTSTOWN, an early sugar port and a living museum of Georgian buildings. *St. Peter's Church* is called the cradle of Quakerism in the New World.

Christ Church (1837) on the south coast is noted for the fact that several coffins in the graveyard have had a habit of mysteriously wandering about, and on an east coast cliff *St. John's Church* has another interesting graveyard containing the remains of a supposed descendant of the Emperor Constantine who sailed here from Turkey and died in 1678. *St. George's* (1784) has an altarpiece by the American painter Benjamin West which, according to legend, was misplaced in an outhouse for many years and found by a thief who was horrified to see a painted face staring up at him.

Near *Bathsheba* on the Atlantic coast are the *Andromeda Gardens*, privately owned but open to the public for a nominal charge. Thousands of wildly colorful tropical plants, interestingly placed over the steep hillside, are identified by instructive labels and descriptions.

Bonaire

Some of the town names are Dutch—KRALENDIJK (coral reef); some, Papiamento—NIKIBOKO (Knickerbocker); and some, outright Spanish—RINCÓN (corner), oldest settlement on the island. None are more than villages, really. Even Kralendijk, capital and port city, is a miniature, an uncrowded collection of clean-lined Dutch houses and public buildings. Here, as in Aruba and Curaçao, the practice of painting window frames and shutters in bright or deep-hued contrasting colors enhances this uncluttered neatness.

The Custom House, the Government Guest House and other buildings along the waterfront all wear a look of complete self-possession. Bonaire has never been a rich island, but it has always taken pride in itself. Some of the vernacular houses along the streets are in grave need of assistance, but here as in so many small islands, three generations of a single family may own a property jointly. They all can't live in the one house, so they shutter it up and let it simmer and wilt in the tropical sun while they wait for something to happen: a buyer who will come along with enough cash to meet their outrageous asking price, which they can't quite agree on themselves. Big developers are the only people with that kind of cash and if the land is finally sold, the house is lost forever. To date, things haven't gone that far in Kralendijk and the town is well worth seeing before they do.

Curaçao

The island that supplies liqueur for crêpes suzette and fuel oil for more prosaic cookery also can boast some of the oldest and best preserved buildings in the West Indies. WILLEMSTAD, the capital and chief port, is really twin cities. It lies on the southwest coast guarding both sides of the St. Anna Bay narrows. *Punda* is joined to *Otrabanda* by the movable Queen Emma bridge,* which is made entirely of pontoons. It was first constructed in 1888 at the urging of a remarkable down-east American named Leonard B. Smith, who became U.S. consul there after a career of transporting north-woods ice to the tropics. (He also was responsible for bringing electricity to Curaçao.) Punda and Otrabanda were old cities by the time Smith arrived.

The prevalent architectural style is more typically Dutch than West Indian. Most of the buildings are familiar in their rectangular shape and steep roofs, but those in town are generally three or four stories high, often with dormer windows. Some have mansard roofs and elaborate scroll or stepped-edge facings. The story goes that one of the Dutch governors suffered from eyestrain in that fierce and unaccustomed sunlight and commanded all houses to be painted any color but white. Willemstad today is a symphony in pink and yellow and creamy beige.

Almost everything in Willemstad is within walking distance of everything else. On the Punda side at *Waterfort*,* on the outer edge of the estuary where a hotel has supplanted the 1837 barracks, one can almost reach out and touch the incoming ships as they pass. Nearby are the *Government Buildings*, the automobile-less *Herrenstraat* (pre-1700) and the *Handelskade* waterfront with its shipboard markets. *St. Anna's Catholic Church* was built in 1751, and the *Mikve*

*A new bridge beyond Willemstad now permits the Queen Emma to be used solely by pedestrians.

*The corresponding location in Otrabanda is the *Riffort* (Reef Fort).

Israel Synagogue was founded in 1730. The synagogue's ark was carved by Pieter de May as early as 1709. Not only is this the oldest synagogue in the West Indies, but its *Beth Haim* cemetery of more than 2,500 tombs was established in 1659 before the Brazilian Sephardic immigrants, who had arrived in Curaçao via the Netherlands, were allowed to worship in a temple.

The oldest structure of all is probably *Fort Amsterdam*, completed as early as 1675 but begun before 1642, when Gov. Petrus Stuyvesant lived above the main entrance. The present-day *Governor's Palace*—the result of numerous additions and changes—is far more elaborate and now has a definite nineteenth-century look. Rectangular, with a central entrance projection, it has elaborate Palladian windows and an arched ground floor colonnade. Among other buildings to see here is the eighteenth-century *Fort Protestant Church.*

On one of the few hills of the island is *Fort Nassau*, built in 1796 as a lookout point for both foreign and domestic intrusions. The fort houses a restaurant now and the view encompasses the vast oil refinery, which at night looks like a fairyland city, as well as the real city of Willemstad. Otrabanda and the *Scherloo* district have street after street of old houses, many with original roof tiles and much in need of repairs. The *Curaçao Museum* is in a nineteenth-century great house in Otrabanda; a handsome seventeenth-century plantation house named Chobolobo is occupied by the Curaçao liqueur plant, which welcomes visitors. All in all, this city, which survives on its tourism, trade and the export of refined petroleum, has done a far better job of continual face lifting than most of the others.

Grenada

No one has properly explained how the apostrophe got into the name of Grenada's wonderful town, ST. GEORGE'S, but any self-respecting holy man would be proud to be its patron, unless he considered beauty sinful. The best and most appropriate approach is by sea, so that one can see the celebrated double harbor divided by a steep wooded ridge come into view through the habitual mist.

Guarding the town is venerable *Fort George*, begun in 1705 by the chief engineer of French forces in the Caribbean. It is now used as police headquarters and may be visited at specified hours. There are subterranean passages and a small military museum, and a hospital now occupies the site of the old barracks.

St. George's first hospital, on *Morne de l'Hopital*,

Spanish Town, Jamaica's original capital, is a collector's despair with its many Georgian buildings in varying states of disrepair. Dominating the square is the imposing memorial to Lord Rodney, his statue rather ridiculously clad in Roman armor.

shared space with fortifications, all of which were built in the early years of the eighteenth-century and are now largely replaced by houses. One of the three redoubts remains as it was when the series of nearby tunnels which were dug in the hillside were presumed to have been used for listening to catch any enemy who might be attempting to blow up the forts.

Fort Matthew, atop Richmond Heights, was once the officers' quarters and mess hall; it had an appropriately elaborate kitchen, which is still in use, although now the complex is a mental hospital. *Fort Frederick* above was the citadel. The old works are still handsome in their state of partial ruin.

On the bay in town, the *Esplanade* and *Market Square* have fine examples of wrought-iron work. The streets of St. George's are lined with relatively undisturbed examples of West Indian-Georgian buildings, many of which still retain their characteristic red tile roofs. Along the *Carenage*, the second part of the double harbor, are the hundreds of schooners and sailboats, yachts and dinghies so often seen in the photographs. They moor at concrete posts containing old spiked cannon.

The townspeople have always taken care that their patron saint received proper respect; the Roman Catholic cathedral and the Methodist (1820) and Anglican churches are all named for him. The latter church was acquired from Capuchin monks, who had built it originally in 1690, but its present Georgian style incarnation dates from about 1825. Being English, it dedicates one of its many plaques and monuments to the victims of Julien Fédon. (See ch. 5.)

Also on Church Street is *St. Andrew's* Presbyterian (1830) with an old clock tower and bell. *Government House*, brooding on the hill above, has been rebuilt several times; it underwent a remodeling in 1802 and another in 1887, when a new facade was added that doesn't make architects happy. The view makes up for it, however.

Guadeloupe

POINTE-À-PITRE on Grande Terre is the arrival point to the island for most people, and much of the harbor area remains picturesque with its island sloops and Saturday market. Three-story, pitched-roofed and shuttered buildings line the streets, and *Place de la Victoire*, venue of Victor Hughes' famous guillotine, is still the official city center. The town prides itself on its "Paris of the Antilles" nickname* and on its boulevards, cafés and shops.

Place de l'Eglise, is named for the Roman Catholic cathedral that faces a landscaped square. The church also has a nickname, "The Iron Cathedral," because of the framework of bolted iron ribs in the walls that are supposed to protect it from earthquakes and hurricanes. No hint of its skeleton is visible on the yellow and white facade, whose decorative panels alternate with columns, stained glass arched windows on the upper story and arched portico.

Overlooking the harbor at Gosier, *Fort de la Fleur d'Epée* has the finest view in Grande Terre. The grounds are well-kept, but there are no guides. The fort has a moat and is pitted with dungeons, which one isn't allowed to visit. Plans are underway to use the original steps as a setting for a *son et lumiere*, outdoor concerts and folkloric shows.

Le Moule and *Massacre Beach*, on the northeast coast of Grande Terre, have been battled over since the first settle-

*Cap Haitien (Cap Français) had the nickname first, before it was burned down by Henri Christophe in 1802.

ment of Guadeloupe by Caribs, English and French. The town was once the entrance from the Atlantic side and its beach the invasion point. Atlantic storms sometimes unearth strange flotsam: human bones of long-ago battle victims. The low-lying, picturesque town has only remains of its old fort and a cathedral.

BASSE TERRE town, capital of both islands wings, is on the southwest coast of Basse-Terre in the shadow of the soufrière. More typically West Indian than its big sister on the River Salée, it trades in bananas, honors Victor Schoelcher with a monument, is guarded by the vast old *fortress of St. Charles* and has a seventeenth-century church, the *Cathedral of Our Lady of Guadeloupe de Estremadura.* A few miles north on the coast is the village of VIEUX HABITANTS, one of the earliest settlements. Its buttressed stone church with a curious Italianate tower was consecrated in 1666, and there are interesting tombstones in the churchyard.

Haiti

Le Cap, Cap François (or Français), Cap Henri and now CAP HAITIEN is a little like a dog-eared memory book. Its monuments and the bits of buildings that have survived from the days of its glory are the faded signatures and snapshots of long-forgotten friends. In the seventeenth and eighteenth centuries it was the Second City of Hispaniola, the reigning queen of St. Domingue. In the nineteenth it was forced to bow to the emerging Port-au-Prince in the south, and now in the twentieth century it is a picturesque grid of long avenues crossed by narrow streets, with multicolored, peeling houses, the all-too-noticeable Haitian open-sewer system, wrought-iron balconies and shuttered doors on the street level. Withal, it has an astounding vitality. Streams of people constantly seem to be flowing in and out of town on foot or astride donkeys, the women carrying tremendous loads of produce and chairs on their heads—for their comfort at the market—the men with oil cans or charcoal or fish. On a Sunday morning, returning from a vaudou ceremony in the hills, many of the participants carry large, half-burned candles as well. The market building in town, like the famous Iron Market of Port-au-Prince, is a scene of much confused activity—high-decibel chattering voices and garbage and trash intermixed with the astonishing array of merchandise on sale.

When a cruise ship makes a call, an informal sidewalk market of bad wood sculpture and paintings is set up near the dock, which is centered on the long *Rue du Quai* running the length of town. Except for up-to-date signs, an occasional horn-tooting traffic tie-up and camera-toting tourists from the cruise ships, Cap Haitien still looks as it must have in the 1840's, when it was rebuilt after an earthquake, although most of it feels much older.

The facade of the *Cathedral* facing the *Place d'Armes*, the fountain and parts of *2 Place Toussaint L'Ouverture*, including the seal of the Marquis de Beauharnais, survive from colonial times, which of course in Haiti means pre-1800. Next to the Cathedral is a handsome nineteenth-century mansion now dedicated to the regulation of the tobacco trade, but known locally as the house where President Franklin D. Roosevelt signed the formal pact in 1934 ending United States occupation of Haiti. Across the street is a small museum filled with documents, statues, paintings and other mementos of the north's original struggle for independence from 1791 to 1804, as well as of the subsequent regime of Henri Christophe. Christophe's spirit is still very much with the northerners. They speak of him as "King Christophé," pronouncing the "e" and pointing out the *Hotel de la Couralle*, where in his youth he was a chef or a waiter. After her husband's violent demise, Madame Christophe moved to Pisa, Italy, where she built a chapel dedicated to her two daughters, one of whom is buried there. The commissioning of architecture seemed to run in the Christophe family. Documents concerning the chapel are in the museum as well as a number of items depicting the *Battle of Vertieres*, the last battle of the Independence War. This event, too, is very meaningful for the Capoises, who erected a monument to the heroes of the battle just outside the city gates.

The chapel and convents of *Notre Dame de Lourdes* dominate the hillside, which backs the city as the harbor fronts it. Two small, pleasant parks are located on the west side near the *Carenage*. Beyond this side of the harbor is a series of ruined forts, bastions and walls, some built over with houses, others currently being broken up into stones for future building projects. The steep roadway hugging the coast passes the sites of *Fort Leclerc, Pauline Bonaparte Leclerc's palace* and *Fort Joseph*, all ravaged by time, earthquakes and weather. Well preserved, however, is the tomb of General Etienne Magny, who defended Le Cap against the English in the latter days of the rebellion. Several cannon remain nearby, where they were mortared by U.S. Marines in 1915.

A narrow and difficult footpath beyond is the only access to *Fort Picolet*, which crowns the point of the Cape. Perhaps that explains why this extensive set of walls, gates and look-

Another evidence of architectural nostalgia—this time, for Paris—is the gleaming white replica of the Basilica of Sacre-Coeur set in the midst of tropical foliage near Fort-de-France, Martinique. The city itself is a melding of French and West Indian influences.

outs is in better condition than the others. Little is known about the origins of Fort Picolet but Albert Mangones, Curator of Haiti's public monuments, says that it is patterned after the style of Vauban, who may have engineered fortifications in the West Indies, although this has not been definitely established. Picolet bears the mark of Vauban's innovative style of low walls built on strategic elevations, with deep foundations allowing for the use of large caliber cannons. The site was probably used for battery emplacements long before the fort was built; it commanded the only waterway free of reefs leading to Cap Haitien's harbor. Indeed, on a clear day, the view is almost limitless and is even better from the top of the gas-lamp lighthouse, a nineteenth-century addition.

Today, Haiti's country people still use their own traditional style of architecture, inherited from ancient Africa. Roads fanning out of Cap Haitien are lined with huts hand-

built out of braided sticks and plastered with mud. Some are whitewashed—others left to weather into a rich orange-yellow. Floors are tamped dirt and roofs are of thatch or tin, which is a sign of prosperity. These wattle-and-daub communities are usually small—clumps of four of five houses lined up along the road or huddled together near the provisions fields. When a man decides to build a new house, his neighbors help him. After the walls have been woven and have stood for a bit, the mud is applied; two or three days later the family of parents, four or five children and perhaps grandparents moves into the house, which is seldom bigger than a standard American room-sized rug.

One sees these houses everywhere, grouped around Cap Haitien's tiny airport and on the road to DONDON, where there are many caves, some with Amerindian petroglyphs of unknown antiquity. (One cave was said to be the sacred site of man's creation. The Arawak Adam descended from heaven through a hole in the cave ceiling.) In one way or another, the history of Cap Haitien spans perhaps twenty centuries.

This span includes Christmas Day in 1492, when Columbus was forced by the wrecking of the *Santa Maria* to found the New World's first European settlement, called La Navidad,* and the day in 1974 when thrice-daily air service to Port-au-Prince was inaugurated.

If Cap Haitien is a memory book, PORT-AU-PRINCE is the book's owner. She is a lady "of a certain age" who still flirts and dresses like a girl even though her face is lined and her once-celebrated figure has gone stringy. Yet in spite of decadence and neglect, she retains a kind of elegant beauty—and lovers who remain loyal.

In the hilly southeast residential district is a superb collection of nineteenth-century mansions—some run down almost beyond repair, others well-kept or restored for use as schools, institutes or hotels. Endless combinations of dormers and balconies with intricate iron patterns or carved wooden scrollwork decorate these houses of wood or peeling stone. Some are shuttered and empty; in others, louvers flung aside afford glimpses through the house of a garden beyond. One five-story castle, a private residence with grounds occupying an entire city block, is like a series of afterthoughts

---

*A methodical search for the site of La Navidad near *Bord de Mer* on the northwestern coast of Haiti is being conducted by local archaeologists, who cite changes in the shoreline around the supposed landing point as a complicating factor. Locations of Indian village middens and alluvial-deposit measurements are of some help, and it is possible that they may already have discovered parts of the original fort, although at this writing, no announcement has been made.

—as if each year the owner had decided to hang a bedroom onto a second floor corner and later to add a balcony, and then part of another story, so that the whole edifice is like a lopsided wedding cake. It is a short walk from there to the district's two resplendent nineteenth-century hotels, the Oloffson and the Splendid. With its turrets and carved wood trim, the Oloffson was once a presidential residence and a hospital; the Splendid, with twenty-foot carved plaster ceilings and Greek revival pillars, was a merchant's town house.

Closer to the waterfront, the buildings are less elaborate but many are just as ornate. As in many other Caribbean cities, the modern slums were once districts of pride.

The first cathedral, *St. Ann's*, has an historic altar. It was built in 1720 in the north central section of the city; Dessalines took his oath of office there eighty-five years later, and it is now opened occasionally for schoolchildren to use as a band rehearsal hall. Curving around the giant nineteenth-century *Cathedral* that replaced it across the street is a section of the original city wall. Other relics of the old colonial period are rare. East of the two Catholic churches is *St. Trinité Episcopal Cathedral*, built in 1928 by descendants of a group of American blacks who emigrated to Haiti in 1861. The church edifice is remarkable for its now-classic murals of Bible scenes, painted on commission during the 1950's by a number of then-unknown primitive artists. The unprepared viewer will be startled to notice that *vaudou* symbols and ceremonies are portrayed openly in many of the paintings. How this unique and wonderful gallery of Haitian art came about through the determination of the late director of the Centre D'Art, De Witt Peters, author Selden Rodman and Episcopal Bishop Voegeli, is best told by Mr. Rodman in his *Haiti: The Black Republic.* More than anything else, the works in the Cathedral helped establish Haiti's reputation as a nation of born artists. A few of the early talents—such as sculptor Jasmin Joseph, whose unique series of terra cotta sculptures depict complete Bible stories—are still tapping their original inspiration. Unhappily, many others are imitating their own early work, and hundreds of purveyors of "airport art," using assembly-line techniques, turn out canvases daily for tourists.

Northeast of St. Trinité is *Fort Nationale*, built by the British during the late seventeenth and early eighteenth centuries. There were once forts around the city that were named for every day of the week except Saturday. Most of them, including *Fort Jacques* in Pétion-Ville, have been destroyed, changed or built over. At the heart of Port-au-Prince is the *Champ de Mars*, a great open, parklike govern-

The ruins of warehouses and fortifications in the "lower town" of Oranjestad, St. Eustatius, are all that remain visible of this once prosperous *entrepôt*. The harbor waters have closed over many of the seventeenth and eighteenth century buildings, including the fort shown in the engraving of Statia in Chapter Three, and the old sea wall.

ment center with monuments and the presidential palace, all rather recently constructed. Along the esplanade at the waterfront, in the section built for a bicentennial exposition in 1946, are the *Théâtre de Verdure, Casino International* and the *Cockfight Arena.* The boulevard passing through this area is named *Harry Truman.* A few blocks' walk to the northeast brings one into the center of a street market as cacophonous as the fabled Iron Market, with its intricate iron roof. In neither area is it advisable to go around snapping pictures, temped as one might be. In fact, most Caribbean islanders, especially market people, resent being photographed without their permission.

Port-au-Prince is as lively and varied as any medium-sized city in North America and, like many, has its upper-middle-class bedroom—tree-lined and filled with handsome villas—a few miles away.

This is PÉTION-VILLE, which is in the hills to the southeast and commands fine views of the city and harbor. General Pétion established it when he built *Fort la Camp* and attempted to take the government away from Port-au-Prince. President Boyer later named it for his predecessor and built a palace, which until recently was a police headquarters. Like so many other landmarks, it has been razed. Not far away a new luxury resort has accommodations designed to look like landmarks—as if they had been built in the time of the property's first owner, Pauline Bonaparte Leclerc.

Almost due south on the Caribbean coast is the town of JACMEL, immortalized in the paintings of Préfète DuFaut and in the folk song, "Going to Jacmel." As DuFaut's works so vividly evoke it, houses are perched every which way on the hills overlooking the harbor. Gardens grow out of roofs at various levels; streets are sometimes ramps with steps. There is a Spanish-looking *cathedral*, an *iron market* and a *Place Toussaint Louverture*, where most of the public buildings and the *Vitale mansion* are. Once the home of Jacmel's leading coffee merchant family, the mansion is a symphony of balconies and gardens.

West of Jacmel is LES CAYES, looking out on *Ile à Vache* (Cow Island), a favorite buccaneer hideout in the seventeenth century.* Like so many of Haiti's provincial towns—JÉRÉMIE, GONAÏVES, MIROGOÂNE, PORT-DE-PAIX—Les Cayes has its private aspect of beauty and desolation, pride and despair, all mirrored in the buildings and the streets and in the faces of the people.

Jamaica

FALMOUTH was a latecomer. MONTEGO BAY, twenty miles to the west, had been the chief north-coast port since Spanish days. Planters in the sparsely settled eastern quarter of St. James parish felt cut off from business and social life until they at last achieved the unusual feat of founding a separate parish named after the then-governor (Trelawny) and a capital named after the principal river (Martha Brae). The parish remained, but the town was not on the sea, and the harbor at the mouth of the Martha Brae was the natural place for the parish seat to develop. It was named for Governor Trelawny's home town in England, and very soon—in the last decade of the eighteenth century—Falmouth began to sprout.

It flowered in the nineteenth century, and its buildings

---

*In the nineteenth century a promoter named Bernard Kock persuaded President Abraham Lincoln to agree on a $250,000 fee for setting up a resettlement project on Cow Island for five thousand ex-slaves. Lincoln never paid him, but many of the would-be settlers did. They are said to have died there of hunger and thirst.

had a symmetry, a harmony reflecting the entire urban picture that has been matched in few places. Unknown architects—amateur or imported via English blueprints—designed buildings that belonged to each other; none was identical to its neighbor, but each was somehow right in the whole. Subsequent shoring up, reroofing and other violations of the original designs have greatly altered this perfect Caribbean town. Miraculously, enough is still there to whet the appetite and raise hopes that the bulldozers won't arrive tomorrow. The persistence of the Georgian Society of Jamaica—a small but articulate group—has been responsible for creating citizen awareness that the town is indeed a treasure.

The Georgian Society has also been able to rescue—or at least postpone demolition of—the old *barracks building* in SPANISH TOWN, Jamaica's first capital. They have not been successful in Montego Bay, where a traffic-relieving highway and landfill project have already begun to duplicate in this historic city what was done to Kingston's waterfront.

A chief characteristic of Falmouth's buildings is their horizontal line. A stringcourse divides two-story structures, emphasizing length rather than height. The old houses all had cedar-shingled roofs, and often there was a series of bays across one roof, as in the majestic *courthouse* built in 1815. When it was remodeled after a fire in the 1920's, a single roof was substituted and the whole look was lost. Other typical features of the Falmouth houses are the main-floor balcony across the facade, usually with graceful iron or carved-wood fretwork.

A walking tour would normally begin at *Water Square*, which is oval in shape. A fountain has replaced the original stone reservoir in the center, and opposite the traditional, iron-roofed open-air *town market* is Sweetie's Supermarket. However this and other modern stores occupy old buildings around the square. Market Street nearby presents a vista of classic houses (including the *Moulton-Barrett* family town house at No. 1), many with zinc roof replacements and some looking as if a strong wind would bring them down. The sea is the giver of life to Falmouth, and the old houses along the waterfront, ruined walls and fishermen's halls are dominated by the courthouse, which is a reminder of times when this town was an international free port. The other dominant structure at the opposite side of town on Duke Street, *St. Peter's parish church,* is also in need of repair and has a spectacular stained glass window. Surrounding residential streets are well worth exploring, although the principal Georgian buildings are generally closer to the harbor.

Despite the fate of MONTEGO BAY's central harbor section, there are still some remarkable Georgian and Victorian houses sprinkled around the old town; many are now used as shops, restaurants, pubs, art galleries and offices. From the *Parade*, go east on Market Street to *St. James Church*, turn south on East Street to Church Street, then east again to Dome. At the corner of Princess, turn northeast to Prince and south to Duke Street. Doubling back on Queen Street, keep going to Water Lane and turn north to wind up again at Church Street. Admirers of gingerbread exterior trim, imaginative colonnades, balconies and gazebos, roof shapes and window treatments need only take this type of walk.

The same kind of discovery awaits walkers in LUCEA, on the northwest coast; PORT ANTONIO on the northeast and a number of villages in between such as RIO BUENO, ANNOTTO BAY and PORT MARIA; HIGHGATE in the hills above; and on the south coast, SAVANNA-LA-MAR and OLD HARBOUR. Experienced explorers will take issue with this selection and add their own favorites, and surely the towns of St. Thomas parish in the southeast and Manchester and St. Elizabeth in the central highlands ought not to be ignored. Jamaica could be visited a hundred times and still not be fully discovered.

A tour of SPANISH TOWN begins at the *Square*, where a collection of large public buildings surrounds a green park. Here are more Georgian specimens on a grandiose scale: The *House of Assembly* and the *Hall of Records*. (For years, Spanish Town battled with Kingston over which town should keep its priceless documents. Spanish Town finally won.) The colonial archives office, which has the most complete and sophisticated system for preserving documents of any island in the Caribbean, is worth getting permission to visit. Next to *Old King's House*, a classic columned facade only, which archaeologists are excavating down to the original Spanish foundations, is the new archaelogical museum (see page 163) and the *Jamaica Folk Museum*. This museum's vivid and worthwhile display of tools and artifacts showing country and slave life in the preceding centuries can be seen for a nominal entry fee.

The most obvious attraction in Spanish Town Square is the imposing, but poorly kept arched *memorial to Lord Rodney,* who is regarded here as the savior of Jamaica because of his victory at the Battle of the Saintes. However, his statue in the rotunda of the monument is a rather ridiculous version of the controversial old gentleman. Barelegged, encased in Roman armor and with a huge cape or toga sweeping his shoulder, he gazes out at Spanish Town—at the trucks and motor bikes and goats snarling up traffic and at the schoolchildren buying colored ice from the Juicy Man, most of whom haven't the slightest idea who that funny statue is supposed to represent. But on the whole, the Square hangs together despite its incongruities as does the rest of old Spanish Town. As in Falmouth, the houses stand directly on the street, with balconies, overhangs or enclosed and louvered galleries providing shade and air circulation. Although the town suffers from the familiar results of ill-considered or pragmatic alterations, enough is left of the original work by unknown artisans with a sense of space and beauty to make it worthy of priority attention from the Jamaican government.

For a walking tour from the Square, follow any of the streets northwest to reach the ruins of *Trinity Chapel*, or southwest to the *Cathedral of Santiago de la Vega* (spelled by the English St. Jago). On Fresh River near Spanish Town, is a place called Ferry, where the inn, which claims to have been operating continuously for three hundred years, serves refreshments and Jamaican food.

KINGSTON, the capital city, is too spread out for the average walking tour. Toward the foothills of the Blue Mountains from the downtown section, Victorian mansions and town estates with lawns and gardens now share the neighborhood with life-insurance towers and convention hotels. Some of the vernacular buildings are being occupied for modern uses, such as the Jamaica School of Art, the School of Music and, most notably, *Devon House*. A vast, three-story nineteenth-century estate house of great beauty and elegance, Devon House was restored and until recently used as a museum for the Jamaica National Trust and Institute, but now has been converted into the official National Gallery of Art. Well-designed shop arcades and a replica of an old Port Royal Grog Shop, serving authentic Jamaican food and drink, are grouped in the gardens outside. Devon House—an oasis and happy example of what people of taste can do when they are allowed to use a building creatively—attracts tourists and locals alike and is economically viable.

PORT HENDERSON, the one historic Jamaican town which has been restored and preserved under the direction of the Jamaica National Trust Commission is also the most neglected. As a collection of native urban architectural achievements from the eighteenth and nineteenth centuries, Port Henderson is of great interest, yet almost nobody goes to see it. Few efforts have been made to publicize it as a visitor attraction, although visually it has far more to offer than Port Royal, which is on every tourist itinerary. A bad reputation is alluring, and who remembers a good one?

In the seventeenth century, *Passage Fort* on the west side of Kingston Harbour was the port for Spanish Town,

Basseterre, St. Kitts, is an exercise in architectural serendipity. Most of the houses are set back from the street and face small fenced gardens; typical arched overhangs of the second floor galleries are trimmed with hand-carved wood. These serene eighteenth and early nineteenth century homes are—and look —lived in.

seven miles away to the northwest. Silt from the Rio Cobre began filling the docking area, and Port Henderson, also then called New Brighton, became the sea link to the capital. Named for John Henderson, a colonel of the militia and owner of Green Castle great house, the town was built on his property. Part of its popularity was due to a natural salt-water spa.*

After Spanish Town lost its long battle to remain Jamaica's capital and the honor was permanently awarded to burgeoning Kingston, Port Henderson began deteriorating. Stones were taken from the buildings, and nature completed the process of turning it into a series of ruins. The town had become a virtual tomb by the time the Jamaica Historical Society and later, the National Trust, took notice and went into action during the 1960's. They had to train their own team of workmen in the techniques of handling dressed stonework, old-style brickwork and trussed timber roofing, and they also had very limited funds. Today a majority of the

*Lady Nugent, wife of Lt. Gen. George Nugent, who was governor from 1801 to 1806, wrote in her much-quoted journal, "Drive to Port Henderson. Both little 'G' and Bonella [her children] bathed in the cold salt water bath there and behaved extremely well."

For more than four centuries, the tradition of the early morning street market has persisted in many West Indian towns. This one is in Marigot, harbor capital of the French side of St. Martin, and the scene is repeated in Philipsburg, on the Dutch side.

buildings have either been preserved or restored as a kind of urban museum an achievement largely unappreciated by the Jamaican public.

Green Castle great house commands the town, overlooking the harbor and Port Royal at the tip of the sandspit to the east. It has been conserved as a ruin along with the smaller *Bullock's Lodge* below the main house, which may either have been the estate attorney's residence or a guest house. Lady Nugent mentioned visiting Green Castle and would have approached the mansion in her carriage by a long, curving driveway.

Another such landmark was the *House of the Two Sisters*, a name which may have referred to its original owners, or perhaps to the landladies of the hotel it became during the nineteenth century. The Commission has used the house—it had decayed seriously by 1960—and its two kitchens as a training school for the restoration workmen. The two-story *Old Water Police Station* once had a pitched shingle roof and an external staircase, but these features had been substantially altered during the years. After the building was returned to its more or less original state, it became the Rodney Arms restaurant. But now a fire has destroyed it; the bad luck which has pursued the town in the last hundred years seems to persist.

The *Longhouse* had been an inn and lodging house until about 1898. It was built in coursed dressed stonework and had timber floors and roof and a verandah on the ground floor where horses, carriages and drivers were all accommodated. The gentry reached the main floor via two external stone staircases at each end of the building. The house's name probably came from the fact that the main floor was one long room with a balcony. In the restoration, timber posts have been used to support the balcony roof, although a technical argument raged for some time among the architects on evidence that it had been cantilevered. They ran into a number of other problems of authenticity and, in the main, had to settle for expediency. (Where does one find 29' x 12" x 12" hardwood floorboards today?)

The old *Chapel*, which had been built within an even older warehouse, was a victim of the 1951 hurricane. The aim of restoration has been to use it again for religious services. Another set of walls has been capped to a uniform level and roofed in the typical hipped shape with shingles, and was designed for modern use as a crafts center. The mineral bath has been roofed but not restored for use as a bathing pool.

At the entrance of the town, the information office is in a small dressed-stone building that was once the public latrine. In many early towns and forts such structures were as carefully and handsomely done as the more imposing public buildings, and this one is no exception.*

Port Henderson is open daily to visitors for a small admission fee and should be included in tours of Spanish Town and the White Marl Arawak museum.

Nevis

Like so many capital cities in the smaller islands, CHARLESTOWN is essentially a village. It winds narrowly along the shoreline, its vernacular houses and public buildings

---

*The latrine in El Morro, San Juan, Puerto Rico, is now used for some of the museum displays.

fronting directly on the streets. The center of town—the covered market, the harbor and the pretty little flowered mall—are crowded and busy. Most Nevisians live in or near town, which was once protected by *Fort Charles*, now only a large complex of ruined walls, cannon embrasures, a deep well, undergrowth and centuries of trash strewn nearby. The *Baths*, an eighteenth-century health resort and making claim as first in the Caribbean—sits in neglect above Charlestown, while *Mount Nevis* rises like a theatrical backdrop over all. The Baths were originally built by Thomas Huggins in 1778, and although it was rebuilt in an interesting style late in the nineteenth century, the ruins of the older structure are still visible.

One of the grander buildings on Main Street is the *Salvation Army hostel*, a large two-story rectangular structure whose facade appears to have been deprived of an earlier street-level colonnade. Upper-story sash windows—ten in a row—are protected by louvered shutters, and the ground-floor entry is arched. *St. Paul's Church* is one of several seventeenth-century structures that have been rebuilt one or more times after hurricanes and earthquakes. The use of large vertical bricks with contrasting light-stone steeple, quoins and arches makes for a sturdy pioneer look that is at the same time graceful. *St. Thomas* was the first Anglican church on the island (circa 1640), but it has also been rebuilt. The churchyards in Nevis are as interesting as the churches themselves, although they are badly in need of proper care. One inscription—that of Peter Thomas Huggins, 1787-1857 —suggests in a time when life spans were generally shorter that Huggins must have taken advantage of the health spa his father built.

No one seems to know how old the badly deteriorated *synagogue* in Charlestown is. The owner of *Morningstar Estate* recently undertook repair of the graveyard—clearing it of undergrowth and rubble and building a concrete wall around it. The oldest tombstones are mostly Portuguese or Hebrew inscriptions and date from 1684 to 1730. Curaçao claims to have the oldest synagogue in the West Indies, but researchers of the Island Resources Foundation for the St. Kitts-Nevis Government raise the suggestion that this one might predate it. There is no mention of it in local records.

The story of *Cottle Church*, on the other hand, is well known. Old Sir John Cottle built it for his slaves, but he attended services right along with them. This didn't sit well with his peers, but he got away with it because he was president of the Nevis Council. Off the main road, the ruins cannot be reached by car and are overgrown, although the walls are in fair condition. The original bell is now ringing from the steeple of *St. Theresa* in Charlestown. *Fig Tree Church* is noted as being the scene of the wedding registration of Horatio Nelson and Fanny Nisbet. Readable tombstones in the churchyard range from the years 1682 to 1800.

Saba

At first sight the towns and hamlets of Saba seem to come straight out of Tolkien or perhaps *Brigadoon*. WINDWARDSIDE, *Hell's Gate, English Quarter* and THE BOTTOM are real enough, though; building anything on Saba's perpendicular landscape has always been a test of strength and required an understanding of realities. For centuries the people had no road. They carved a stairway out of the living rock from the sea up the mountainside and hauled everything up those three hundred and fifty steps.* Today, the road that begins at the STOL landing strip on the lower north side of the cliff and winds up over the pass at Windwardside to swirl down the other side and end at Fort Bay was also built by hand; the herculean labor must have taken a gritting of the teeth in the face of landslides and washouts and the knowledge that it could all go in the course of a single hurricane. After one such storm when the road to Fort Bay was blocked, a heroic Saban drove his jeep as far as he could, dismantled it and carried the pieces across the rocks to the other side, put the jeep together again and brought supplies from the waiting ship below.

The typical Saba house—a small rectangular wooden cottage with pitched roof, stout wooden hurricane shutters and stone bake even—also represented the most practical way to build. The bright painted trims and the neatness, the immaculate cobbled steets and well-kept stone retaining walls all bespeak a pride that continues through times of economic hardship and isolation. New building tends toward the flat-roofed, stuccoed nonentity. However, Saba is not likely to find its economic salvation in big industry, so it may not be ruined environmentally and architecturally by inappropriate factories with smoking chimneys (although oil is said to lie under the sea at the Saba banks where the island's fishermen now make their difficult living).

Tourism, limited as it will probably always be, is one solution to Saba's economic problems, and the welcome given visitors is genuine. Recently a suggestion was made

*Much of the stairway at *Ladder Bay* remains, but it takes a true hiker to descend to the sea and climb back up again.

that the Dutch government, through the structure of the Netherlands Antilles, declare the entire island a national park, which in its green natural beauty it deserves to be. If this does come to pass, perhaps Saba's unique architectural style can be preserved, as well.

The Bottom, the capital "city," nestles in a cup of hills about halfway down the south slope. Its homes, churches, school and the administrator's headquarters and the old government guest house, now a small hotel are scattered around winding streets that can all be covered on a walking tour. To reach The Bottom, most visitors would have to drive; only the nimble Sabans walk from one village to another. Windwardside is all steep lanes clinging to hillsides, and in some places, the old stone steps remain, especially on the climb to the top, which is appropriately named Mount Scenery. The island's one swimming pool at the Captain's Quarters hotel in Windwardside is set beside a cliff twelve hundred feet straight up from the sea. Views of the seascape from English Quarter and Hell's Gate and Booby Hill have an unreal quality, and when the fog slides in on the wind and one can't see beyond the island, it is easy to believe that the centuries haven't passed at all—that out there in the mist are the frigates of the Spanish, the English or the Dutch pursuing their perpetual voyages of conquest, piracy and slave trading.

St. Croix

Built in 1734 under the direction of the Danish West India and Guinea Company, CHRISTIANSTED was a planned community from the very beginning. The French had sold St. Croix to Denmark the year before and settled it with colonists from St. Thomas and St. John who immediately began building a fort—*Christiansvaern*. Frederick Moth, who later became governor of all three islands, ruled as to how the streets would be laid out, who could live where and how the houses were to be built.

The fort was the center of town, and the Company buildings, residences and warehouses surrounded it. The *Customs House* was directly on the waterfront. Thirteen years later, a building code went into effect which was meant to segregate the "good" sections from the "poor class" areas on the outskirts. Good houses were to be of masonry or wood and face the street in a straight line, with a passage of three to four feet between each house. Everywhere but in *Strand Street*, houses had to be placed on footings or foundations; Strand Street buildings could be on pilings. All houses within the city limits had to have shingle roofs; thatched roofs were allowed only on the western outskirts or on the waterfront. The town surveyor had the right to decide where free-colored persons might build their homes, and their lots could be no larger than 30' x 30'. Slaves were not allowed to live among the free-coloreds under any circumstance.

Everybody had to get a building permit (street overhangs were regulated), and ordinances decided the locations of taverns and other commercial establishments. Property owners had to build fences, and their hearths and ovens had to be of approved masonry.

Until the decline of sugar in the nineteenth century, Christiansted's population grew rapidly to between five and six thousand. The town's only major fire, in 1866, was not particularly devastating. The restored buildings one finds today are similar in many ways to those of FREDERIKSTED on the western shore of the island.

In Frederiksted, which was named for King Frederik V and built on land claimed from the La Grange estate, a fort and warehouses were begun, but nobody seemed to be very much interested in building homes there. By 1766 there were still only 341 residents. In contrast to Christiansted, most were dock wallopers, free-coloreds, poor whites and officials stationed there. Following von Scholten's proclamation of emancipation in 1848, many of the newly freed slaves moved into the town. Building codes were strict here, too, but Fredericksted suffered a series of calamities that ranged from fires to worker riots, hurricanes and a tidal wave. The present-day reconstructions and preservation efforts in both towns are a remarkable achievement; they have made them living and working communities attuned to twentieth-century life, not dead museums.

Fort Frederik, begun in 1752, is typically Danish in architectural style. The first foreign salute to the United States flag was given here, although St. Eustatius claims the honor of being first to recognize U.S. sovereignty on a military vessel. Restoration of the fort is being planned by a department of the Virgin Islands government in conjunction with the V.I. Bicentennial Commission and the Fort Frederik Commission.

South of the fort is the late eighteenth-century *Customs House*, which is still being used for its original purpose. A two-story gallery was added to it in the nineteenth century. *On Strand Gade* are a series of arcaded buildings facing the water; *Victoria House* is of especial interest for its elaborate gingerbread trim. On *Kongens Gade* (King Street) at 32-33 and 37B; are two notable late-eighteenth-century buildings; *Dronningens Gade* (Queen Street) contains five buildings that typify the progression of architecture from the eighteenth to the late nineteenth century; 58-60 *Hospital Street* is an eighteenth-century two-story masonry building which once was a private residence, then a school and is now a police station. The *Anglican Church*, King's Street, is a combination of classic and gothic revival architecture; the *Catholic Church* at Prince and Market Streets is a mid-nineteenth-century rebuilding of the eighteenth-century cathedral; the *Lutheran Church* on Hill Street dates from the late eighteenth century and is the oldest standing church edifice in Frederiksted. Outside of the town on Creque Dam Road is the *Mount Victory School*, one of eight built about 1840 as a result of the Governor-General von Scholten's proclamation of compulsory education for all children in the Danish Virgin Islands.

In Christiansted, the *Friedensthal Moravian Mission,* which played such a strong part in education, will be found near the mid-nineteenth-century *Anglican Church*. At the waterfront is the *National Historic Site*, which includes *Christiansvaern* and *Government House* with its grand staircase. Nearby is the *Alexander Hamilton House* at 55 King Street; it was originally built in the 1750's and recently rebuilt after a fire. Hamilton is said to have worked here as a clerk. The *Lutheran Church*, 4 King Street, was originally the 1840 Dutch Reformed Church. Some relics remain from the original building; the tower and front porch date from the 1830's. At 46 King Street is the *Pentheney House*, an early nineteenth-century town house. Fifty-two King Street, occupied by a gift shop, was an early eighteenth-century residence. Next door is the old *De Nully House*, now the Lutheran Parish Hall.

St. Eustatius

ORANJESTAD, the only town on this once very prosperous island, reflects a combination of three centuries. The fourth century—the twentieth—is beginning to show its face, but most of the houses on the winding cobbled streets of the Upper Town, which is perched on the edge of a cliff overlooking the bay, were originally built in the 1600's and then rebuilt during the 1700's and 1800's. Some of those currently occupied are well kept in typical Dutch-clean style, others have deteriorated and suffered jerry-built changes, while those which have been closed and boarded up by their absentee owners are falling into ruin, their yards covered with litter.

A number of these old town houses show the result of

estate division in which a family would build separate houses for various members around a compound with cut stone walls on the street and alley sides. *Fort Oranje* remains the civic center, with streets fanning out from it. A walking tour in the area will reveal the graceful yellow-brick town house of *Governor de Graaff* (see ch. 5), much in need of maintenance and restoration but with a delicate hand-carved roof trim; the old *Government Guest House*, now used as a court house and soon—it is hoped—to become a museum of the island's newly formed Historical Foundation; and the so-called *"Three Widows" Corner* across the narrow street whose three one-story wooden houses are the aforementioned well-kept ones. The *Judson Library* occupies the second story of a private family compound that still has remnants of its seventeenth-century origins, such as a stone oven and a water-filtering stone. Ruins of the *Synagogue* built in 1738 and of the Dutch Reformed Church (1775) are stark and neglected. The churchyard of the latter, the *Anglican church-yard* minus its edifice and the Mikvah Jewish cemetery all have tombs and gravestones from the early 1700's. Several traders from New England—particularly from Rhode Island —and their families were buried near the Jewish cemetery where the names on the stones are mostly Portuguese, an indication that they were Sephardic Jews who had emigrated to Statia from Brazil. Trading as they were with the American colonies, they had to learn English and all but a few of the inscriptions are in both Hebrew and English.

The life once lived in the mysterious houses lining Oranjestad's Upper Town streets seems almost tantalizingly within one's reach. An eighteenth-century engraving shows members of Statia's upper classes in white wigs and brocades dancing the minuet at a ball. But today's realities are donkeys and goats and blaring rock radio music, the children selling slave beads to tourists,* the broken steps and shattered roofs and the need for a sustaining economic life base.

Near Fort Oranje a fieldstone road with its original retaining wall winds precipitously down the cliff to the Lower Town, ending near the *Old Gin House*, a ruin that once housed a cotton gin and now provides a tasteful setting for an inn. The other buildings along the shore are remains of brick warehouses and stone military installations, some of which have slipped under the harbor waters. Earthquakes and rock-

---

*A few years ago a cache of blue glass beads of various sizes and shapes was found in a half-submerged ruin near the Lower Town called Crook's Castle. They were identified as barter beads used by slaves and were probably brought over on a slave ship, perhaps to be distributed throughout the Caribbean.

slides did much to destroy the earliest buildings here; Admiral Rodney did the rest. The building of the new pier has revealed seventeenth-century structures embedded in the walls of the cliffs, and there are military installations all along the shoreline that remain unidentified. All the islands need funds and expertise to carry out a program of exploration-preservation-restoration, but Statia needs this kind of immediate attention the most. *English Quarter*, the ruins of a plantation house and sugar works, is situated on the opposite side of the island near the vast, deserted span of beach known as Zeelandia. Many of the stones here and in the dry walls flanking the old roads are constantly being vandalized for building. A floor of old Dutch tiles—each with its separate hand-painted picture—was recently broken up for scrap. If this sad and wondrous place begins to oppress the spirit, go hiking up the Quill, the volcanic cone with a rain forest inside. Better still, wait until a moonlit night when the young men of the island take torches and hunt land crabs. Even "crab-back," a pâté cooked in the shell, may date back to the seventeen-hundreds when Statia was known as the Golden Rock.

St. Kitts

A walk through BASSETERRE is an exercise in serendipity. The two most rewarding squares, *The Circus* and *Pall Mall*, are lined with the kind of town houses that gladden the heart of a Georgian buff. Most of the houses are set back from the street and face small fenced gardens or are shaded by fruit trees. Typical arched overhangs of the upper stories are trimmed with hand-carved wood. The sidings are of shingle, while ground-floor walls are usually of stone or brick. Sometimes the slate or tile roofs remain; even the tin imitations are in fair repair. These homes are lived in, and the air of old-family serenity is almost a reproof to eager beavers with snapping cameras.

A park replaces the old slave market. Of the church steeples that dominate the skyline, the principal one belongs to the peripatetic Anglican St. George. This church, whose steeple was damaged in the 1974 earthquake, has been repeatedly struck by disaster since its original construction in 1670. In the churchyard, which is badly in need of upkeep, some gravestones of planters and their families date from the first half of the eighteenth century. In the center of the warehouse district on the waterfront is the garishly night-lit, big *Harbour House*, an amusing, unintentional caricature of Victorian pretentiousness.

On OLD ROAD, which is now a small village, are the remains of England's first permanent settlement in the Caribbean; private houses occupy most of the area. Not far away is *Middle Island Church* (also damaged in the 1974 earthquake), where the pioneer Sir Thomas Warner is buried. His tomb is cared for, but the church and churchyard, which has legible inscriptions from as early as 1727, are neglected. A recent survey of these and other ruins on St. Kitts and Nevis by the Island Resources Foundation for the Government resulted in recommendations for preservation or restoration, but at this writing it is not known what action will be taken.

St. Lucia

When one of the worst hurricanes in recorded history struck CASTRIES in 1780, many planters simply abandoned their holdings and moved on. As had happened in Bridgetown, Barbados, it destroyed many of the seventeenth- and eighteenth-century buildings, so that most of what is left of historical and architectural interest dates from the nineteenth century.

New development of the pier area makes it difficult to visualize what Castries once looked like, but it probably re-

Gustavia, the toy-like capital of St. Barth's, was notorious for a brief period in the late eighteenth century as an anchorage for corsairs recruited by Victor Hugues, French Republican Governor of Guadeloupe. His pirates preyed on United States ships in the Caribbean and nearly triggered a war between the U.S. and France.

sembled Kingstown (St. Vincent) and St. George's (Grenada). The present *Cathedral of the Immaculate Conception* was built in 1894, but survived the next hurricane to hit town. These disasters, coupled with the constant French-British battles over St. Lucia, left the "Helen of the West" architecturally confused. *Morne Government House*, also built in 1894 and overlooking the town, reflects the mélange, but the building is visually pleasing and offers interesting displays of St. Lucia's history for the casual visitor.

VIEUX FORT, situated on the south coast at the head of a peninsula called *Moule-a-Chique* (probably meaning Peninsula of the Chiggers) was the first spot to be settled. The English came, then the Dutch and, finally, the French, but none of them could cope with the resident Caribs. The fortifications they built have been destroyed by time. The district became the island's sugar capital in the eighteenth century, and the surrounding estates built mills and used the fine natural port for shipping. It was also an important Roman Catholic parish, and the stone tower on the cathedral built by members of the La Rose Folk Society is of special architectural interest. The town had its adventures during and after the French Revolution: Victor Hugues sent a force to recapture St. Lucia from the British, who retreated to Vieux Fort, then escaped back to Castries in a Dunkirklike fleet of small boats, leaving the French to control the southern parish, and eventually the entire island. When the British returned in 1796, they faced a long period of guerrilla warfare, and the upheavals virtually decimated the sugar estates around Vieux Fort.

Aside from the vernacular buildings of the historic town, and the old lighthouse at Moule-a-Chique, Vieux Fort has a special meaning for Americans. During World War II the United States took a 99-year lease on 1,200 acres of land in the vicinity, establishing an air base—called Beane Field—in 1941. The main section of the base was returned to the St. Lucia government in 1960 after a good many American-style improvements had been made on access roads and in the harbor. The development of Beane Field made it possible to build an international airport there which has since been further improved by the Canadian government under the Canadian Commonwealth Caribbean program.

St. Maarten/St. Martin

Within thirty-six square miles of green hills and expanses of inland waters and salt ponds are two nationalities and eight communities, including the capitals of the Dutch and French sides respectively, PHILIPSBURG and MARIGOT. The various settlements literally wander; houses dot the hillsides and cul-de-sacs all over the island so that the villages themselves—*Simson Bay, Prince's Quarter, Orleans, Grande Case*, French and Dutch *Cul de Sac* in addition to the capitals—are no more than a main street or two. Everything is in miniature and there is no sense of crowding.

There is no way of separating the centuries architecturally. Mounds of field stone, broken walls and old estate houses are everywhere if one looks out for them, but they are undated and largely ignored. The spine of the hill, *Mount Concordia*, on which the French and Dutch signed their hopeful first agreement in 1648 making a sharing of the island official, has a view both of the French and Dutch sides, but the only memento from the past is a ravaged dividing wall disappearing into the mountain bush. Elsewhere on the border a small monument does commemorate the historic occasion; however, no mention is made that subsequently the island changed hands sixteen times before it settled into its present unique, customsless division.

Although towns on the Dutch side give off some of the Dutch ambiance and, as always, the French have left their imprint on the colony they acquired, the "island house" one sees everywhere is the stone-and-wood rectangular, sash-windowed, shuttered, pitch-roofed, porched classic. Some houses still have hand-carved wood lacework decorating the main-floor gallery. Almost all have lost their original shingles and tiles; the pink roofs of today are painted tin. There seems to be neither the money nor the inclination on this island to encourage preservation of landmarks or urban character. None of the forts on either side—such as *Amsterdam, Willem, Point Blanche, St. Louis*—have been cared for or interpreted for visitors. In most cases, it is impossible to reach them except by hiking up to the rugged top of some hill.

When the Dutch West India Company got down to serious business in the early seventeenth century, it discovered salt was the commodity it most wanted besides slaves. The ideal situation for undercutting the Spanish price for salt was to establish strategic bases on various eastern Caribbean islands where salt was available. St. Maarten had great "pans" or flats of land open to the flow of sea water which deposited the precious stuff in little peaks as the water evaporated. The Dutch merchants were determined to get St. Maarten back from the Spanish both for its salt and its favorable-wind position. So the director of the Dutch West India Company himself, Petrus Stuyvesant—a rugged-looking man with a hawk nose and a cocked eye who was stationed at Curaçao—was given command of an expedition in 1644 to go up and take back St. Maarten. At the head of a fleet of ten ships, Stuyvesant sailed to St. Kitts, where he picked up a few eager volunteers, had a seventeenth-century version of an LCP built and got to St. Maarten on Palm Sunday. The Spanish at Fort Amsterdam (so named later) on the long rocky western arm of Great Bay may have been observing the religious holiday, for the Dutch passed them by and were able to establish a beachhead at nearby Cay Bay. They built a battery on the hill above and while Stuyvesant was waiting for an answer from the Spanish governor to his demand that the island be turned over to him, an advance reply came in the form of a cannonball that struck him in the right leg. He was carried aboard his flagship and there relieved of the offending leg. The mishap was to be the end of the Dutch campaign to get back St. Maarten but the beginning of Stuyvesant's career as Director-General of New Netherland (New York). As it turned out, he lost his leg in vain. When the war between the Spanish and the Dutch in Europe finally reached the eighty-year mark, the Spanish left St. Maarten anyway and the Dutch and French started contending for it.

Before the final settlement in 1816, the Dutch and French were driving each other out periodically and then signing new treaties while the British pounced in whenever the opportunity presented itself. In 1791, when Lord Rodney made his famous raid on St. Eustatius to rid it of its "nest of vipers," he also wreaked a good deal of havoc in St. Maarten. Not having the basic natural resources to pick itself up economically without the profitable trade that had made it so important to the United States, Statia never recovered from the devastation. St. Maarten, on the other hand, was well established by that time in sugar and tobacco as well as salt. Plantations in the central valleys, Dutch Cul de Sac and Lower Prince's Quarter, were dotted with the sugar mills and great houses that were a familiar sight in other islands.

The owner of one great house in Cul de Sac called *Retreat* (now a privately owned ruin) was a doctor of laws named Willem Hendrik Rink, a handsome Dutchman who became commander and governor in 1790. Dr. Rink apparently was not only a man of incorruptible political character (his predecessor had been accused of malfeasance in office), but he was able to keep commerce going in a time of depression while convincing the Dutch Government that a central courthouse was needed in Philipsburg, the south shore capital founded by John Philips in 1737. The *Courthouse*, built in 1793, is St. Maarten's only architectural salute to its busy history that is supervised by the government. Restored twice and tenderly nurtured today as the Post Office for the Dutch side, it stands at the head of the square leading from the Great Bay pier—immaculate, not quite authentic, but as close to the original as any of the island's buildings will ever be. It had a balcony upon which the entire island council could appear to the public on important occasions; a weighing room, vital in the island's trade; various guard and meeting rooms; and a jail with an "airing" yard which Governor Rink said must be included since it was unhealthy for the prisoners not to have a daily dose of sunshine.

At the age of seventy-five Rink tired of being a widower and married the daughter of his neighbor, Diederik Johannes van Romondt, whose estate house was across the road from Retreat. Exquisitely restored, it is now a hotel called Mary's Fancy. Susannah von Romondt, by the way, was nineteen at the time of her wedding, and three years later the marriage was annulled for being "without issue."

Rink's beautiful courthouse was partially destroyed in 1819 during a hurricane and wasn't restored until 1826. At that time a certain Michiel de Rudder was hired as bell ringer,* gravedigger, court messenger, bailiff, sexton and schoolteacher. He received an additional five pesos (about five dollars) for tolling the bell during a funeral procession along Front Street to the cemetery. The modern restoration completed in 1969 is modeled after the 1826 version and, among other things, has lost its airing yard.

In the public cemetery at the west end of Front Street (Philipsburg still has only Front and Back Street with the later addition of "The Other Street" for traffic diversion), tombstones may be found dating back to the time of John Philips himself. Most of the gravestones beyond the gate reading "*Memento mori*" are poorly cared for, but one handsome and still legible stone bears the names of five Quiller family-members, all of whom perished between 1748-49; the oldest was forty-eight years old, the youngest eight months.

Standing alone at the opposite end of Front Street a classic island house observes the increasing traffic and bustle of the town. Square, with a long flight of steps up to its main story and replete with lacework, it seems to long for the days when the only accommodations for important visitors was the *Government Guest House*, called a "pasanggrahan" by the

---

*At nine o'clock each evening, the bell was rung as a curfew for slaves still working at the salt ponds or on plantations.

East Indian Dutch. The hotel, near the east end of Front Street, uses the restored guest house for its lobby, bar and dining terrace, and shops nearby, such as the Windward Islanders, are built on foundations of old Philipsburg homes that occupied this area when it was the posh residential section. Across the street behind a restored cedar house—now the West Indian Tavern—is a yard filled with buried brick walls; some of the outcroppings show the early yellow ballast brick. Nearby is one child's grave, and island old-timers claim that this was the site of a seventeenth- or early-eighteenth-century synagogue. Since no scientific digging has been done and there appear to be no records of the building, the mystery will probably remain as unsolved as it is in Nevis. Philipsburg's other showplace is its 123-year-old *Methodist Church*, and its remarkably elegant manse that was built later. The property, which is on the west side of the pier, runs from Front to Back Street.

French St. Martin can boast three settlements that retain tantalizing remnants of their earlier character. MARIGOT, a busy fishing and market port, lacks Philipsburg's neatness but has its own rakish French charm and a number of good French restaurants and delicacy shops. GRANDE CASE on the north coast is a miniature Philipsburg—both curve along beautiful beaches and are backed by salt ponds—and ORLEANS, the first French settlement on the island, is a village most visitors drive through and hardly see. Walking tours through these places would be impractical; the sudden views of old houses as one drives over the hilly roads are more rewarding. One wonderful farmhouse, that must surely be haunted, is set in a meadow just over the border of the French side. It has captured hundreds of imaginations, and the owner has probably had as many purchase offers for it as any in the West Indies. But rather than sell, the owner lets it sit there, prey to succeeding generations of termites. Other such great houses seem either too costly to restore or have been allowed to be claimed by the earth. The ruins of Retreat, Rink's mansion, is the prime example.

French St. Martin can lay claim to the newest ghost "town" in the Western Hemisphere. Built in the 1960's as a luxurious hotel patterned after a Mediterranean village, this battered child of a promoter's imagination was always just about to open but never quite did. Successions of fund-raising efforts sank as the water table rose, and the towers and arcades and landscaping and fine Spanish furniture were vandalized and left to disintegrate as every new rescue attempt went the way of the earlier bankrupt angels. If the caretakers of the *Auberge de la Belle Créole* would take a hint, they might recover a modest amount of the vast total investment; tours through the place would at least pay for its maintenance. As it stands now, it is an apparition best seen from the deck of the yacht *Maison Maru* on a dreamy day-cruise around the island.

St. Thomas

During the great sugar boom of the late eighteenth and early nineteenth centuries, St. Croix and St. John were the producers, while St. Thomas delivered the goods. In CHARLOTTE AMALIE, the island's one real city, the dockside warehouses attest to this fact. Before the harbor received a strip of landfill for a modern road, the long rows of storage houses at right angles to the quay made it possible for goods to be directly loaded into or unloaded out of the buildings.

Although commerce began in the seventeenth century, the usual catastrophes such as fire and hurricanes swept through the town from time to time, so that most of the restored warehouses in the area now renowned as the Caribbe-

Santo Domingo de Guzmán, founded in 1498, is shown here in a city plan of 1671. It is an almost perfect guide for a walking tour today to many of the places shown in the old city, particularly the Plaza, the area along the river and the old wall.

an's most popular free-port shopping center are no more than a hundred years old, give or take a few decades. Many were put up on old foundations and walls after a fire.

With its orderly rows of arched doorways and wrought-iron balconies, this stone, brick and stucco waterfront section of Charlotte Amalie (named for a Danish princess and pronounced Ah-mal-yeah) is like a gussied-up version of Cap Haitien. Twentieth-century tradesmen, with an eye for merchandising the West Indian architectural flavor, have tried to do the kind of job here that cultural agencies are accomplishing in Santo Domingo and San Juan. If the results aren't as carefully authentic, "atmosphere" is what sells, and St. Thomas remains as commercially minded today as it was under the Danish West India and Guinea Company and the Danish Crown.

The waterfront is about the only flat section of town. A series of tall, rounded hills curve around the harbor that once sheltered pirates as well as legitimate merchant vessels. (See chs. 4 and 6.) Dubbed "Blackbeard" for his luxuriant and beribboned whiskers, the nineteenth-century pirate Edward Teach would be astounded if he could look down today from his hilltop stone tower at the scene below, where on a typical day as many as seven cruise ships lie at anchor.

Steep old cobbled streets, some aided by stairs, fan up to the north of the warehouse district, and from *Christiansfort*, the *post office* and the venerable *Grand Hotel*. The hotel was built in 1841 but claims to be the oldest structure in continuous use as a hostel. The richest source of fine buildings is on *Government Hill*, directly above. This hill, flanked by Garden Street on the west, is dominated by *Government House*, still used by the current governor. It is an elegant brick and wood three-storied mansion of noble proportions. A balcony, supported and based by slim columns and running across the second-story, provides an overhang for the first-floor arcade. Both have delicate wrought-iron railings. The building and its balcony have pitched roofs, and the many windows on all three levels are bordered by decorative wood panels. Inside, among a collection of paintings by St. Thomians are two by the island's native-son Camille Pissarro, who was born Jacob Pizarro in 1830 of a union considered illegal by the Jewish community. He was later declared legitimate; to the credit of the congregation, this happened before he became famous.

Nearby is *Crown House*, dating from 1750 but noted most as having been the residence of Peter von Scholten when he was governor of St. Thomas in 1827, before he had been named governor-general of the Virgin Islands and went to live in St. Croix with Anna Heegaard at Büllowsminde.

(See ch. 5.) As part of its furnishings the interior of Crown House has eighteenth-century Chinese wall hangings, an authentic four-poster bed and a French crystal chandelier supposedly from Versailles.

To the southwest is the *Frederick Lutheran Church*, with a two-hundred-year-old parsonage claimed to be the second oldest Lutheran building in the Western Hemisphere. Until 1793 services were held at the chapel inside the Christiansfort. (See ch. 6.) The present church building was reconstructed a few months after the devastating fire of 1826. Above Main Street and west of Garden is the *Dutch Reformed Church*, which has had a continuous congregation, if not the same building, since 1660 before the island was recognized as "settled." The *Anglican Cathedral* is reached via Garden Street and the Sephardic *Synagogue* is at the center of hilly Crystal Gade. Although there was a Jewish congregation in St. Thomas from 1665 on, the first synagogue was yet to be completed in 1782 when large numbers of Jews from St. Eustatius fled here in the aftermath of Admiral Rodney's revenge on that island. A building was completed in 1796 but was destroyed by the 1804 fire that took more than twelve hundred houses. A new one was built in 1812 but it proved to be too small, so another went up in 1823. After still another fire in 1831, enough donations came in from congregation members and abroad to build the present part-neoclassic, part-Moorish structure. Ionic capitals are on supporting columns inside and out, fine plasterwork decorates the dome, lancet arched windows are set into the thick walls and dark wooden louvers extend into the arches.

The tour of historic houses of worship ends with the old *Moravian Mission* at Nisky near Crown Bay. Here a ceiba still stands; the noted missionary Augustus Gottlieb Spangenberg of the Bethlehem, Pennsylvania, Moravian Mission is said to have preached his first island sermon under it. (See ch. 5 for more on the Moravian Missions in the Virgin Islands.) The seminary, school and church are built around the ruins of the church, which is dated 1777.

There are some sugar estate remains in the hills surrounding the city, whose old houses look particularly attractive at sunset. If St. Thomas could overcome the symptoms of its emergence into modernity, such as traffic tie-ups and pollution problems, the beauty of Charlotte Amalie might not seem so anachronistic. The culture shock was inaugurated in 1917 when the United States paid twenty-five million dollars for the Danish islands as a hedge against foreign invasion. United States armed forces had moved into Haiti and the Dominican Republic during the first part of the twentieth century but however controversial these occupations may have been, they were not permanent. The effects of annexation in Puerto Rico and outright purchase in the Virgin Islands were quite different; these acquisitions were to continue. Mainland values arrived and stayed on. The black islanders were mostly ignored or exploited although many were absorbed into the general pursuit of the American Dream. A middle class sprang up with typical booster rivalries; St. Thomas and St. Croix are as competitive as New York and Chicago. With the coming of tourism—the logical chief industry for a nonagricultural island—identity was almost entirely plowed under, and only recently has a movement toward recognition of Virgin Islands heritage taken form.

This resurgence for St. Thomas means a past-due recognition of the effects of polluting industries on the island with its physical limitations, and on its surrounding waters. It also means coping with huge numbers of day visitors from the cruise ships who have little or no personal human contact with the shop salespeople and other inhabitants. The social pressures imposed by every American subculture, from Wall Street to Main Street to Haight-Ashbury and Chelsea, have had their consequences. It remains now for this lovely island to remember who it is.

St. Vincent

KINGSTOWN is being discovered by increasing numbers of cruise passengers and longer-staying visitors, so it is to be hoped that the eighteenth- and nineteenth-century architectural treasures lining the hilly Bay, Middle and Back Streets won't go the way of similar buildings in Antigua's St. John and St. Lucia's Castries. Its *Market Square* rivals the one in St. George's, Grenada, for color and liveliness, and *St. Mary's Cathedral*, built in sections by a Flemish padre, is a rich gingerbread wedding cake right out of an architectural student's nightmare. Every two years the priest would visit Europe, pick up a few new styles in arches and return to add a layer or two. Somehow, it does stick together. *St. George's* Anglican church on Back Street is where Alexander Leith is buried. (See ch. 2.)

At *Fort Charlotte* (1805), above the northern side of the harbor, work has been done in restoring the site, and a museum is being established. The famous *Botanic Gardens*, said to be the oldest continuously planted and grown in the Caribbean, received the first plants in 1793 from Captain Bligh's mercy ship, *Providence*; these included the breadfruit,

The Cathedral of Santa María de Menór, in Santo Domingo, houses the supposed remains of Don Cristóbal Colon (Christopher Colombus) as well as those of his brother, his son, and grandson. Whether one believes the story or not, this lovely gothic structure is an astounding testament to the building zeal of the sixteenth century Spanish settlers.

brought from the south Pacific to be planted as a cheap and easy food for the starving slaves. Descendants of the original shoots still grow here. These beautifully kept gardens, which are a visual and olfactory delight, contain the *Spachea perforata*, the world's rarest tree, giant double banyans, lily ponds, all varieties of palm, a complete nursery and representatives of every tropical fruit tree found in the islands. *Government House*, a white Georgian mansion perched on the wooded hill above, may soon be converted into a museum.

Trinidad and Tobago

Before achieving independence in 1962, Trinidad-Tobago had a little more than a century and a half of British rule. Before that, Spain—or more accurately, Spanish Venezuela—dominated the cultural life of the larger island, even to the name given the capital—Port of Spain; the style of this town is now largely nonentity modern with fascinating dollops of gingerbread *mit schlag*. There were a number of French settlers in the north, as well, and they, along with the Spanish, have left more of architectural interest than have the British. The *Town Hall* is an exception. It combines a block of eighteenth-century Spanish houses with an interior design of later English styles—an odd but successful mixture. The huge *St. James Barracks* were built from designs under "C" for "Columned Facade" in some British War Office filing cabinet and had the good fortune to turn out well. The *Deanery* in Queen Street is Georgian from the early nineteenth century, while in *Marine Square*, most of the buildings look French rather than English.

Roman Catholic churches prevail, with a few Protestant ones. But, as in no other Caribbean island, Trinidad can boast Moslem mosques and Hindu temples which, if not ancient, are at least characteristic of those other Indies.

Tobago's influences were mainly English, Dutch and French; its towns are small and modest, with no architectural pretensions, but interesting enough to explore if one grows weary of the beaches and Buccoo Reef. The most characteristic feature in Tobago houses is the so-called "Demerara" window, named for the Guyanese river and rum, and probably brought from Trinidad. Its features are a double sash flanked by set-in louvers and a solid overhang.

THE SPANISH ISLANDS

The ghetto approach to housing known as "low-income apartment complexes"—all seemingly stamped from the same upended paper-clip file—is beginning to overrun the islands. Adequate housing for island people should take priority over other building, but none of the new architects (assuming the builders have employed any for these projects) seem to have listened at all to the lessons of the past. In the Spanish islands—Dominican Republic and Puerto Rico—the early settlers thought big and spacious. Their men may have continued to clothe themselves in sweaty armor and thick, uncomfortable doublets and boots, but in the houses they built, their women floated on cool tiles through airy Moorish-style galleries, their mantillas dwarfed by high, arched ceilings. Windows were placed to send breezes across to other windows; public and private structures in the new world were memories of vaulted and soaring medieval cathedrals. Thick walls kept the heat away; central patios trapped the sun, and the greenery grown was to be observed from the darkened inner chambers.

Back in Spain this kind of building may have been chilly in winter—hence that traditional heavy clothing—but in the Caribbean it was ideal. With today's economics erecting thick walls and high ceilings to survive centuries may be untenable, but much of what *is* being built will be ready for the trash heap in twenty years.

The government buildings, churches, fortresses, warehouses, city walls and mansions of SANTO DOMINGO and SAN JUAN were made of large "cold" stone blocks or of what was called "tapia," a mixture of crushed stone and earth which produced a rich, rough stucco effect. Some tapia was quickly and cheaply put together; in other cases it has outlived solid brick and stone. The three-foot-thick walls were often left to acquire a yellowish patina, but just as often they were whitewashed to an eye-shattering white whose glare was relieved by heavy dark-wood beams, doors and shadowed ells and galleries. Windows were numerous and generous in height. Heavy wooden shutters could be closed against storms or attack and opened for serenades and keeping cool and keeping watch. Pairs of triangular stone seats were placed under the inside sill, so sheltered, chaperoned ladies could sit there and view the passing parade of the town, or perhaps so a maid could warn the señora of a returning husband if she happened to be occupied with something other than her household duties.

Such amenities were restricted to the gentry, but in the meaner houses of Spanish towns at least some of the adaptive principles were employed. Walls along the streets were high, and houses were built around central patios and gardens. Iron gates admitted one to a corridor as high as the building itself, but open to the sky. If it acted as a sound box, echoing the quarrels and other private business of several families, it also admitted cool air to all the apartments.

Unlike other European settlers, the Spanish built their kitchens inside their houses, and they resembled a decorator's dream-kitchen for a woman's magazine. The stove consisted of a pair of brick arches with a flat top. Wood burned in the arches provided heat for cooking on the surface. A triangular flue, also of brick, was suspended above to carry smoke and fumes through the ceiling. Floors were of tile, and utensils and smoked meats hung from hooks. A porous stone filtered the drinking and cooking water. Probably also present in all Spanish kitchens was a tall ceramic oil jar.

Spanish colonial life and culture closely resembled that

of the mother country not only because of a speaking acquaintance with the subtropical climate but because an intimate relationship between church and state was immediately established in the colonies. The Cathedral, the Audiencia and the Fortress were inextricably bound to one another; taut chains held the colonies to the Crown which was—in the early days at least—also the spiritual and military leader. Whereas those in high places regarded missons with suspicion in other European colonies, almost every church in the Spanish islands had its mission brother- or sisterhood functioning in the daily life of the town. So there was always a cathedral, its plaza, the mission, its residences, a rectory, smaller chapels and other religious buildings.

Santo Domingo

The plan, repeated in cities throughout the Spanish colonies, was inaugurated in the oldest living city in the Western Hemisphere, SANTO DOMINGO DE GUZMÁN, which was founded on Hispaniola's south coast by Bartolomé Colón, the admiral's brother, in 1498. Here, Bartolomé established a chapel where the first mass was celebrated on the east side of the *Rio Ozama*, which flows into the Caribbean from the heights of the Cordillera Central. The river widens at the mouth to form an estuary. Building soon began on the west side, of the river, and a street called *La Calle de las Damas* took form along with a street of warehouses known as *La Atazarana* (an Arabic word). Latter-day historians insist that great ladies of the town took the air of an evening along Las Damas, but the street's proximity to the area of ship anchorage and unloading into the warehouses suggests that this premier port city had a rather more vernacular night life.

A city wall with appropriate fortifications along the river and the sea was soon built to guard the proliferating structures which began to cluster around the *Cathedral de Santa María de Menor*, begun in 1514. Combining elements of the gothic and the baroque but lacking a bell tower (it would have provided an easy lookout over the entire city), this glorious building now houses the supposed remains of Don Cristobal himself, along with his brother, his son Diego and his grandson. The adventures of the admiral's bones have received full literary treatment elsewhere; he was supposed to have been buried in Sevilla and Havana, but Dominicans insist that he is now at rest, at last, in the place he wanted to be. His statue was erected much later in the plaza outside. For visitors from the modern section of Santo Domingo, it is an easy landmark for locating the cathedral, which sits in the center of the busy Old Town, as raffish and unheeding as any other decaying commercial center.

Hundreds upon hundreds of interesting houses and shops in various stages of neglect are sandwiched between structures of no character along narrow streets. But at a single, haphazard turning, one finds a restored building such as the *Casa de Tostado*, done to perfection by the *Oficina de Patrimonio Cultural*. Under the direction of Manuel E. del Monte, this office has achieved a purposeful extensive (and expensive) program of rehabilitation in the old city since the passing of Rafael Trujillo and the changing of the city's name back to its original.

The Casa is now a museum that exacts a modest entry fee. Built around a large patio, it exhibits a superb sample of a Renaissance loggia, restored to its sixteenth-century glory —the first such find by the archaeologists and architects exploring their ancient city. In the original facade was a Moorish-style window with a single fluted column in the center, probably unique in the islands. The first stone portico and stone tower also were uncovered by the workmen. A mahogany spiral staircase on the second floor is authentic, but the Casa's furnishing are examples of various periods in Santo Domingo's history. Colonists must have been overcome by nostalgia for their homeland, and their furniture was either imported or precise copies of what they remembered. The bedroom of the señora of the house has been imaginatively recreated with a handmade ecru lace spread on the big carved wooden bedstead, a chair with her mantilla and evening slippers, and a low stool beside the bed with her utilitarian day shoes and shawl.

Other displays are: swords of the period, hangings, inlaid wood sixteenth-century mirror frames and the reconstruction of those triangular-stone "waiting seats" called *poyenas*. Similar exhibits are to be found at *Casa del Cordón*, a building used for very modern purposes, as headquarters of the Banco Popular. It was originally built in 1503 by Don Francisco de Garay, whose given name echoed his principal interest, the Franciscan Order. So devoted was he that he had the entrance decorated by a huge carved-stone knotted and tassled cord such as was worn by the padres. The cord is arranged like a swag over the door frame, which has a basket-handle arch, itself intricately carved with roses. The great door is of characteristically polished, almost-black mahogany with authentic hardware.

The two-story palace—said to be the first in the new world to be constructed entirely of solid rock, although it would be difficult to prove this—was the scene of many dramatic events. Don Francisco loaned it to Don Diego Colón, the admiral's son, when he arrived as Viceroy of the Indies with his consort, Doña María de Toledo. While their own palace, the Alcázar, was being built, they occupied the Casa del Cordón and installed the audiencia (the Supreme Court for all the Spanish islands) there. Later, when Sir Francis Drake invaded and ravaged Santo Domingo in 1585, the upper-class women brought their jewels to the palace in the hope of persuading *El Draqui* to take their ransom and go away and leave their beautiful city alone.

Restoration of Casa del Cordón was under the direction of the Oficina de Patrimonio Cultural, with help from the Organization of American States; the decor was done by Felipe Goico. The bank which financed the work has used it since 1974 for its officers' headquarters, board meetings and other executive functions. English-speaking guides take visitors through free of charge if the bank officers are not in residence. Every detail has been perfectly recreated, from the fifteenth-century cathedral tile stair-rises to examples of sixteenth-century *arcols*—treasure cabinets—finely worked iron gates and brick-framed doorways and windows. The high ceilings are beamed in black hardwood and the floors tiled in combinations of square and hexagonal shapes. The second-floor arcade has a series of stone columned arches which once sent cool air circulating through the rooms. Now they are paned in a deceptively tinted glass to allow for artificial air conditioning—a concession to modern requirements that looks authentic but could be a danger to man or bird trying to pass through what looks like nature's own air.

When Diego Colón and his Doña María finally moved into the Alcazar they had a place of their own as magnificent as the borrowed one, but it looked far more fortresslike and it had a Moorish air. Overlooking Rio Ozama and facing the Atarazana, it had psychological value as a symbol of authority. The Columbus family had been unpopular in Santo Domingo from the beginning, and it may be remembered that Don Cristobal himself left the city in chains after his third voyage. Not that it was much of a city yet in 1500. Most of what there was, crumbled in an earthquake in 1502, and it was Nicolás de Ovando who began building what we see now in original construction or in restoration.

Ovando was appointed governor by King Ferdinand when strife between the Colón family and opposing elements in the new colony developed into a serious power struggle. The new governor must have been a man of great sensitivity and determination; in what was still mostly a wilderness he launched a building boom that culminated in the most impressive collection of urban buildings found anywhere in the islands. Sensitive or no, he was the inaugurator of the *encomiendas* system of land division which amounted to slavery of the Indians; to those lost people must tribute be paid for the architectural beauty in which they had no part except for their labor.

Ovando's residence, servant's quarters, the *Ozama fort* and *Powder Magazine* were close to the river mouth in an area now industrialized but also being rehabilitated into a completely restored neighborhood destined for adaptive uses. It faces the Calle de las Damas and is near the Atarazana, which has already become a major attraction with its cafés, shops and art galleries. One of the giant warehouses—one that has a vaulted ceiling and was originally used for boat building—will be turned into a nightclub. Diego Colón's Alcazar, among the first of the structures to be restored, was badly damaged during the 1965 civil war. A two-story rectangular building of stone and tapia with original classic arches in the ground-floor loggia, it was reconstructed on the upper floor with a carved-stone balustrade, basket-handle arches and Moorish stone carvings along the roof line. If a description of the interior, with its solid beamed ceilings, massive arched doorways with decorative wrought-iron gates and harlequin tiled floors, sounds ornate, the use of space dispels this effect. As in all of these palaces and official buildings, simplicity was the key.

Among the recreated plazas, streets and buildings in Ovando's city are *El Convento de los Dominicos* in *Plaza Pablo Duarte; Plaza de Billini; Universidad de San Tomas de Aquina*, which with its library is reputedly the oldest university (1538) in the Western Hemisphere; the charming pedestrian mall *La Plazaleta de las Curas* (Little Square of the Friars) with its original arched gateway; and the *Pantheon*, once a Jesuit residence and church, later a warehouse, then a bordello and now housing tributes to the nation's heroes. The building has a curious cupola that is entirely lined with beautiful mosaics. Along the old city sea wall are the remains of *Fort San Felipe* and *Puerta de la Misericordia*, whose outer gate is now dedicated to a hero of the independence war against Haiti in 1844. *Independence Square* includes plaques paying tribute to three of that war's leaders.

Returning to the *Plaza de Colón*, one will see two Renaissance-style palaces bordering the cathedral: the *Borgella* and the *Viceroy's Residence*. On the other side of the cathedral is the *Mercy Gate*, so called because if a political or criminal fugitive could outrun his pursuers and make it to the gate, he would get "special consideration" by the audiencia.

All of these neighborhoods and buildings may be discovered on foot in the old city; Columbus's statue and the cathedral mark the ideal starting and ending places.

What has been accomplished in the brief time since a feasibility study on restoration of historic sites was commissioned by Esso Oil Company in the 1960's could be a model and inspiration to other islands. Especially significant was the study's emphasis on restoring whole neighborhoods rather than single buildings. The necessary money has come from a number of public and private sources, as well as from the Organization of American States. Architects, engineers, archaeologists and other specialists have overcome incredible obstacles, not the least of which has been the need for agreement on details of construction or ornamentation where no precedent existed. What it took most of all was the will to do it, and although it is far from completion, now that the people of the city can see what is being accomplished, they feel a robust new pride in their heritage.

Puerto Rico

Why the Colón brothers picked Santo Domingo, for all its beauties, as the location of their crown city remains somewhat of a mystery. It was the central point in the northern Caribbean, but Don Cristobal was looking for a passage to the Indies, and almost any island other than Hispaniola would have served as capital and principal settlement for colonists. Havana, indeed, did become more important. *Puerto Rico*, the "rich port"—a name first given by Ponce de Leon to the city of SAN JUAN BAUTISTA (Puerto Rico later became the name of the entire island)—could have been *la ciudad primada*. Standing at the head of the Lesser Antilles landfalls and at the beginning of the great complex of northern islands, it was closer to home than Santo Domingo.

But except for a brief period of prosperity in the first two decades of the sixteenth century, when gold still poured out of the island's rivers, Puerto Rico was always a kind of stepchild among the Spanish colonies. San Juan was established after Santo Domingo; it was not permitted a university or a people's hospital, and none of its constructions, with the eventual exception of El Morro, achieved the architectural magnificence of a Santa María de Menor or an Alcazar. Nevertheless, as often happens with the runt of the litter, San Juan developed a distinctive personality of its own and, in spite of official neglect, put up a town full of buildings unique and beautiful in their own right. Among these were *El Convento Dominicano*, which should not be confused with the Carmelite convent and church built first in the seventeenth and converted in the mid-twentieth century into a fine hotel known as "El Convento." The Dominican Convent, begun in 1523 on land donated by Ponce de Leon, is a marvel of arched loggias on all four sides of a large central courtyard. Located near the Fort Brooke gate to El Morro, with an entrance from the *Plaza de San Jose*, it is now a working headquarters for the Institute of Puerto Rican Culture. Over a greater period of time this organization has matched the corresponding one in the Dominican Republic, for restorations, discoveries, and useful adaptations of historic sites. Concerts, ballets and art exhibits are held here, and authentic handicrafts are on sale in one section.

The Instituto de Cultura Puertorriquena was created as a public corporation by the Commonwealth Legislature in 1955, a year when the famous "Operation Bootstrap," or *Fomento*, was bringing hundreds of industries to the island. Some foresighted people in the administration began trying to combat the effects of this swift industrial revolution on a predominantly agricultural society; already the English-speaking mainland values and mores, fast foods and gimmickry were replacing traditional ways, and more than one visiting American sneered, "*What* culture?" when told that Puerto Rico had a cultural renaissance program.

As in Santo Domingo later, Institute personnel wisely realized that preservation and conservation goals should involve entire urban zones; thus the program for San Juan covers almost half the old city-island. Recently, a second zone in the city of PONCE on the south coast was declared a national monument, and planned for the future are YAUCO and SAN GERMÁN, early settlements near the southwest coast.

Under the continuing direction of a remarkable man named Ricardo E. Alegría, the program covers pre-Columbian Indian sites, (the *Taino* ball court at *Utuado* is now a public park and museum), historic buildings, parks and the arts, and also encourages private owners in the declared zones to restore their properties in an authentic manner. Not only do they receive tax relief for this kind of undertaking, but they have the benefit of free advice from the Institute's staff on everything from the facade designs to balconies, cornices, hardware and decorative elements. Private restorers can buy at cost the materials they need for the work, and although some San Juan building owners complain that maintenance costs are soaring and that tax relief should be given for that, as well, the fact is that since 1965, 229 buildings in the old city have been completed and at least 16 more are in construction.

Santos displaying the island's traditional art rendering of carved wooden saints.

Anyone who has negotiated that hike up Cristo Street on a sunny day, with all of those stop-offs for investigations along the way, should find it easy to make one more historic stop before resting in the *Plazuela de las Monjas* (the Little Plaza of the Nuns) facing the cathedral or taking more specific solace in *El Patio de Sam* or the *Hotel el Convento*. Walking toward the bay from *Cristo Street* along *San Sebastian*, one comes to the house on the outer wall known as *Casa Blanca*. Until 1974 it was not possible for the casual visitor to see this house of the Ponce family; now the Institute of Culture has restored it superbly so that it is a blessing to the eye and imagination. The Spanish Crown awarded the property to Ponce's family sometime after 1521, and when Don Juan's son became *alcalde*, or military governor of San Juan, the original wooden building was made into a fortresslike mansion. After that, Casa Blanca was always the residence of governors, and when Puerto Rico became part of the United States, the U.S. army commander carried on the tradition by living there.

More than a museum, *Casa Blanca* will have concerts and other indoor and outdoor events. This serene complex of buildings and gardens, following sundial time rather than airline schedules, seems as far from the commotion of Santurce, Río Piedras and Bayamón as the centuries that gave it form. From one terrace the view encompasses the entire bay. How could old Ponce have ever thought Caparra was the place to live?

Ponce's original home at *Caparra*, however, is included in the restoration program. In digging around the site, numerous artifacts were found that are now in the museum adjacent to the preserved ruins of the mansion. The birthplace of national hero and journalist Luis Muñoz Rivera in *Barranquitas* is another Institute restoration project which includes a typical Puerto Rican village museum and library. At *San Germán*, the church of the hermitage of *Porta Coeli*, architecturally reminiscent of the Spanish missions in California and Mexico, has been turned into a museum of religious artifacts. The old town itself is a mine of rural colonial architecture, still almost unchanged.

7

Hymns and Dread Children

If you are enjoying the great good fortune of being on an island at sunset where you can look westward across the Caribbean Sea as the sun, a giant orange disk, sinks into the water, watch for the phenomenon known as "The Green Flash." For a second the uppermost part of the sun looks green, a trick of atmospheric optics that infuriatingly seems to occur only at the moment you have involuntarily blinked your eye. It is not an illusion; it really happens, but almost nobody ever sees it.

The transition of the islands from feudalism into today's world has been almost as swift. In comparison to the centuries it has taken North America and Europe to evolve into an industrialized society, the time of wrenching adjustment in the Caribbean has been a green flash.

As they have been required to do everywhere since their importation from Africa, the people have had to try to learn new skills instantly. In the Caribbean they had to build the new-style factories, hotels, roads and public buildings, with strange and monstrous machinery, function in hotel services and coexist with conspicuously affluent strangers.

Because the money and direction for all this development has come from the outside or from wealthy local landowners or a combination of both, and because so many island workers are still underpaid, polemicists have a handy slogan: The New Colonialism. The comparison is so easy that it has long since taken hold of the minds of those who do not care to think further or try to grasp the complexities of the problem of how their island should be developed.

It has also offered an opportunity for mainland demagogues to move in and capitalize on cases of exploitation. In the 1960s the press played up the so-called Black Power movement in the Caribbean to the fullest with sensational newspaper stories and TV documentaries that made the West Indies appear ready to explode in a black versus white revolution. The menace they depicted struck trepidation into the heart of many a potential white tourist, and because crime—as elsewhere in the world—has been increasing in the islands, such a traveler has understandably hesitated before putting a toe in Caribbean waters (at a good deal of expense to himself) for fear of coming face to face with the violence he has avoided at home.

If, in this mood of suspicion, the tourist does decide to go, he looks for surliness on every face and complains about the slow service in his hotel or the inability of the dinner waiter to understand his needs. If some untoward event does happen, that—not the joys of his travels—is what he remembers to tell his neighbors when he returns.

Casual visitors tend not only to be amused but scornful at the spectacle of some island man's defeat by a mysteriously nonfunctioning motor. Mainlanders trying to run a modern business in the islands may dine out for months on hilarious stories of ineptness they have encountered among their employees. In his wry and humorous novel, *Don't Stop the Carnival*, Herman Wouk depicted islanders turning their fecklessness and secrecy into a conspiracy to frustrate an American expatriot trying to run a tropical hotel. That secrecy—or privacy of communication—is not very different from the methods Africans used against their masters during the centuries of slavery. What they were doing in the Wouk novel was a form of rebellion against further intrusion by outsiders. The paradox for most islanders today is that while they desire twentieth century comforts—as who does not?—the means of achieving them, usually through tourism, are often too costly in terms of personal independence and inappropriate for the realities of island life.

The most visible example of the dilemma has been the policy of many island governments regarding tourism. The word "tourist" is divisive in itself, implying a nameless outsider, too insensitive—or too rich—to mind being shoved around. A "visitor" implies a guest who deserves everyone's hospitality. But Tourism has been the word used by governments and hotel enterprises and too often has been considered both a strictly dollars-and-cents industry and a miraculous solution to unemployment. For example, a hotel building program would be launched, usually without regard to or study of the environment that was being disturbed, and people would hastily be trained on the job in the building trades. Once the hotels were up and the roads and shops put in and an airport constructed, workers had to be found who could staff these amenities, and they were seldom the same people who did the building. In order to keep the international loans coming and the building trades employed, new

hotels had to be added. But to fill the hotels, convenient transportation to the island became necessary. That meant either enlarging the airport or finding new space that would accommodate international jet aircraft. It also meant training personnel to deal with flight schedules, car rentals, irate travelers, complex baggage systems and more machinery. A great many people now had jobs.

But the natural attractions of an island aiming at tourism usually need to be adapted to suit foreign tastes: Swamps must be cleared to get rid of mosquitos and old buildings destroyed or built over to make way for banks, airline offices and shopping centers. In the hope of finding jobs, people are drawn into the cities where the excitement is, abandoning the countryside where nothing much ever happens and nobody is making any money. If the island where all this is happening were a place of unlimited space and resources, the hurtling expansion might go on indefinitely.

Then suddenly, there are too many hotels and con-

Because close to 95 percent are of African ancestry, this does not mean that island people are a homogeneous mass. The mix of color gradations, educational distinctions, aristocracies, peasants, middle classes, and a burgeoning intellectual elite is further complicated by a wide generation gap.

dominiums for the size of the island. In order to feed the visitors the steaks they demand, costly imports of produce and equipment unobtainable on the island begin upsetting the trade balance. By now the farms which might have been supplying local foods are inadequate because no one wants to work there anymore. Towns that were once familiar and comfortable gathering centers for their districts become overcrowded with the unskilled and unemployed, riddled with slums and filled with strange people in shorts and funny hats who are presumed to be rich. The beaches where islanders once bathed themselves and cooled their horses and donkeys at will are now reserved for hotel guests only. But still the

building boom must continue or heavy industry be introduced, or both, if the increasing population is to find employment.

Each island, being different from all the others, has its own set of problems, and the picture is not necessarily as grim everywhere. Nevertheless, enough islands began to worry about what seemed to be a collision course to meet under the banner of the Caribbean Tourism Association in 1972 in Puerto Rico for a massive general discussion of where they were all headed. Under the guidance and inspiration of the CTA's then executive director, Herbert L. Hiller, they launched the idea of establishing a tourism research

The older generations sometimes hike for miles to attend church services or revival meetings, and many church buildings have been in continuous use for centuries.

center, a kind of permanent seminar for the exchange of ideas and planning concepts. Among the organization's ambitious goals is to "find ways to use tourism in strengthening other key sectors of the economy with special reference to agriculture, with the long-term objective of reducing the dependence on tourism." Another is "to promote the consciousness of the need to preserve both the natural and man-made beauty of the Caribbean environment and to demonstrate its direct relationship to the development of an attractive tourism product."* A third is to seek economic solutions that suit the physical limitations inherent in islands and the unique cultural qualities of the people.

And the people are by no means a homogeneous mass simply because in most islands close to 95 percent are of African ancestry. The mix of color gradations, educational distinctions, island aristocracies, peasants, newly created middle classes and a burgeoning intellectual elite is further complicated by a generation gap that amounts to a chasm.

Turn on a radio to the local broadcasting station. Half of the programming is rock, reggae, sports reports—language for the young; the other half is hymns, church services, exhortations, and bible stories. The most powerful radio transmitter in the Western Hemisphere belongs to a religious station in Bonaire.

While the older generation attends revival meetings by hiking for miles or driving cars with bumper stickers reading, "Don't be caught dead without Jesus," their teen-age children in knitted caps and shades are doing nothing much in the vicinity of the blaring record shops, absorbing their own message. Some are rebels calling themselves Rude Boys or Dread Children and have taken the external trappings of the Ras Tafari movement in Jamaica, which protests against a materialist "Babylon" society, and use them as an excuse for violence and mindless vandalism. Yet the Rastas, with their wild "dread locks" hairdos, mystical worship of Emperor Haile Selassie,* and ritual smoking of the cannabis weed are a religious sect whose motto is "Peace and Love." Many are artists or craftsmen of exceptional talent and skill.

In the 1860's, when the United States had at last declared emancipation, those who had been taught by Baptist and Moravian missionaries began moving toward present-day revivalism with its involvement of entire congregations in worship services. Many American freedmen came to the is-

*Caribbean Tourism Research Center Quarterly, Vol. 1, No. 1 (September, 1975). Barbados, West Indies.

*Following the Emperor's death in 1975, the Ras Tafarians have either refused to believe he is dead or are sure that he will rise again.

After the Civil War, American freedmen came to the islands as missionaries to establish "native Baptist" societies. Variations began to appear, some extreme, depending strongly on the old African rituals and the experiencing of "possession."

lands to establish "native Baptist" churches. Variations appeared, some extreme, depending strongly on the old African rituals and the experiencing of "possession." Receiving messages from the Spirit, losing one's senses in ecstasy became an expected part of the ceremonies. This also happens in *vaudou* rites but it is not similar to other cults or a substitute for established religions. In Haiti, celebrants may be Catholics or Episcopalians and still believe in *vaudou* with no apprent confusion.

Two leading revival-possession cults in Jamaica are called *Pukkumina* (or Pocomania) and *Zion* and enjoy wide participation among adults, especially in the Kingston area, which is also a center of younger-generation unrest.

Roman Catholic, Anglican, Dutch Reformed, Baptist, Congregational, Presbyterian, Jewish and Christian Science organizations have continued through all of this, with the Catholic Church retaining its sovereignty through its school systems and its seniority. Gaining ground fast are the Church of God, Pentecostal, Four Square, Jehovah's Witness and Seventh Day Adventist proselytizers, who have established meeting houses and fund-raising programs. Teaching and social work are being done by the Friends and the Salvation Army, and there are philosophic offshoots such as the Bahai movement.

Such intense religiosity and the widespread feeling for the land, for property, does not make for sentiment favoring communism, even in islands (excluding Cuba) where there is pressure for land reform. How the youth cults—the grab-it-all, it's-my-turn-now avalanche—so highly publicized abroad will settle into middle age in the years to come will be largely influenced by what happens in the struggle for cultural iden-

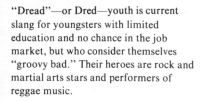
"Dread"—or Dred—youth is current slang for youngsters with limited education and no chance in the job market, but who consider themselves "groovy bad." Their heroes are rock and martial arts stars and performers of reggae music.

It may be that the outcome of the race into the future will be determined by understanding of the past.

tity and the overcoming of poverty. The present religious forms may phase out with the passing of the older generations. But the core of tradition does have a chance to survive because there are similarities of expression between the old and the young despite their differences. The creative exuberance that has always refused to be kept down is in the "roots theatre" of Trinidad and Jamaica, in an increasing body of work by relevant island authors and in the music of reggae, a genuinely original form. Reggae rose out of Ras Tafari protest and early revivalism, rock and country-and-blues, but it has its own beat and its own message. It is heard on records, backyard sound systems, radio, nightspots and street corners, and everybody—including those who worry most about the younger generation—dances to it. But reggae is essentially the voice of deprived youth, crying out for change. In an area where children are universally cherished, the expression of their need will have to be listened to and acted upon. That need is for a world that will somehow erase poverty without

resorting to the systems now in control. In view of a general resistance to birth control movements, the solution at the moment seems obscure.

One hopes that goals in the islands—and indeed, in all those areas calling themselves the Third World—will eventually develop along lines that do not use the present criteria of the big industrialized nations as a model to be followed literally. Islands remain islands, forever fecund and green when they are allowed to be. Agriculture, the losing industry of the modern world, cannot be shunned much longer if the world is to survive. Where else but in the islands—even those which have turned their soil hostile—is agriculture more appropriate or more traditional? Where else is there more opportunity to experiment with farming of the sea?

It may be that the outcome of the footrace into the future will be determined by an understanding of the past.

Bibliography

Abrahams, Peter. *Jamaica, an Island Mosaic*. London: Her Majesty's Stationary Office, 1957.

Acworth, Angus W. *Buildings of Architectural or Historic Interest in the British West Indies*. London: His Majesty's Stationary Office, 1951.

Augelli, John P., Ed. *Caribbean Lands*, Grand Rapids: the Fideler Company, 1965.

Barada, Bill. Treasure salvage-archaeology. *Skin Diver*, July 1975, pp. 56-60.

Bass, George F., ed. *A History of Seafaring Based on Underwater Archaeology*. New York: Walker and Company, 1972.

Battick, John F. Richard Rooth's sea journal, 1654-55. *Jamaica Journal*, published quarterly by the Institute of Jamaica, Dec. 1971.

Bryan, Patrick. *Emigres*. Fourth Conference of Caribbean Historians, University of the West Indies, Mona, Jamaica, Apr. 1972.

Buisseret, David. Edward D'Oyley. *Jamaica Journal*, Mar. 1971.

———. The Morant Bay Fort. *Jamaica Journal*, Dec. 1970.

Cargill, Morris, ed. *Ian Fleming Introduces Jamaica*. The Netherlands: Andre Deutsch, Ltd., 1965.

Clarke, John Henrik. Slave revolt in the Caribbean. *Black World*, Feb. 1973.

Concannon, T.A.L. *Jamaica's Architectural Heritage*. The Georgian Society of Jamaica, 1971.

———. Kenilworth ruins. *Jamaica Journal*, Mar. 1974, pp. 21, 22.

————. Our architectural heritage. *Jamaica Journal*, June 1970.

Connell, John, and Sheppard, Jill. *Caribbean Conservation News*. Barbados: Caribbean Conservation Association, Sept. 1975.

Connell, Neville. Colonial life in the West Indies as depicted in prints. *Antiques*, May 1971.

Cotter, C.S. "Sevilla Nueva, The Story of an Excavation." *Jamaica Journal*, June 1970, pp. 15-22.

Coulthard, G.R. The supreme being of the Arawaks. *Jamaica Journal*, March 1969.

Craton, Michael. Dr. John Quier. *Jamaica Journal*, no. 4, Dec. 1974, pp. 44-47.

————. The oldest Jamaican sugar estate. *Jamaica Journal*, Sept. 1970.

Devaux, Robert J. *St. Lucia Historic Sites*. Castries: St. Lucia National Trust, 1975.

Dominican Republic. *National Park System Report*. Santo Domingo, 1975.

Easter, B.H. *A Guide to Morne Fortune, St. Lucia.* St. Lucia Archaeological and Historical Society, Feb. 1966.

Elkins, Stanley. *Slavery, A Problem in American Institutional and Intellectual Life.* New York: Grosset & Dunlap, 1963.

Exquemeling, A.O. *The Buccaneers of America.* London: Penguin Books, 1969.

Figueredo, Alfredo E. *The Archaic Period of St. Thomas, Virgin Islands: New Evidence and Interpretations.* Report S 41, Society for American Archaeology, 39th Annual Meeting.

————. *The Virgin Islands Archaeological Society Report.* Vol. 1, 1974.

Fremmer, Ray. Jonathan Barnet, pirate-hunter. *The Gleaner.* Kingston, Jamaica, Sept. 13, 1970, p. 31.

Gjessing, Frederick K. *Observations on the Architecture of Reef Bay Estate*, report, St. Thomas, U.S. Virgin Islands, 1968.

Golding, Morton J. *A Short History of Puerto Rico.* New York: New American Library, Inc., 1973.

Green, Timothy. Roosting birds and the dangers of a gas barge. *Smithsonian*, May 1975., p. 34.

Greenberg, Jerry and Idaz. *The Living Reef.* Miami: Seahawk Press, 1972.

Guadeloupe, Department of. *Bulletin*, L. Gruner, INRA station de zoologie el de la lutte biologique, 97 170.

Hancock, Ralph. *Puerto Rico—A Travelers' Guide.* Princeton, N.J.: D. Van Nostrand Company, Inc., 1962.

Hannau, Hans W. *Guadeloupe.* Andermann, for the Tourist Board of Guadeloupe.

Harrigan, Norwell, and Varlack, Pearl. *The British Virgin Islands, a Chronology.* Tortola: Research and Consulting Services, Ltd., 1970.

Hart, Ansell. Colour prejudice in Jamaica. *Jamaica Journal*, Dec. 1970.

Hartog, Johann. *Aruba* and *Bonaire* and *Curaçao.* De Wit, N.V., Aruba, 1962.

———. *The Three S's—Saba, St. Eustatius, St. Maarten.* De Wit, 1975.

———. *Die Bovenwindse Eilanden.* De Wit, 1964.

———. *The Courthouse of St. Maarten.* Government of the Windward Islands, St. Maarten, 1974.

Hatch, Charles, E., Jr. *Reef Bay ("Par Force") Estate House and Sugar Factory.* Virgin Islands National Park Historic Structures Report and History Data (Office of History & Historic Architecture, U.S. Department of the Interior), June 1, 1970.

Howard, R.A. St. Vincent Botanic Gardens, 1765-1955. Reprinted from *The Geographical Review*, Vol. XLIV, No. 3, 1954, pp. 381-393.

Institute of Tropical Forestry. *Bulletin.* Forest Service, U.S. Department of Agriculture, Rio Piedras, Puerto Rico.

IUCN. *Bulletin*, Dominican Republic Marine Park, Vol. V, No. 2, Feb. 1974.

Jesse, Rev. C. *Outlines of St. Lucia's History.* Castries: St. Lucia Archaeological and Historical Society, 1970.

Jesse, Rev. C., and Easter, B.H. *A Short History of the Town and District of Vieux Fort.* St. Lucia Archaeological and Historical Society, 1971.

Kay, Frances. *This is Grenada.* St. George's: Carenage Press, 1971.

Keown, Ian M. *The KLM/ALM Guide to the Dutch Caribbean*, 1972.

Keur, John Y., and Dorothy L. *Windward Children*. Assen: Royal Vangorcum Ltd., 1960.

Kirby, I.A. Earle. *The Sugar Mills of St. Vincent, Their Sites*. St. Vincent Archaeological and Historical Society, 1973.

Lewin, Olive. Cults in Jamaica. *Jamaica Journal*, June 1969.

Lightbourne, Jno. *The Story of Fort Christian*. St. Thomas: Bureau of Libraries and Museums, 1973.

Martinique Local Council. *Martinique, Richesse de France*, 1971.

Marx, Robert F., *Port Royal Rediscovered*. N.Y.: Doubleday and Co., 1973.

———. *Shipwrecks of the Western Hemisphere*. N.Y.: David McKay, 1975.

Metraux, Alfred. *Haiti*. New York: Universe Books, 1960.

Mikesell, Marvin. Essays on the Problems and Prospects of Research in Foreign Areas. In *Geographers Abroad*. Chicago: Univ. of Chicago Press, 1973.

Mitchell, Carleton. *Isles of the Caribbees*. 2nd ed. Washington, D.C.: The National Geographic Society, 1971.

Morris, Richard B. The declaration was proclaimed but few in Europe listened at first. *Smithsonian*, July 1975.

Murphy, Patricia Shaubah. *The Moravian Mission to the African Slaves of the Danish West Indies*. Caribbean Research Institute, College of the Virgin Islands, St. Thomas, 1969.

Nevins, Allan, and Commager, Henry Steele. *The Pocket History of the United States*, New York: Pocket Books, Inc., 1945.

Osborne, Francis J., S.J. Ysassi, last Spanish governor of Jamaica. *Jamaica Journal*, March 1971.

Paiewonsky, Isador. *Jewish Historical Development in the Virgin Islands*. St. Thomas, 1959.

———. *La Trompeuse in the Harbour of St. Thomas*. St. Thomas, 1961.

Proceedings of the International Congress for the Study of Pre-Columbian Cultures of the Lesser Antilles. Barbados, 2nd: 1968. Grenada, 3rd: 1969, St. Lucia, 4th: 1973, Antigua, 5th: 1974. Florida State Museum, University of Florida, Gainesville.

Puerto Rico. *Programa de parques y museos del Instituto de Cultura Puertorriqueña. National Park Service Bulletin.* Introduction by Ricardo E. Alegria. San Juan, 1973.

Radcliffe, Virginia. The city that fell into the sea. *Pastimes*, Sept. 1974.

Rainsford, Marcus, Esq. *An Historical Account of the Black Empire of Hayti Comprehending a View of the Principal Transactions in the Revolution of Saint Domingo with Its Antient and Modern State.* London: Albion Press, 1805.

Reckord, Carol. Jamaica's sugar industry. *Jamaica Journal*, Dec. 1969.

Reckord, Mary. The slave rebellion of 1831. *Jamaica Journal*, June 1969.

Reynolds, C. Roy. Tacky and the Great Slave Rebellion of 1760. *Jamaica Journal*, June 1972.

Robinson, Alan H. *Virgin Islands National Park.* St. Thomas, 1974.

Robinson, Carey. *The Fighting Maroons of Jamaica.* Jamaica: William Collins and Sangster Ltd., 1971.

Roiman, Selden. *Haiti: The Black Republic.* N.Y.: The Devin-Adair Co., 1954.

St. Clair, James. Problem oriented archaeology. *Jamaica Journal*, March 1970.

Seaga, Edward. Revival cults in Jamaica. *Jamaica Journal*, June 1969.

Severin, Timothy. *The Golden Antilles*, N.Y.: Alfred A. Knopf, 1970.

Smith, Bradley. *Columbus in the New World.* N.Y.: Doubleday and Company, 1962.

Somerville, Delores. *Old Forts of Montserrat.* University Voice-ZJB, Sept. 6, 1972.

Taylor, John. *Manuscript.* Institute of Jamaica, West India Library, Port Royal, 1685.

Tyson, George F., Jr. *Toussaint L'Ouverture*, Englewood Cliffs, N.J.: Prentice-Hall, Inc., 1973.

Tyson, George F., Jr., and Carolyn. *Inventory of the Historical Landmarks of St. Kitts-Nevis.* St. Thomas: Island Resources Foundation, Inc., 1974.

————. *Preliminary Report on Manuscript Materials in British Archives Relating to the American Revolution in the West Indian Islands.* St. Thomas: Island Resources Foundation, Inc., 1973.

Van Meeteren, N. *De Oude Vestingwerken Forten en Batterijen van Curaçao.* Willemstad, 1921.

Waugh, Alec. *A Family of Islands.* N.Y.: Doubleday and Company, 1964.

Wilgus, A. Curtis, and D'Eça, Raul. *History of Latin America.* N.Y.: Barnes and Noble, Inc., 1953.

Wood, Peter. *Caribbean Isles.* N.Y.: The American Wilderness/Time-Life Books, 1975.

Wright, Philip, and White, Paul F. *Exploring Jamaica.* London: Andre Deutsch, 1969.

Wynter, Sylvia. Jonkonnu in Jamaica. *Jamaica Journal*, June 1970.

Photo Credits

Grateful acknowledgment is made to the following persons or organizations to reproduce the following photographs: frontis, St. John's Tourist Bureau; page v, Frank Pistone; page 2, Saba Tourist Information Office; page 3, Trinidad-Tobago Tourist Board; page 5, Bob Wands for the United States Virgin Islands; page 7, Virginia Radcliffe; page 9, Charlotte Frieze Blum for Island Resources Foundation; page 11, French West Indies Tourist Board; page 13, French West Indies Tourist Board; page 16, Virginia Radcliffe; page 20, Bonaire Tourist Information Office; page 23, Explorers Club Library; page 24, St. Lucia Tourist Office; page 26, Milton Machlin; page 27, Jamaica Tourist Board; page 28, French West Indies Tourist Board; page 31, Fritz Henle for the United States Virgin Islands; page 36, French West Indies Tourist Board; page 38, Puerto Rican Institute of Culture; page 45, Fritz Henle for the United States Virgin Islands; page 47, Virginia Radcliffe; page 49, Virginia Radcliffe; page 51, Virginia Radcliffe; page 59, Institute of Jamaica; page 63, Jamaica Tourist Board; page 71, Jamaica Tourist Board; page 73, Institute of Jamaica; page 77, Johnny O'Brien, Jamaica Tourist Board; page 82, French West Indies Tourist Board; page 93, Charlotte Frieze Blum for Island Resources Foundation; page 94, Richard Steedman for the Jamaica Tourist Board; page 95, Institute of Jamaica; page 97, Bonaire Tourist Information Office; pages 98 and 99, Institute of Jamaica; page 101, The United States Virgin Islands; page 103, unknown; page 104, Johnny O'Brien, Jamaica Tourist Board; page 107, Johnny O'Brien, Jamaica Tourist Board; page 108, Virginia Radcliffe for the National Trust for Historic Preservation; page 109, French West Indies Tourist Board; page 111, Jamaica Tourist Board; page 119, French West Indies Tourist Board; page 125, Air France; page 133, Fritz Henle for the United States Virgin Islands; page 148, Virginia Radcliffe; page 150, Virginia Radcliffe; page 152, Russell Keune, National Trust for Historic Preservation; page 155, Virginia Radcliffe; page 157, French West Indies Tourist Bureau; page 160, Helen Marcus for St. Eustatius Tourist Information Office; page 163, Virginia Radcliffe; page 164, Virginia Radcliffe; page 169, Virginia Radcliffe for National Trust for Historic Preservation; page 172, French West Indies Tourist Board; page 177, The United States Virgin Islands; page 183, Virginia Radcliffe; page 184, Virginia Radcliffe; page 193, James Hakewill, engraved by Sutherland, sold by Jamaica Polio Trust; page 194, French West Indies Tourist Board; page 197, Virginia Radcliffe; page 201, Jamaica Tourist Board; page 205, French West Indies Tourist Board; page 208, St. Eustatius Tourist Information Office; page 213, Virginia Radcliffe for National Trust for Historic Preservation; page 214, French West Indies Tourist Board; page 223, French West Indies Tourist Board; page 229, Institute of Jamaica, city plan from Arnoldus Montanus "De Nieuwene Ondenuende Weereld"; page 247, Patrick Harty for Jamaica Tourist Board; page 248, Richard Steedman for Jamaica Tourist Board; page 249, Virginia Radcliffe; page 251, Richard Steedman for Jamaica Tourist Board; page 252, Edward Kritzler; page 253, Virginia Radcliffe; page 254, Virginia Radcliffe.

Index